WHEN CIMARRON MEANT WILD

Also by David L. Caffey

Head for the High Country (Nashville, 1973)

The Old Home Place: Farming on the West Texas Frontier (Burnet, Texas, 1981)

ed., *Yellow Sun, Bright Sky: The Indian Country Stories of Oliver La Farge* (Albuquerque, 1988)

Land of Enchantment, Land of Conflict: New Mexico in English-Language Fiction (College Station, Texas, 1999)

Frank Springer and New Mexico: From the Colfax County War to the Emergence of Modern Santa Fe (College Station, Texas, 2006)

Chasing the Santa Fe Ring: Power in Privilege in Territorial New Mexico (Albuquerque, 2014)

When Cimarron Meant Wild
The Maxwell Land Grant Conflict in New Mexico and Colorado

DAVID L. CAFFEY

UNIVERSITY OF OKLAHOMA PRESS : NORMAN

Library of Congress Cataloging-in-Publication Data

Names: Caffey, David L., 1947– author.
Title: When cimarron meant wild : the Maxwell Land Grant conflict in New Mexico and Colorado / David L. Caffey.
Description: Norman : University of Oklahoma Press, [2023] | Includes bibliographical references and index. | Summary: "Describes the epic range war over control of the Maxwell Land Grant, some two million acres in New Mexico Territory, and its resources between 1870 and 1900. The conflict involved miners, a foreign corporation, local elites, Texas cattlemen, the haughty 'Santa Fe Ring' of lawyerly speculators, and indigenous Jicarilla Apache and Mouache Ute people"—Provided by publisher.
Identifiers: LCCN 2022046304 | ISBN 978-0-8061-9179-9 (hardcover)
ISBN 978-0-8061-9477-6 (paper)
Subjects: LCSH: Land tenure—New Mexico—History—19th century. | Land tenure—Colorado—History—19th century. | Maxwell Land Grant (N.M. and Colo.)—History. | New Mexico History—1848– | Colfax County (N.M.)—History—19th century. | Las Animas County (Colo.)—History—19th century. | BISAC: HISTORY / United States / State & Local / Southwest (AZ, NM, OK, TX) | HISTORY / United States / General
Classification: LCC F802.M38 C34 2023 | DDC 978.92—dc23/eng/20221031
LC record available at https://lccn.loc.gov/2022046304

The paper in this book meets the guidelines for permanence and durability of the Committee on Production Guidelines for Book Longevity of the Council on Library Resources, Inc. ∞

Copyright © 2023 by the University of Oklahoma Press, Norman, Publishing Division of the University. Paperback published 2024. Manufactured in the U.S.A.

All rights reserved. No part of this publication may be reproduced, stored in a retrieval system, or transmitted, in any form or by any means, electronic, mechanical, photocopying, recording, or otherwise—except as permitted under Section 107 or 108 of the United States Copyright Act—without the prior written permission of the University of Oklahoma Press. To request permission to reproduce sel ections from this book, write to Permissions, University of Oklahoma Press, 2800 Venture Drive, Norman OK 73069, or email rights.oupress@ou.edu.

To the memory of
Ann Dunwody
Clovis Bradford
Lawrence R. Murphy
Charles Leland Sonnichsen
Teachers—devoted, wise, and generous

Contents

List of Illustrations ix

Preface xi

Introduction 1

1. The Plains People and the Cedar Bark People 7
2. Lucien Maxwell, Master of the Cimarron 22
3. Gold on the Maxwell Grant 35
4. In Pain and Trouble 44
5. A Brew Made for Mayhem 57
6. Unsettled 70
7. The Tolby Murder and Its Aftermath 86
8. A Town in Turmoil 101
9. Rumors of an Indian War 112
10. The Whirlwind 122
11. The Coming of the Law 135
12. A Most Audacious Ring 149
13. A Reckoning 161
14. Settling the Maxwell Grant Conflict 175
15. Time and Change 193

Notes 209

Bibliography 237

Index 249

Illustrations

Figures

Treaty council participants   20

Lucien Bonaparte Maxwell   27

Hydraulic mining in the Moreno Valley   40

Lucien Maxwell, Charles Holly, and John Watts   45

Elizabethtown, New Mexico   59

Cimarron, New Mexico   72

Francisco "Pancho" Griego   78

Franklin J. Tolby   88

Robert Hamilton Longwill   98

Stone jail, Cimarron, New Mexico   108

Issue Day at Maxwell's ranch, Cimarron, New Mexico   114

David Crockett, Gus Heffron, and Henry Goodman   131

Henry Ludlow Waldo   140

Mary Tibbles McPherson   151

Samuel Beach Axtell   157

Cimarron News and Press "Extra"   170

Jicarilla camp on the Mescalero Reservation   177

Oscar Patrick McMains at Stonewall, Colorado   191

Abreu family at Rayado   201

Mary Tolby Smith and family in Indiana   203

Maps

The Maxwell Land Grant as surveyed and confirmed **xvi**

Colfax County, the Maxwell Land Grant, and adjacent areas of New Mexico and Colorado **xvii**

Table

1. Aggregate Homicide and Lynching Rates in Colfax County, New Mexico, 1870 to 1880 **195**

Preface

An Iowa native, C. L. Sonnichsen devoted time during his career as an English professor in Texas to studying feuds in the nineteenth-century West. Contrary to assumptions, he observed, many people who got involved in violent conflicts were not so much rebelling against the law as improvising to redress grievances in circumstances in which usual instruments of law and justice were nonexistent or too weak to effectively settle civil disputes or to rein in people who were stealing, bullying, or otherwise preying on their neighbors. When people were left to their own resources, he reasoned, feud law might be better than no law at all, but not much better. His objection to the handling of outrageous violations outside the legal system was that "all forms of self-redress, but especially hanging and ambushing, are both catching and habit-forming." "Once men take the law into their own hands," he observed, "they seem unable to lay it down," until compelled to do so by whelming force in the hands of a superior authority.[1]

Something like this occurred in Colfax County, New Mexico, and on the storied Maxwell Land Grant, which covered a large portion of the county and extended into southern Colorado, in the last three decades of the nineteenth century. During that period, at least eleven lynchings took place in Colfax County, and murders—from ambush and otherwise—were common. There were substantive disputes at the root of many confrontations, but frequently they spawned quarrels that became personal. There was also, in this time and place, a steady background of saloon shootings and other violence unrelated to the larger issues.

I first learned about the episodes related here while tenting and hiking in the mountains of northern New Mexico, first as a consumer, then as a teller, of campfire stories. The tales attracted me, as did the mountains, to a lifelong love of New Mexico, its varied landscapes, and its history. The stories were entertaining, full of exotic Native cultures, daunting explorations and conquests, rebellions, murders, gunfights, and a multicultural cast of colorful characters. But they were only stories, and the people in them characters in an imaginary landscape. I felt little sympathy for the parched travelers on the Jornada del Muerto, and no pain for victims and survivors of conquests, shootings, hangings, and all the other calamities. They were just characters in a story.

Much later, I became a chronicler of these events, writing conventional narratives of the Colfax County War for chapters in books on New Mexico's territorial times, focusing on the period between 1875 and 1878. These accounts still kept a safe distance from the bygone days of the nineteenth-century past. Historical context was minimal, and little or no attention was paid to enduring impact on the people, or on later times. Other accounts of these proceedings have been written, most following the conventional pattern.

There is little reason for revisiting these events, if not to provide information not found in previous accounts, or to apply other interpretive perspectives. These are the aspirations that have driven the present work. Its focus on violent conflict in Colfax County, New Mexico, and on the Maxwell Land Grant as finally surveyed, confirmed, and adjudicated, begins with the sale of the Maxwells' claim to a corporate entity in 1870, marking a regime change as significant locally as those of the Spanish conquest of the upper Rio Grande, or the U.S. occupation of New Mexico. This account extends to the end of the nineteenth century, by which time violence over claims of the Maxwell Company had largely subsided. Further intentions for this study were to explore the encounters among cultural and economic factions competing for resources in the region between 1870 and 1900, and to explore and reveal human dimensions, responses, and experiences of those involved, insofar as letters, court testimony, memoirs, contemporaneous reporting, and other credible sources allow.

Did the trouble in Colfax County add up to a war? This question sent Stephen Zimmer, a historian and resident of the county, to the *Merriam-Webster* dictionary, where he pondered two definitions. Seen as "open and declared hostile conflict between states or nations," he concluded, "war" did not fit the sort of blowup that had occurred in the 1870s; but looked at in the broader context of an alternate definition, as "a state of hostility, conflict, or antagonism," the disorder in the Cimarron country qualified easily.[2] But the phrase, "Colfax County War," did not appear for some time, and was not common until the middle of the next century.

The Colfax County War has been characterized by at least one authoritative source, the *New Encyclopedia of the American West*, edited by Howard Roberts Lamar, as "a series of single murders." That is true enough, but it can be stipulated that during its most intense phase, in 1875–1876, murders came thick and fast, and it was fortunate that there weren't more of them. The less frequently mentioned "Maxwell Land Grant War" was a better fit for the "war" metaphor, in that it involved two organized factions engaged in a sharply defined conflict, with multiple incidents and skirmishes taking place over many years. This work embraces the entirety of the conflict that kindled so much violence in the region between 1870 and 1900. The geographic scope of the narrative consists of Colfax County and the Maxwell Land Grant, parts of which lay in southern Colorado. The total region is sometimes referred to here as the "Cimarron country."

Subjects inviting examination include (1) the clash of cultures, including systems of land tenure, law and governance, the economy, and the disposition of conflicting claims on resources; (2) the nature and impact of racial prejudice in intercultural contact and conflict in the American West; and (3) causes and permissive factors that resulted in extraordinary violence in the western territories. Also of interest are federal management of public land and Spanish and Mexican land grant claims, U.S. policy and practice in engaging and containing Native American people in the West; the impact of foreign investment in the Maxwell grant claim; the arrival of the railroad and its effects; and the influence of Gilded Age federal policies in western U.S. territories.

Spelling, especially spelling of proper names, is inconsistent in period newspapers, court records, census rolls, and correspondence, including holographic writings, which provided much of the original source material for the work. The intent has been to spell each name as the person named spelled it, or to determine from varied sources the correct or most common spelling, then use that consistently. Spellings in direct quotations are as found in the quoted material.

The subject matter of this book necessarily involves repeated references to several groups for which cultural or racial identity is pertinent to the discussion. In this respect, multiple options are available for reference to persons by race, cultural group, or origin, but advice concerning use of specific terms has a way of shifting over time. Usage in this work is sometimes suggested by context, with one term more apt in a detached or analytical reference, a different term preferable when relating an event as a story in its historical context, in language as understood by people of the period and place. In all instances, the intent has been to acknowledge the dignity of all groups respecting variations in culture, language, appearance, and other value-neutral characteristics.

The author is beholden to numerous institutions and individuals for their assistance with research as well as sharing of thoughts on the topic. Much of the final work was done during the pandemic of 2020–21, during which several professionals went above and beyond to help with access to documents and images while their facilities were closed to the public. Grateful acknowledgment is extended to professionals and staff specialists at the Center for Southwest Research, University of New Mexico, Albuquerque; Special Collections, New Mexico Highlands University, Las Vegas, NM; Rio Grande Historical Collections, New Mexico State University Special Collections, Las Cruces; Special Collections, Eastern New Mexico University, Portales; New Mexico State Records Center and Archives; Western History Department, Denver Public Library, Denver; Old Mill Museum, Cimarron, NM; Metropolitan Library System, Oklahoma City; Southwest Collection and General Library, Texas Tech University, Lubbock, TX; DeGolyer Library, Southern Methodist University, Dallas; Arthur Johnson Memorial Library, Raton, NM; Church History Library of the Church of Jesus Christ of Latter-Day Saints, Salt Lake City; and History Colorado, Denver.

I am grateful to Chuck Hornung for sharing materials and directing me to the importance of the Springer court house fight in relation to the history of violence in Colfax County; to Linda Davis and Julia Davis Stafford for use of materials in the CS Cattle Company collection; and to Stephen Zimmer and Randolph Roth, who shared insights and pertinent materials. Special thanks are due to Veronica Velarde Tiller and Malcolm Ebright, who each read portions of the narrative and shared their expertise and comments; and to the readers who reviewed the work for the University of Oklahoma Press and provided useful, well-informed advice. Sharon Niederman and James Abreu spoke with me about topics upon which they have special expertise. Quentin Robinson, Lisa Reichard, and James Klaiber permitted use of family photos in the book. Thanks to Frank R. "Skitt" Trujillo for lending pertinent manuscript materials, and to Tai Kreidler for calling my attention to the 1872 Hittson cattle raid. Inspiration for the title of this book came from Agnes Morley Cleaveland, who titled a prefatory note in her book *Satan's Paradise*, "Cimarron Means Wild." The staff at the University of Oklahoma Press and the assigned copyeditor, Kelly Parker, made the book better through application of their diligence and stellar professional skills. A thousand thanks to Mary Caffey for patience, love, and support.

This book is dedicated to four teachers, all deceased. Ann Dunwody was a second-grade teacher in Abilene, Texas, who through her kind encouragement, made me believe I could write. Clovis Bradford taught civics at Abilene's Cooper High School, urging her students to prize and practice citizenship and to engage constructively in affairs of the community and beyond. Lawrence R. Murphy and Charles Leland Sonnichsen were respected university professors, but known to me as friends and role models who encouraged my interest in history and cultures of the Southwest. My thanks to these, and for others who teach or have taught.

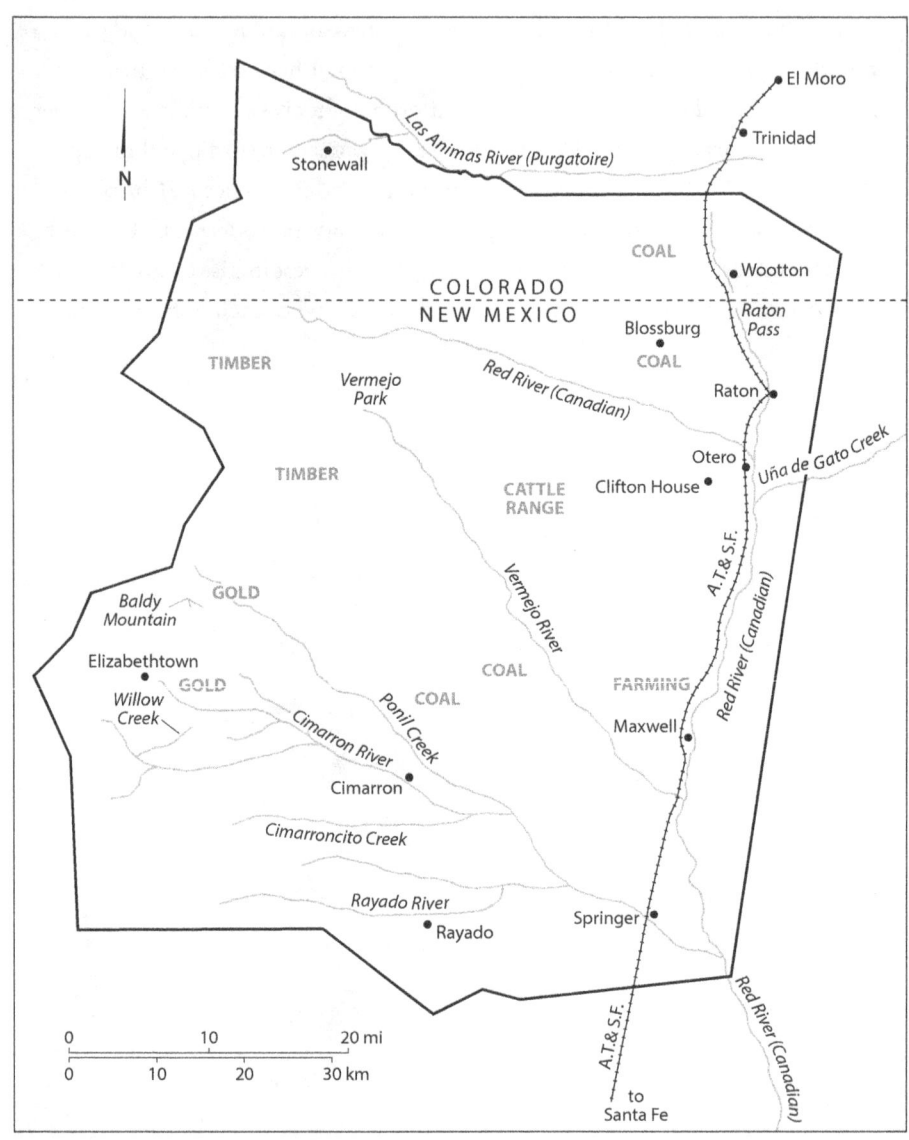

The Maxwell Land Grant as surveyed and confirmed. Cartography by Bill Nelson.

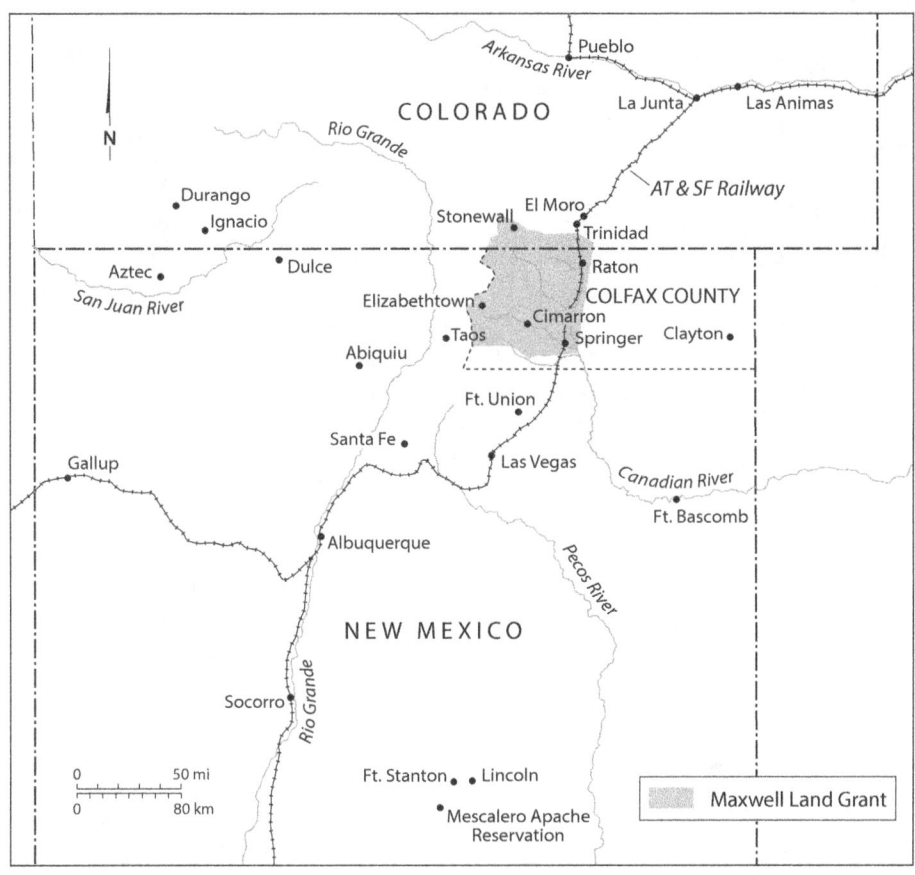

Colfax County, the Maxwell Land Grant, and adjacent areas of New Mexico and Colorado. Cartography by Bill Nelson.

Introduction

When the Northwest Indiana Conference of the Methodist Episcopal Church met in 1873, the presiding bishop called for a missionary to go and work in a region in the northern mountains of New Mexico, a U.S. territory first peopled by Native American tribes, then centuries later by Spanish-Mexican settlers. Population around the Moreno Valley and the Canadian River drainage was growing with an influx of miners and other Euro-Americans, and church elders felt called to send a missionary to preach, teach, build churches, and take the Word to people in need. When a call went forth for a good man to go, there were no takers until the timely appearance of Franklin James Tolby, a young preacher with a wife and two daughters, infant and toddler. Tolby would take the appointment. The *Chicago Inter-Ocean* later explained the hesitance of other men to volunteer: "New Mexico seemed so far away, and the difficulties to be overcome and the trials to be endured so great, that it required an unusual amount of Christian fortitude for the minister to sunder his relations and remove to this far off land."[1]

Franklin and Mary Tolby, with Rachel and Grace, were soon off to make their home in a place they had never seen, one beyond the terminus of the nearest railroad, in a land of high sky, soaring mountains, and wide extended plains. In that fair-seeming land there were many dangers, toils, and snares, and few amenities. Soon after the family's arrival in New Mexico, Tolby sent a letter home to acquaint his sister with the new surroundings, writing, "Cimarron is destined to be the leading city of New Mexico. The word Cimarron is the Spanish for wild, and the city takes its name from the river."[2] The name was also descriptive of the country in a broader sense, for it was a rugged mosaic of mountain and prairie

I

landscapes, remote from the population centers of the United States or Mexico; and it was largely untamed as to the frequent occurrence of violent episodes so common in frontier communities of the late nineteenth-century American West.

As Oliver La Farge would write concerning one of New Mexico's treasured ironies, "It is a land full of the essence of peace, although its history is one of invasions and conflicts."[3] Tolby and his family would too soon experience New Mexico's penchant for violent conflict. In a scant two years, his stricken widow and their precious girls were on their way back to Indiana, leaving husband and papa in a cold grave on a hill just out of Cimarron. His offense? He had spoken and written truth about crime and corruption in the Territory of New Mexico. Tolby's deplorable and untimely murder in September of 1875 became the flashpoint for the most intense convulsion in a long season of turmoil in Colfax County. The crime touched nerves already raw from a variety of causes.

A witness to some of the incidents recalled years later, "It was the killing of the preacher Tolby that got the Colfax County boys up in arms against the official ring at Santa Fe. Of course the interminable fight over the validity and ownership of the Maxwell grant was at the bottom of the assassination, as it was at the bottom of most killing in northern New Mexico in those days." Previous to the murder, "There had been two parties in Colfax County, one representing the grant claimants, backed by the authorities at Santa Fe, and the other consisting of sheep and cattle men and prospectors claiming possession as squatters."[4]

In the 1870s, the West was awash in wars: land grant wars, railroad wars, cattle wars, salt wars, and more, in addition to an ongoing array of Indian wars. Colorado had a Grand Cañon War to decide which railroad company could build in the Grand Cañon of the Arkansas River, upriver to the booming silver-mining town of Leadville. In Texas, El Paso had a Salt War, and in Mason County, the "Hoodoo War" broke out over cattle rustling. In New Mexico, a fight for domination of commerce ignited the Lincoln County War. An antecedent, the Horrell War, was so named for a family that had left recent trouble in Texas to find and make more in New Mexico.

In these days, a "war" was as easily declared as a political ring. All that was necessary for a violent feud to enter the annals of history as a war was to have someone to call it that, preferably in print, and to have the name adopted for general use. The Lincoln County War clearly deserved the designation, as a savage struggle waged by armed cohorts of "House men" and "Regulators," with each side intent on conquering or destroying the other. The paradigm was a good fit, and the expression "Lincoln County War" caught on even as it was in progress. The credentials of some of the other conflicts designated as wars were subject to greater scrutiny.

In the case of the Colfax County War, with its diverse groups and interests, and persistent violence over a longer time period, the picture was not so clear. Some observers of the unfolding rebellion of miners and settlers found the word "war" fitting. With passions running high in the mining camps in 1871, a traveling reporter considered the possibility of "a war in Colfax County, New Mexico."[5] Another paper later informed readers that "a little speck of war" had broken out.[6] But the title "Colfax County War" was slow to catch on. Whatever the turbulence was called, it rolled out over a longer time span that witnessed extraordinary levels of violence, and deaths due to violence, in Colfax County and across the old Beaubien and Miranda Land Grant, later known as the Maxwell Land Grant. The struggle was waged over issues involving ownership and use of the Maxwell property and political control of local governing institutions, but it was, as much as that, a struggle among factions, each having critical interests at stake, complicated by racial and cultural differences and prejudices.

There is some confusion, and substantial overlap, between the Colfax County War and a related conflict, the Maxwell Land Grant War. The two notions correspond in topics, incidents, and persons considered, but there are distinctions. The major struggle in the Colfax County War was one pitting local residents against a powerful political faction known to its detractors as the "Santa Fe Ring," in a battle for control of Maxwell grant resources and local political affairs. The Maxwell Land Grant War was more narrowly concerned with the legal status of the land grant claim. Contending parties in the Maxwell Land Grant War were the Maxwell Company and the miners and settlers and who disputed the company's claim of ownership. The Colfax County War is most often described as having occurred between 1875, when Reverend Tolby was murdered, and 1878, when the so-called Santa Fe Ring was effectively booted from Colfax County after an investigation. The Maxwell Land Grant conflict was a longer slog, eventually involving the more remote Colorado portion of the property in which, for years, settlers not holding any lease or title could build homes and farms or ranches in entirely agreeable isolation, expecting that they would one day be able to claim them under the public land laws.

An attribute of the approach to western American history advocated by Patricia Limerick and others in the late 1980s and early 1990s, as an alternative to the long-revered but problematic notion of a frontier advancing westward across an unsettled wilderness, involves consideration of perspectives and experiences of varied groups that have converged in the North American West. Limerick has detailed the failure of the celebrated Turner thesis as a context for comprehending New Mexico, including the Cimarron country of the 1870s. Wrote Limerick, "The old concept of the frontier—that bipolar opening and closing operation—never looked sillier than it did when applied to New Mexico."[7] She wonders how one would establish when "the frontier" opened and closed in New Mexico, where Spanish settlers traveled north from New Spain in 1598 and where waves of Euro-American settlers and fortune seekers migrated south and west from Missouri and other states across the Santa Fe Trail beginning in 1821. These were preceded by fur trappers and traders who ventured into the Southern Rockies in the early decades of the nineteenth century. In the Cimarron country, many cattlemen and cowboys came from homes in the deep South by way of Texas, after a Civil War that had left some men bitter and demoralized. The original managers of the Maxwell Land Grant and Railway Company came from England, but most of the investors who had put up money for the purchase remained in Europe. Throughout these varied incursions, the Jicarilla Apache and Mouache Ute Indians had been on the defensive on multiple "frontiers," resisting conquest of their homeland as best they could.

The collision of cultures and interests that played out in northern New Mexico and in the Colorado portion of the Maxwell grant between 1870 and 1900 was a major cause of an eruption of violent acts that included assassination, lynching, shoot-outs, score settling and other species of murder, and countless non-lethal injuries. Prevailing conditions in the Cimarron country after the sale of the Maxwell grant pointed to a likely collision. New Mexico before the railroad came was susceptible to Ring rule, involving domination by an elite combination that could wield inordinate sway over federal appointments while sustaining the efficient political machine that facilitated its control in the territory. The federal government contributed to instability in the region through its failure to offer clear decisions regarding the Maxwell grant's legal status and boundaries, leaving competitors to fight it out among themselves for far too long. But this was northern New Mexico in the early 1870s—Colfax County an isolated precinct, minimally or ineffectively policed and, according to wary residents, dominated by local agents of the Santa Fe Ring, who held key public offices and acted as directed by their leaders in the capital.

By 1871, the Maxwell Land Grant, formerly a backwoods estate ruled, more or less, by a former guide and hunter noted for his idiosyncrasies, was newly owned by a foreign corporation motivated by visions of treasure flowing from west to east and across the Atlantic. The "English company" aspired to colonize the estate with farmers, miners, and other settlers from the British Isles, and foresaw railroads crossing the grant, bringing prosperity and generating a hefty return for the capitalists who had many Dutch gilders or pounds sterling invested in the company.

But the vision of the British administration was a contested one. Ute and Jicarilla Apache Indians clung, desperately and futilely, to a homeland that embraced the mountains and plains of the Maxwell Land Grant; and a variety of resources attracted other claimants who were prepared to dispute the questionable and legally unsettled claim of the Maxwell Land Grant and Railway Company. Into the Moreno Valley and Ute Creek, and up the sides of Baldy Mountain, came the hopeful miners. Home seekers desiring free or cheap land on which to establish farms or small ranches migrated in hopes of homesteading or otherwise acquiring tracts of land that they believed belonged to the public domain. Ranchers with larger herds, increasingly cramped in north-central Texas, came seeking cheaper, more abundant grass, and in some cases, a respite from scrutiny of the law. Such men found these things, for a time, along the Red River and its tributaries, grazing their herds on valley and prairie lands that, while legal claims were being sorted out in courts and Congress, could pass for open range. The estate claimed by the English company was vast, but it was too small to accommodate the divergent aspirations of all interested parties. For many sturdy and independent-minded men of the western territories, resort to force was the reflexive response to conflict, so something resembling a war was practically inevitable.

As distant as the chaotic events of the Colfax County War and related conflicts may seem today, their history provides a backward glance at issues that continue to confound Americans in the twenty-first century: the scourge of gun violence and the vexing question of what to do about it; the stubborn curse of racial prejudice and its manifestations; and a tension between democratic ideals and the selfish motives that so frequently afflict the institutions and processes intended to empower those lofty aspirations. Whether there are lessons to be drawn from the experiences of a disordered past in an isolated southwestern territory, or whether readers are simply to understand that the best and worst impulses of human nature are enduring, and perhaps beyond the power of societies to change, is a question left to be pondered by each and all.

CHAPTER I

The Plains People and the Cedar Bark People

Long before the coming of Spanish conquerors, or of traders, troops, and settlers from the United States, Jicarilla Apaches and Mouache Utes inhabited the southern Rocky Mountains and the plains east of the mountains in present-day northern New Mexico and southern Colorado. With a land base of several million acres and a variety of landscapes and climatic zones, they moved about, influenced by the climate and the availability of resources, including water, useful plants, and wildlife that provided sources of food, shelter, and clothing. While these bands did not attain the notoriety of the southern Apaches, Plains Indians, and other indigenous peoples whose deeds and reputations gave them starring roles in stories of conquest and resistance, their fighters were quite capable of defending them against enemy bands in the region. Jicarilla and Ute people were unavoidably important in relation to the Cimarron country and the violence that occurred in the 1870s, because much of the conflict was over possession of ground that lay in the ancient and historic homeland of these Native people.

The Jicarillas, whose heartland encompassed a region drained by the Rayado, Cimarron, Ponil, and Vermejo basins, were comprised of two related but distinct bands. Those who lived in the Cimarron country at least part of each year were known to the Spanish as Llaneros or "Plains people." These indigenous people observed tribal beliefs and traditions, cared for their children, traded, hunted, and managed relationships with other tribes in the region and with their kinsmen of the Ollero band, the "mountain-valley people," who mostly lived farther west.[1]

The Llaneros were friendly with the Mouache Utes, the "cedar bark people," with whom they shared a homeland that was sacred to all.[2] The affinity among the Jicarilla and Ute Natives included amiable social and economic relations, intermarriage, and a durable alliance in warfare, and extended to the Ollero band of the Jicarillas and the several Ute bands that shared a common homeland in the southern Rocky Mountains and adjacent plains. In the mid-1800s, the Llaneros and Mouache Utes normally made winter camp in the lower elevations of the Cimarron country. With the approach of warmer weather, the Utes usually packed their belongings and relocated to the eastern slopes of the Sangre de Cristo Mountains in present-day southern Colorado. There the people could hunt, gather food, and harvest hides for their own use and for trade. Routes of travel were increasingly influenced by the incursions of soldiers and settlers coming to the region under Spanish, Mexican, and U.S. auspices. For the Mouache Utes, this later meant traversing the land claimed as part of the Beaubien and Miranda (or Maxwell) Land Grant, from the southern Rockies through the Stonewall Valley, and southeast to reach the Indian agency at Cimarron, from which provisions were distributed.[3]

The Jicarillas, of Athabascan origin, coalesced over centuries in which several culturally related bands were scattered across a wide area of northern New Mexico and adjacent mountains and plains, but combined to assume one tribal identity. Over some three centuries of exploration, conquest, and settlement, dating from the Coronado expedition of 1540–1542, Spanish authorities and the Mexican regime that followed added to their store of information regarding the divisions, cultural characteristics, and alliances of the indigenous people. By the time U.S. troops and officials imposed their authority on New Mexico in 1846, the Jicarilla tribe had taken on the enduring structure of two bands united by culture, familial relationships, and alliance, occupying distinct but proximate orbits.[4] Divisions among the Ute people, characterized by differences in geographic domain and governance, were also recognized by the newcomers.

Through centuries of change, the indigenous people of the Cimarron country, particularly the Jicarillas more closely identified with northeastern New Mexico, have exhibited remarkable resilience and flexibility as a people, helping them preserve their tribal identities and cultures in spite of various threats and encroachments on the homeland. "Indeed," observed anthropologist and historian Dolores Gunnerson, "Jicarilla history illustrates the Southern Athabascan talent for adapting to changed circumstances without losing the hard core of their cultural integrity; in fact, it is probably to this talent that the Jicarillas owe their survival."[5] It was an attribute that would be severely tested.

Through nearly three centuries of contact with the Spanish regime preceding the Mexican Revolution, the Jicarillas were able to adapt, adjust, and coexist. Veronica E. Velarde Tiller notes that her ancestors' way of life did not change radically with the coming of Spanish colonists. The Jicarilla people lived peaceably apart from, but in proximity to, Spanish settlers, and added words from the Spanish to their own vocabularies. They welcomed Spanish material goods and quickly adapted to the use of horses for work and warfare.[6] As described by B. Sunday Eiselt in her study of Jicarilla archaeology and ethnology, *Becoming White Clay*, their success was partly attributable to their capacity to persist in "enclaves" amid immigrant peoples who were culturally and racially different, remaining "intact, distinctive, and discernible" as indigenous people, while interacting constructively with newcomers.[7]

With the arrival of explorers, traders, trappers, prospectors, soldiers, and settlers from the United States, Canada, and western Europe came successive waves of change, including changes that would ultimately prove devastating to indigenous people in New Mexico and across western North America. Differences between the Natives and non-Hispanic white newcomers in language and appearance were notable, but differences in values, technology, and regulating norms in laws and customs were still more consequential. Differences in the weapons made by the Natives and those brought by the American military were daunting. Advances of foreign intruders into spaces previously controlled by Native people were threatening and confusing, and sometimes provoked determined resistance.

Spanish-Mexican colonizers and westering white Americans and Europeans implemented different strains of oppression and exploitation, including the sanctioned use of Pueblo Indians in forced labor.[8] Most unnerving were white American attitudes concerning exclusive ownership of property and a habit of making and breaking treaties based on political pressure. The intruders' systematic and unstinting decimation of beaver in the mountains and great buffalo herds on the prairies must have been horrifying to Indian eyes, destroying the essential food staple and threatening the very survival of Native peoples. The destabilization of traditional lifeways increased the vulnerability of the Jicarillas, Utes, and other Native peoples, and their seasonal migrations and movements for purposes of trade and hunting gave the impression that the land they used was unsettled and open for claims by immigrant settlers. Public land laws often provided legal cover for appropriation or theft of land occupied by Plains or nomadic Indians, who had not been regarded by the American government as historic and rightful owners of western lands.

There were significant differences among the Pueblo people inhabiting villages along the Rio Grande and mobile tribes like the Utes and Jicarillas. The village dwellers occupied durable structures and raised corn, squash, and other crops. They were peaceful unless severely provoked, but were vulnerable to the abuses of *encomenderos* who, by authority of the Spanish Crown, were granted use of Native labor. However, the Spanish government offered some protection for Native territory, acknowledging land rights of the Pueblos as early as 1704 in law through which each of the pueblos was entitled to four square leagues of land, informally known as the "pueblo league," a measure equal to about 17,350 acres.[9] Even earlier documents have been offered as proof of the intent of the Spanish to protect Pueblo lands in perpetuity.[10]

Utes and Jicarilla Apaches living in the rugged, sparsely peopled mountain country north of Taos were less vulnerable to abuses, but neither did their nomadic lifestyles invite the kinds of acknowledgment of ownership that came to the Pueblos in the form of legal title to the lands they were living on. The Utes and Jicarillas suffered a progressive diminution of their homeland and the resources that sustained them, and they would not be situated on satisfactory reservations until nearly two centuries after the earliest formal allocations of land to the Pueblos.

A distinction between the relatively stable Pueblos and the more nomadic tribes was still notable in 1870, when special agent William Frederick Milton Arny conducted a census of Native populations, grouping tribal entities under two classes: "the Indian Pueblos of New Mexico" and "the Wild Tribes of New Mexico," including Utes, Apaches, and Navajos.[11] Despite its common use prior to 1870, the descriptor "wild," in preference to a more benign term reflecting the Native tribes' mobility and use of freestanding family habitations like tipis and hogans, was unfortunate, likely reinforcing for readers distant from Indian country the impression of indigenous people as savages unworthy of acceptance as equal beings.

The year 1858 has been identified as a critical turning point for American Indians of the western mountains and plains.[12] In that year, in the estimation of William Bent, Indian agent for the Upper Arkansas Agency in Colorado and member of a prominent frontier trading family, the discovery of gold in Colorado had set off a rush of at least sixty thousand fortune-seeking immigrants.[13] Already pressed by the encroachments of gold seekers and an advancing mass of settlers moving westward beyond Kansas and the Platte River, the Indians of Colorado and the greater West were about to see a snowballing of the forces that decimated their land base and food supply, and that aggravated the nearly inevitable violence accompanying such intrusions.

An Enduring Alliance

By the 1870s, the Mouache Utes and Jicarilla Apaches found themselves equally unwelcome in their homeland, living several months each year in the cauldron of economic and cultural conflict that was Colfax County, New Mexico. They had long been on friendly terms—distinct peoples, but allies in war and increasingly related by intermarriage between their bands and, more broadly, among both the Llanero and Ollero bands of the Jicarillas and the numerous bands comprising the Ute people.

Together and separately, the Apaches and southern Utes first resisted Spanish attempts to settle in the mountains and valleys north of Taos, which they had long regarded as their homeland. They fought off Hispano settlers through the first half of the eighteenth century, sometimes allied with Plains tribes, other times with Navajos.[14] By the mid-1700s, the Utes had turned away from some of their historic allies, including Comanches, and were gravitating toward the Jicarillas. The friendship between the Utes and Jicarillas would endure down to modern times.[15] By 1779, when the Mouache Utes and Jicarillas joined Spanish forces of Governor Juan Bautista de Anza to fight off Comanche raiders, the alliance was well established. An accommodation had been reached with the Spanish, whereby Indian and Spanish forces fought common enemies when cooperation was mutually beneficial.[16] Further, Spanish settlement had not threatened the way of life or survival of the Utes and Jicarillas who, in fact, benefitted from increased trade with the Spanish.[17]

When Mexico had attained independence from Spain in 1821 and New Mexico had come under a new regime, the initial impact was minimal. During the quarter century of Mexican rule, however, authorities became concerned with growing threats on New Mexico's northern frontier, from the Navajos, from Comanche, Kiowa, Arapaho, and Cheyenne Indians, and from the upstart Republic of Texas, which was eager to extend its boundaries and influence.[18] In defense of Mexican territory, and often in a spirit of self-dealing, governors of the Mexican province of

New Mexico, including Manuel Armijo, awarded large grants in the north beyond Taos and nearby settlements, in the homeland of the Utes and Jicarillas. Actions of the Santa Fe administration were subject to Mexican law, but oversight was minimal, and liberties were taken. Government officials in Santa Fe dispensed more land in a quarter century than Spanish officials had in two centuries.[19] Grants were initially restricted to Mexican citizens, but aliens later could petition for land in partnership with Mexican citizens. Government officials, Armijo and others, sometimes obtained personal interests in these prized emoluments.

The grants, ostensibly transferring property claimed by Mexico to private parties, marked the first "taking" of these Ute and Jicarilla lands, without consent or compensation, by a colonial power. Among the Mexican grants was one awarded to Charles Hipolite Trotier Beaubien—Don Carlos—a man of French Canadian origin; and Guadalupe Miranda, a Mexican citizen. The grant was approved in January 1841. Rites of possession conferred formal custody on the recipients in 1843. Under Mexican law the tract should have included no more than eleven square leagues for each grantee, or approximately ninety-seven thousand acres.[20] Confirmed, patented, and litigated to a conclusion by the American government years later, the grant grew to several times that size in the hands of creative speculators, and was made to conform to the Euro-American notion of absolute ownership, notwithstanding the prior continuous occupation by indigenous people.

The American occupation of New Mexico in 1846 brought further trauma and a new and confusing amalgam of values and attitudes, expressed in assumed cultural and racial superiority, use of military force to maintain control, and aggressive settlement. Within a few years, the Mexican-American War, the Mexican Cession of territory including much of the present-day American Southwest, and an act of Congress giving New Mexico territorial status made U.S. governance a permanent fact of life for people of the American-occupied borderlands.

While the size and boundaries of the Beaubien and Miranda grant remained in dispute for some years, Maxwell understood it to include, at a minimum, the settlement on the Rayado River at which Maxwell and Kit Carson had first built homes and established agricultural enterprises, the mountains and plains drained by the Cimarron River, streams and grasslands to the north, and Maxwell's headquarters on the Cimarron. Indigenous people continued to occupy their historic homelands, even as settlers and fortune seekers came expecting to find lands that they could own and use. The years between 1846 and 1887, when the Ute and

Jicarilla people were at last settled on reservations, marked a time of vulnerability, instability, and loss of land and resources, posing a severe test of cultural resilience and tribal strength.[21]

Fighting the Frontier Army

Contact between the U.S. Army and the Apache, Ute, and Navajo Indians of New Mexico began almost immediately following the military occupation of New Mexico. Forts built in the 1850s and 1860s were strategically located in areas of concentrated Indian-settler contact. In the heart of the Jicarilla-Ute country was Fort Union, built in 1851 near the junction of the mountain branch of the Santa Fe Trail, a route that brought travelers over Raton Pass; and the "Cimarron Cut-off," a more direct route across the plains from Missouri. For four decades, from the 1850s through the 1880s, Fort Union's central mission in New Mexico was to protect travelers from the states, and to help make the country safe for settlement and commerce. American troops actively pursued Indians of the mobile tribes to suppress raiding or force confinement to reservations; and they acted to keep or restore peace between angry settlers and Native Americans. Sometimes the Jicarillas and Mouache Utes were among the "hostiles" pursued and engaged by cavalry soldiers. At other times, warriors of these groups were enlisted as willing scouts, who were ready to help the U.S. troops fight Comanches, Kiowas, and other enemies who mostly stayed on the plains farther east.

Positions on "the Indian problem" seemed to vary with the role and proximity to Indian country of the observer; even so, firsthand experience with indigenous people did not guarantee enlightenment. Extremes in proposed federal policy could be found in Washington and on the frontier, even among officers commanding posts and troops in zones of contact. Countering civil officials who advocated humane accommodation of displaced Indians were territorial governors and legislators demanding early and complete removal of the Natives from regions coveted by white settlers and speculators. Twenty years past his term as commissioner of Indian Affairs, George Manypenny issued a harsh judgment on U.S. military commanders, and specifically on General James Carleton. Carleton was quoted as ordering Kit Carson, as an officer in service of the army, to make war on the Mescalero Apaches and other Native men his troops might encounter. "All Indian men are to be killed," he specified, "whenever and wherever you can find them."[22] Some field officers gave contrary opinions, disputing the accuracy of charges against the Native people and declining to unjustly attack or punish them at the behest of self-interested whites.

Though opinions varied widely, even among responsible officials in the territories, there were usually at least a few who understood the root of most difficulties between the Native tribes and settler populations. With increasing immigrant populations claiming land, killing or scaring away game, and otherwise reducing the base of subsistence for Indians, the usual skills no longer sufficed to sustain them. In 1854, acting governor William Messervy stated the matter plainly to his contacts in Washington: the choice left to the Jicarillas of New Mexico was to "steal or starve."[23] This situation was reported time and again over two decades before any stability for the Utes and Jicarillas was attained. No apparent thought was given to the notion that the indigenous people, by virtue of historic occupation, should be regarded as rightful owners of the land, entitled to their territorial integrity or just compensation.

Conditions leading to the "steal or starve" conundrum had been worsening for some time. The change from Mexican to U.S. administration put added pressure on the roving Native bands, bringing regular surveillance and more effective military response as more forts were built. After a period of resistance, the Pueblos made peace and received assurances respecting the security of their lands. The "wild" or more mobile tribes, however, were left to fend for themselves, leading to trouble with settlers and soldiers.

The Ute-Jicarilla alliance and the U.S. Army were essentially on a war footing for nearly a decade, from the American occupation to the end of hostilities in September 1855. When U.S. officers determined the necessity of punishing or defeating the Indians, they dispatched troops of horse soldiers to trail the moving bands, attack, and inflict death and discouragement. The forays worked, as judged by depletion of Native populations; they were not so effective in extinguishing cultures or the will to survive. In March 1854, a band of Jicarillas, including approximately one hundred fighting men, gave the U.S. military one of its worst defeats in the West in an encounter between Cienguilla—later called Pilar—and Picuris Pueblo, inflicting heavy losses and sending a force of approximately sixty dragoons into in a hasty retreat. Success was brief, as the U.S. forces soon mounted an attack and established control in the region; the engagement, however, demonstrated the capacity of the Jicarilla warriors to counter a superior force using sound tactics and a mastery of local geography.[24]

The Utes and Jicarillas fought the pursuing soldiers from the Arkansas River to Taos and Abiquiu; from Rayado and Maxwell's ranch to the Chama Valley and beyond. By August 1855, suffering had taken its toll and the Native chiefs were ready to end the fighting. The Capote Utes living near Abiquiu were the first to agree to peace terms, meeting with Governor David Meriwether and the Indian agent, Lorenzo Labadie, on August 8, 1855. Treaties with Mouache and Jicarilla Apache leaders followed.[25] Instances of raiding, hunger-induced pilferage, and settler complaints persisted, but, wrote one historian about the Utes, "Never again did any of the three Southern Ute Bands engage in warfare with the United States."[26] The treaties of 1855 were never ratified by Congress, so a viable plan ensuring security and cultural survival for these indigenous people in a permanent homeland remained painful years away.[27]

Exiles in Their Homeland

The Office of Indian Affairs, operating under a commissioner of Indian Affairs, occupied a critical position in representing Washington to the western tribes and administering its policies and services. The agency was organized under the Department of War, but in 1849 was moved to the Department of the Interior. To the government in Washington, the Ute and Jicarilla people of New Mexico and southern Colorado were essentially homeless until settled on reservations in the late 1870s and 1880s. Meanwhile, the assigned Indian agent served as a link to centers of power and the distributor of rations and "presents" provided to sustain them and avert trouble with non-Indians. The agent's capacity to resolve issues involving Indian residents was limited. The agent could participate in the drafting of treaties, but ratification by Congress was uncertain, and often did not follow.

The tenure of Indian agents was generally short, and agents varied greatly in their ability and zeal for the work. A few were highly competent, dedicated, and thoughtful as to the nature of Native cultures, ethical issues at hand, and measures likely to yield favorable results. Others were job seekers and political appointees with no particular calling for the work and little interest in educational and other activities not expressly required of them. Some were openly disparaging of Native people, denigrating them as lazy, morally degraded, and unlikely to be worthy members of a civilized society.

The grant made to Carlos Beaubien and Guadalupe Miranda, later owned by Beaubien's son-in law, Lucien Maxwell, proved favorable, at least for a time, for the Apaches and Utes who had lived in and around the Cimarron country for generations. Presumably Maxwell valued the business that came his way as a contractor selling beef and other supplies to the government for distribution to the Indians, and for consumption by military forces stationed on the frontier for purposes of protecting settlers, deterring conflict, controlling the Indians, and keeping the peace. As the claimant to a tract of uncertain dimensions and with vaguely defined boundaries, Maxwell may have felt he had no choice but to accommodate the Natives whose use of the land had endured through many generations, predating the arrival of the Spanish explorers. In any case, Maxwell's influence likely delayed the day of final displacement and dispossession, when the Utes and Jicarillas of the Cimarron country would be sent to distant reservations.

Following the American occupation in 1846; victory in a war with Mexico, 1846–48; annexation of the Mexican Cession; and an interval of doubt regarding the boundaries and future status of the newly claimed lands, New Mexico was made a U.S. territory in 1850. Between the end of open war with the U.S. troops in 1855 and relocation of the tribes on reservations—1878 for the Mouache Utes and 1887 for the Jicarilla Apaches—these bands, each numbering several hundred people, were tossed from pillar to post, while an ineffectual bureaucracy struggled to meet their needs and negotiate the rugged terrain of Washington politics. The leading strategy in Congress was to consolidate Native people on as few reservations as possible, but Indian politics also played a role, as some tribes refused to share a homeland with certain others, and all wanted to be located in their home country. Various schemes, such as sending the Jicarillas to live with the Mescaleros and locating all Utes on a vast reservation in western Colorado, were proposed but failed for one reason or another.

Without a protected legal home, Utes and Jicarillas moved about an increasingly crowded range. Many gravitated to agencies at Abiquiu or Taos for scheduled distributions. Some endured temporary exile on proposed reservation lands, by order of federal officials who appeared to be most concerned about pacifying impatient settlers. Many Jicarillas and Mouache Utes returned to Maxwell's ranch. Despite increased settlement by Hispanic farmers and Euro-Americans, Natives for whom the Cimarron country was a familiar home expected at least some degree of protection from starvation and attack. They would return to the heartland repeatedly until they were offered a satisfactory alternative or forced to leave.

Beginning in January 1854, Kit Carson had assumed the office of Indian agent, headquartered in his adopted home village of Taos.[28] He continued in this capacity until 1861, when he resigned to accept a commission in the Union army. His replacement was William F. M. Arny, an idealist and reformer with a penchant for personal and political conflict.[29]

Concurrent with Arny's appointment as agent for the Mouache Utes and the Jicarillas, the decision was taken to relocate the agency from Taos to Cimarron—across the high mountains to a country preferred by many of the Indians and where, it was hoped, intoxicating spirits would be less readily accessible. Maxwell was eager to supply the agency with beef, flour, and other goods, and he may have regarded the Indian population as a valued buffer to more hostile bands.

Arny believed he might fashion a model agency that would do more than dispense rations and try to curtail conflict with settlers. The Cimarron Agency, he thought, could supply the means for and instruction in farming, and could establish a school for Indian children. Arny detailed this approach in his annual report to the commissioner of Indian Affairs, dated September 24, 1861, when he had been on the job for two months.[30] In his report to the commissioner a year later, he could claim surprising progress toward realization of his vision. He had obtained federal funding, two thousand dollars for purchase of supplies and construction of an office, warehouse, and schoolroom. He had obtained, from Maxwell, a lease on a tract of 1,280 acres on Ponil Creek. The layout was complete, and the agency was ready to test Arny's concept.[31] It was not the ultimate solution to the problems of the Natives or the government, but it expressed an optimism for the futures of the Indian people that most agents could not have conceived.

The report was Arny's last as Indian agent for the Utes and Jicarillas, for he had already accepted appointment as territorial secretary for New Mexico. His intentions were undoubtedly honorable, and perhaps practical for an agent of his ability and vision, but his successor, Levi J. Keithly, was not possessed of much vision or zeal, nor were most of the ones who followed. The facilities on Ponil Creek were soon abandoned, along with the hopeful policy they were intended to support.[32] For the Native people of the Cimarron country, the times ahead offered a reversion to the familiar experiences of insufficient support, neglect of social needs, negation of ownership rights, unremitting calls for removal, and repeated false starts in designating viable reservations.

War and Uncertain Peace

History accords the Chiricahuas and other Apaches in southern New Mexico and Arizona distinction as fighters of epic ferocity, ruthlessness, and cunning. Apart from the Navajos, northern New Mexico's Natives are not so renowned in this regard, but the bravery and resourcefulness of the Jicarillas and of the Mouache Utes were well established in the hostilities ending in 1855. Although they had recently been at peace, these warriors still knew how to fight. With trouble afoot in the form of attacks by Plains Indians in the summer of 1864, word reached military commanders that the tribes at Cimarron were willing to help the army fight their old enemies. Having delivered the Navajos into captivity at Fort Sumner, Kit Carson was directed to Maxwell's ranch to enlist a company of scouts who would fight with the soldiers in a campaign to subdue and punish the Comanche and Kiowa hostiles.[33] When the force departed Fort Bascom on the Canadian River, some seventy-five Ute and Jicarilla scouts were there to join the march.

The Indian scouts and the soldiers, including infantry, cavalry, and a battery of howitzers, marched downriver under Carson's command. Two weeks later, they came upon Comanche and Kiowa villages scattered along the Canadian near the old fort known as Adobe Walls. With just over three hundred fighting men, mounted and afoot, and the fearsome howitzers, Carson's force faced upward of a thousand Comanche and Kiowa warriors, perhaps as many as three thousand, encamped in the villages along the Canadian.[34] Badly outnumbered, Carson directed a strategic fight, backtracking to an enemy village where powder was destroyed and buffalo robes and other goods were carried off by the Ute and Jicarilla scouts or were burned. Approximately sixty of the enemy were killed, compared to two soldiers and a scout among the bluecoats.[35] Though not an outright triumph, the fight dealt a hard blow to the Plains Indians, persuading at least some of the leaders that peace on the white man's terms might be their only option. In the view of an eminent historian of the Comanches, Rupert Norval Richardson, the moderate success of the troops and their Ute and Apache allies had proved that a once formidable obstacle to white settlement "was being broken down." However remote their camps, the lords of the South Plains would not again feel safe "from the terrible vengeance of the soldiers."[36]

The Utes and Apaches had already faced the same reality. They returned to their families to await the determination of their own uncertain future, having experienced the exhilaration and the ultimate risk of battle with their mortal enemies, for perhaps the last time.

Into the Unknown

Francis A. Walker was a brilliant economist, statistician, military historian, educator, and public servant of the nineteenth century. In a brief tenure as commissioner of Indian Affairs, he sized up the ethical issues raised by the rush to settle and develop western lands as no one before him had done. For him, the great migration amounted to a great taking of lands owned by Native people and created a clear obligation requiring that the American people provide some means for those displaced in the process to have a viable livelihood in place of the one destroyed. "Had the settlements of the United States not been extended beyond the frontier of 1867," he declared, "all the Indians would to the end of time have found upon the plains an inexhaustible supply of food and clothing." Even as he wrote in 1872, Walker thought that a halt to settlement could give the indigenous people hope of a sustainable traditional lifestyle, but he warned that another five years would leave them "reduced to an habitual condition of suffering from want of food."[37] Walker knew his views were at odds with the national mood and political realities, and that useful policy probably was not forthcoming. He moved on in his career, but the Jicarilla Apaches and the Mouache Utes were left to face the future that Walker had described.

Federal authorities had attempted to negotiate treaties, including provisions for relocation to one or more reservations, to accommodate the diverse bands making up the Ute nation. Efforts were made to do this in 1863 and 1868, but the Mouache Utes were wary of these proposals and wanted to remain near the Cimarron Agency, in a homeland that was increasingly compromised by white settlement and diminishing sources of food and shelter.

In September 1866, A. B. Norton, superintendent of Indian Affairs for New Mexico, put forth a suggestion more likely to please the Utes and Jicarillas, but less likely to pass muster with the Office of Indian Affairs. "Upon the supposition that they will not voluntarily consent to leave their present locality," Norton wrote, "would respectfully recommend that they be located on a reservation in the region of country now occupied by them, in order to save trouble, expense, or warfare in removing them."[38] Norton pointed to a tract on the Rayado, south of Maxwell's ranch headquarters, that he thought could be purchased for fifty

In June 1868, Indian Agent William F. M. Arny (*back center*) met with Ute and Jicarilla chiefs at Santa Fe to talk about a proposed treaty of peace with the Navajos. Jicarilla men were Huero Mundo (*back row, first from left*); Panteleon (*front row, first*); and Vicenti (*back row, fourth*). Among several Utes were Martine (*front row, third from left*); Corinea (*front row, fourth*); and Sobotar (*back row, sixth*). Photo by Nicholas Brown Studio. Courtesy Palace of the Governors Photo Archives (NMHM/DCA), neg. 045814.

thousand dollars, complete with good water, timber and farmland, and buildings suitable for a variety of uses. Norton likely realized that the idea had little chance of acceptance, but the seed had been planted.

As long as the Utes and Jicarillas remained near Cimarron, it was considered necessary to maintain troops in the area to keep the peace. In council with the army officers, chiefs of the two bands made clear their attachment to the land. "We are separate and never made any treaty with the Great Father," the leaders insisted; "We travel over no lands but this; we know no other land and want to stay here. Sometimes we go off but we come back here to this land again."[39]

In his 1867 annual report, Superintendent Norton put forward a specific and impassioned proposal for purchase of the Maxwell grant as a reservation for Utes and Jicarilla Apaches still living near Cimarron. The entire grant, approximately 1.5 million acres, Norton stated, could be bought for $250,000, or about 16¢ per acre, and the Natives would be self-sustaining within a year.[40] Norton's assumption may have been excessively hopeful, but if based on serious talks with Maxwell, the proposition offered an opportunity to avoid displacing the Indians, while improving their capacity for self-support.

The proposal was a long shot at best, and it went nowhere. That no such possibility could be seriously considered or worked out with Lucien Maxwell, who manifestly had more sympathy for the Indians than anyone else in a position to help locate a permanent reservation, is more than regrettable, especially considering that Maxwell ended up with little to show for the claim only a few years after making a high-profile, high-dollar sale of the grant to brokers, who in turn flipped the property to British capitalists. Norton's idea was quashed, in part, by the discovery of gold in the Moreno Valley, a rush of prospectors to the area, and radical new ideas about the value of the property under consideration. For the Plains people and the Cedar Bark people, time was running out. As the homeland was being overrun by miners and settlers, and the end of its administration under Maxwell's casual benevolence was approaching, a durable solution to the settlers' "Indian problem" and the Native peoples' homelessness problem remained conspicuously elusive.

CHAPTER 2

Lucien Maxwell, Master of the Cimarron

Lucien Bonaparte Maxwell would have lived a remarkable life had he done no more than participate in two of John C. Frémont's expeditions in the American West and form a lifelong friendship with Christopher "Kit" Carson. As it happened, greater distinction, related to his own deeds and good fortune, was yet to come. As a young man, Maxwell had set out from the family home in Illinois, heading west and southwest. Eventually he landed in the village of Taos, near the ancient Pueblo of Taos, in the early 1840s. The border region was then under authority of the Republic of Mexico. It was in connection with the immense but vaguely delineated Beaubien and Miranda Land Grant, across the mountains northeast of Taos, that Maxwell had his life's most improbable adventure, attaining legendary status in his own lifetime.

The secret to Maxwell's success? There were many. He was willing to risk and to try the unknown. He was a shrewd man, not afraid of work, a person at ease among people of languages and cultures different from his own. Most of the time, he was a good judge of character. He was able to live in extraordinary comfort, or in the most primitive of circumstances. Also, he married well, taking as his wife María de la Luz Beaubien, the eldest daughter of Charles, or Don Carlos, and María Paula Lobato Beaubien, in May 1842.

Beginning in 1848, when he led an advance party in planting a settlement on the banks of the Rayado River, Maxwell was the dominant figure on the Beaubien and Miranda grant. At that time he was acting essentially as an agent for his father-in-law, Beaubien, who was authorized on behalf of others with financial interest in the grant to work toward settlement and development of property. Tentative efforts to establish a ranch at Rayado began as early as March 1848, but were thwarted, first by severe winter storms, then by the unfortunate Manco Burro Pass incident, in which Maxwell and a party of merchants and laborers were attacked by Jicarilla warriors while returning from business in southern Colorado.[1] Maxwell was severely injured and lost valuable mules, horses, and deerskins in the attack, and was in poor shape when his party was helped to safety by a detachment of soldiers directed to the area. Maxwell did not give up on the Rayado venture. In 1849, he took up the effort with renewed determination, working with Carson to establish a permanent settlement. Lucien and Luz Maxwell and their young family made a home at the Rayado crossing on the mountain branch of the Santa Fe Trail. There Maxwell and Carson worked to establish farming, ranching, and trading enterprises.

Relatively little is recorded of Maxwell's time at Rayado between 1849 and 1857, but his activities, with Carson and then alone or with other partners, included raising sheep and cattle, trading to travelers on the trail, and leasing space to and selling provisions to the U.S. Army for its operations at Rayado and elsewhere in the region. The 1850 census listed Carson as a farmer, but farming developed slowly at Rayado. Carson and Maxwell were often away from the settlement in the early years, leading a trapping party to Colorado and Wyoming in 1851 and spending most of 1853 driving sheep to market in California.[2] Carson soon returned to his home in Taos and left Maxwell to develop the property on his own. Despite the intermittent assignment of a garrison of soldiers from Fort Union to protect settlers, security from Indian raiding was a threat throughout the family's years on the Rayado. By 1857, for this reason and others related to business matters, Maxwell determined to move his headquarters from Rayado to a location on the Cimarron River. The Rayado tract, conveyed to Maxwell by his wife's parents, was first sold to José Pley. After a divorce, Pley sold the property to Jesús Abreu and his wife, Petra Beaubien Abreu, sister of Luz.[3]

Maxwell's Ranch

Maxwell and his wife, Luz, stood to inherit a portion of the Beaubien and Miranda grant, and in 1858, they purchased the large interest owned by Guadalupe Miranda, who had fled to Mexico ahead of the American occupation. At some time Maxwell must have devoted his effort to acquisition of the entire claim, including all shares owned by Luz's siblings and those held by descendants of the slain governor, Charles Bent. Lucien purchased remaining family shares after Beaubien's death in 1864, and by 1867, the Maxwells had purchased all shares, notwithstanding a lawsuit waged on behalf of one of the Bent heirs.[4] According to Lawrence R. Murphy, Lucien Maxwell encouraged use of the name "Maxwell Land Grant" beginning in 1867.[5] Newspapers promptly adopted the usage, but government entities were hesitant to use a term varying from the "Beaubien and Miranda" title associated with the property in public documents. Federal agencies and courts later began referring to the property as the "Maxwell Land Grant," endowing the term with official recognition as it came into more general use.

The legend indicated by comparisons of Lucien Maxwell to a duke, baron, king, or feudal lord, is strongly associated with his years on the Cimarron and the great house that was the center of business and social life in the world that Maxwell made and ruled. The house was built about 1858 under supervision of John Holland, long a fixture in the Maxwell household, who had built a home and outbuildings at Rayado before 1850.[6] In 1864, a visiting writer described Maxwell's home as "one of the biggest and best, nicest and neatest" in the territory. He observed,

> The building is of mud or adobe walls, but so architecturally exact and elegantly finished, whitewashed, shingle roofed, large windows, handsome fences, *portales* or porticoes, with a *placita* or courtyard in the rear, containing dining rooms, cooking rooms, store rooms and servant's rooms, carpeted parlors, mammoth mirrors, &c., surrounded on the outside by handsomely fenced lawns, avenues, gateways &c., that it seems at a distance and indeed near at hand, many times more remarkable than any one of those large two-story frame or stone structures that one could see in the suburbs of Lancaster, Pa. or Independence, Mo.[7]

When touring the Maxwells' home a few years later, the wife of a Fort Union officer noticed a grand hall, the general gathering place in the home. The visitor, Olive Ennis, whose husband was a cavalry officer stationed at the fort, also admired a tastefully decorated sitting room identified as "Virginia's parlor," for Maxwell's most favored daughter.[8] Across the placita, Ennis visited the kitchen overseen by Dinah, a Black woman who had cooked for the Maxwells for more years than she could remember. Others who visited the home remarked on the separate dining rooms for men and women, set in expectation of thirty or more guests who might have a meal there during a normal day.

Maxwell's revenue-producing enterprises also expanded. On the Cimarron, he engaged in farming, stock raising, and selling goods to travelers and settlers. When Cimarron became the agency for Ute and Jicarilla Apache Indians in the area, his contracting business with the federal government greatly expanded. He also continued selling beef to the government to supply troops at Fort Union, who were routinely dispatched to Maxwell's whenever there was conflict with the Natives, or between Natives and settlers. In 1864, he built the stone mill in which grain was ground into flour. He built a sawmill to produce lumber. After gold was discovered on the grant in 1866, Maxwell had another lucrative resource to develop. He invested in quartz mills and in the "big ditch" meant to bring needed water to placer sites.

According to several witnesses, it was Maxwell's standing practice to welcome visitors to his table, sometimes offering a bed or shelter. He expected and took no payment for the courtesy and did not want be bothered with handling money for gestures that he saw as incidental costs of rural hospitality. Colonel Henry Inman's *The Old Santa Fe Trail* (1897), the most widely circulated and borrowed account of Maxwell's lifestyle, is sometimes criticized for descriptions viewed by some historians as romanticized portrayals of a life, in Inman's words, "lived in a sort of barbaric splendour, akin to the nobles of England at the time of the Norman conquest."[9] Many of Inman's depictions of life at "Maxwell's Ranche," however, are corroborated in accounts that preceded his early portrayals of Maxwell, as published in 1891.[10]

In 1864, O. J. Goldrick of the *Daily Rocky Mountain News*, told readers that "nearly a hundred" people regularly were fed at Maxwell's tables, requiring daily rations of "one whole ox, three or four sheep and nearly a sack of flour, a sack of sugar and one of coffee."[11] As a child, Agnes Morley Cleaveland, the young daughter of an officer of the Maxwell Company in the mid-1870s, had the run of the former Maxwell home. She recalled being told that an average of twenty persons had been served at each meal during Maxwell's time, not counting "those who were fed directly from the kitchens," which when included, might have brought the total nearer the hundred diners cited by Goldrick.[12] Proud of the single grand piano that graced her family's home on the frontier, Agnes told of her wonder at seeing four grand pianos, two each upstairs and down, in Maxwell's great house.[13] The instruments presumably had been purchased by Maxwell, but were still present some years later, when Agnes reported seeing them.

Maxwell's ranch headquarters, during its long heyday, had to be a bustling place, with his family, servants, storekeepers, millers, and livestock handlers. Cavalry soldiers from Fort Union were often in the area, sometimes passing through, sometimes encamped for peacekeeping duty. Ration days brought crowds of Jicarilla Apaches and Mouache Utes, but peaceful Indians were welcome and could be seen around Maxwell's home on most days.[14]

Maxwell's orbit extended from the headquarters ranch to distant pastures and the fertile valleys of the Cimarron and adjacent drainages. Along the agricultural section of the Cimarron, Goldrick observed in 1864, "There are over a hundred Mexican laborers, tenantry or peones pro tem of Maxwell's, who live or rather subsist by cultivating small patches, on the shares."[15] Estimates of Maxwell's workforce varied. Said William Ryus, a stage coach driver who stopped at Maxwell's ranch in the 1860s, "The system existing in the territory at that time was the system of peonage. Lucien Maxwell was a good master, however, and employed about five or six hundred men." Of Maxwell's fortune in livestock, Ryus recalled, "During my travels across the plains, I do not believe that for a distance of forty-five miles I was ever out of sight of the herds—cattle, horses, goats, sheep, etc.—belonging to Mr. Maxwell."[16]

The subject of peonage or "condition of servitude" as an element of Maxwell's operation surfaces periodically in the narratives of writers who visited the property or later heard stories of his management of the grant. Certainly Maxwell and Carson experienced as normal practices that were later deemed unacceptable—such as the taking of captive women and children in war by enemy tribes for use as slaves. While spending a week at Maxwell's in early fall, 1865, Irving Howbert discovered that the female servants were Navajo. "We were told that Mr. Maxwell had purchased these squaws from Apache Indian warriors, who had captured them in various raids in the country of the Navajos, with whom they were at war," he noted.[17]

Maxwell's world was mostly isolated from the warfare between "free" and "slave" states during the 1860s, but the halcyon days of "Maxwell's Ranche" spanned the national regimes that ruled before and after the Emancipation Proclamation. Olive Ennis, the officer's wife from Ohio, noted that among Maxwell's peons were several Navajo women who made beautiful blankets for him, and said

Lucien Bonaparte Maxwell. This portrait, in the Maxwell family for some years, depicts Lucien Maxwell as multiple sources have described him, in the informal attire that he was said to wear around his ranch. Artist unknown. Photo courtesy of the Victor Grant Collection, Arthur Johnson Memorial Library, Raton, N.Mex.

with reference to their service, "I do not believe he ever recognized emancipation." The ranch's Black cook, reminded that war had made the slaves free, responded with indignation, telling Ennis that "Marse Lucien" was not, in fact, her master, and affirming her loyalty to him.[18]

Concerning the nature of peonage on Maxwell's estate, it is uncertain exactly what sort of arrangement prevailed. Cleaveland thought that Maxwell might have improperly collected tribute from Hispanic farmers already living in the area when he moved onto the grant, since it could not have been said with certainty that all of those working the land were on the yet unsurveyed grant. That Maxwell had little conflict with presumed tenants, Cleaveland supposed, was attributable to the prior experiences of the *paisanos*, many of whom had lived in villages in which relationships between peon and *patrón* were understood. Maxwell, she conceded, "was a good *patrón*."[19] Most observers shared the opinion that Maxwell was a good and respected manager of the domain, but stories of his whipping servants indicate that he could be a stern and demanding master as well.[20]

Some aspects of Maxwell's style and manner struck observers as peculiar and contributed to his legend as noteworthy qualities. In formal portraits, Maxwell strikes a distinguished pose in business attire, but Goldrick, visiting the home ranch in 1864, found him knocking around "from store to mill and from wheat fields to corn rows," now showing his hands how to hitch up a mule team, then surveying his cattle, heedless of appearance, displaying "carelessness about pride and indifference about wardrobe."[21] Melvin Whitson Mills, who upon his arrival in the territory as an attorney in 1868, was introduced to Maxwell, was more thorough and graphic in his description, telling an audience in 1922, "He looked slouchy, if not dirty and often had one pant leg in one boot and the other pant leg out, wearing an old cotton belt with a baggy dirty shirt hanging over his cotton sash with a broad brimmed smashed up hat, with a face only now and then shaved, leaving his big black mustache."[22]

Maxwell generally did not go in for politics in a visible way. In his only pursuit of public office, he was elected probate judge of Colfax County, newly created out of a northern portion of Mora County in fall of 1869, but he resigned a year later, presumably in anticipation of his move from the county following his sale of the grant. Still, Maxwell's hold on the grant and his success as a supplier to the military and to Indian agencies was very much dependent on the government and called for some dexterity in securing favorable decisions and sustaining useful relationships. He was careful to give attention to such matters. In 1858, Captain Randolph Marcy wrote to his brother, telling of a visit to Maxwell's ranch, in which his men were invited to "two balls or fandangoes." Of the circumstance, Marcy explained, "The ball was given exclusively for our benefit, and of course we were duty bound to attend. The proprietor of the ranche had received a large sum of money from me for mules and horses and he wished to make our stay with him agreeable."[23]

A feature of his home that Maxwell was pleased to show off was the room in which two or more Navajo women wove beautiful blankets, reportedly completing one every six weeks. In 1866, a traveling writer for the *Daily Rocky Mountain News*, probably frontier editor John T. Russell, reported, "They are now at work on one that Maxwell proposes to send to the Secretary of the Interior." The secretary, as it happened, had much to say concerning the validity and status of land grants in general, and Maxwell's in particular.[24]

An intriguing facet of Maxwell's career concerns his relationship with money. During the heyday of his ranch on the Cimarron, money seemed to flow freely, both in and out of Maxwell's coffers. He profited handsomely from federal contracts—a partial but incomplete explanation for his ostensible indulgence for the Indian residents that many white settlers and potential investors were eager to have removed to reservations. Visitors to the ranch describe an extensive farming operation, decentralized among the small plots of Hispanic New Mexicans. Maxwell shared in the production of all or nearly all such farms, taking his part in tons of hay, bushels of wheat, or whatever tenant families could produce by labor.[25] Stores at Rayado, and later on the Cimarron, sold goods in the region and to travelers on the Santa Fe Trail. Railway transportation was much anticipated, but the old trail would continue as the primary route for freight and immigrants until long after Maxwell had sold and left the grant. He could well afford the hospitality offered to his guests. Surely he could afford to assist in providing the sustenance that kept peace with resident Utes and Jicarillas, whenever the inevitable lapses in federal support for the Indians occurred. In Maxwell's later years on the ranch, a discovery of gold and the rapid development of mining led to an upward jolt in revenue.

O. J. Goldrick, who seems to have functioned as a regional correspondent or travel writer for the *Rocky Mountain News*, wrote of Lucien Maxwell, "His wealth is said to be the greatest of any man in New Mexico, at least, so large that he himself has no definite or exact idea about it."[26] Neither could Maxwell's superintendent estimate the number of acres under cultivation or the number of sheep in his flocks. Goldrick estimated the Maxwells' worth at some $200,000 to $250,000, including land, livestock, and other assets. If the immense size of the grant, as it would eventually be determined, and the value of its minerals could have been known, the figure would have been far greater. Indians living on the grant insisted that the land was theirs, but it had been "translated" into property as regulated by governments—divided into parcels that were conveyed legally by sale or otherwise, first by the Mexican government, then by an American regime that proved flexible as to titles and boundaries, depending on the creativity, influence, and audacity of attorneys and speculators.[27]

The popular image of Maxwell depicts him as a casual, if not careless, manager of money. Several sketches refer to the chest or "bureau" that was against the wall of a nearly empty room, in which Maxwell reportedly kept a large stash of cash in an unlocked drawer. Fear of his wrath, should he learn of any theft, apparently provided adequate security. Much of Maxwell's reported casual dispersal of money occurred in acts of generosity—such as collecting gambling debts but refunding the money in the form of a "loan," particularly if one of the guests had put himself in a bind by losing heavily at cards.

E. H. Bergman, who had been associated with Maxwell in ownership of the Aztec Mine and as superintendent of the stamp mill in which their ore was processed, was more severe in his critique of Maxwell's personal financial management. Interviewed years after Maxwell's death, Bergman recalled that when Maxwell had gone to New York to close on the sale of the grant, he received $650,000 for the bulk of the property and another payment for the home ranch that was reserved as a separate holding. With $750,000 credited to him in one of the city's banks, he took $50,000 in cash for walking-around money and soon left New York having spent some $30,000 on gifts for friends in New Mexico. In a conversation with one of Maxwell's relatives, Bergman was asked, "How long do you give him to spend that money?" "Five years," Bergman replied. The relative disagreed, saying, "He'll get rid of it in less time than that."[28] A visitor interested in Maxwell's life story was told that his last years "were embittered by the treachery of false friends and dishonest dealings," likely referring to an investment of at least $250,000 in a company organized to extend the Texas and Pacific Railroad across southern New Mexico and Arizona. Maxwell had invested heavily at the urging of his old employer, John C. Frémont.[29] The Panic of 1873 set the venture on a course for bankruptcy, however, and Maxwell reportedly lost his entire outlay.[30]

Maxwell and Native Peoples

A consensus among observers of Lucien Maxwell's life and career credits him as a man whose affinity and experience allowed him to get on well with American Indians. He had been in mortal conflict with Utes and Apaches, but his relations with Natives on the grant were generally peaceable. He seemed to enjoy having Indians on the place and welcomed them in his home. Ute visitors sometimes slept on the floor of Maxwell's large hall following an evening's conversation that included their host, and on occasion, Kit Carson and other frontiersmen known to them.[31] To Melvin Mills, the attorney, it seemed that Indians on the grant were one of three idols revered by Maxwell, along with his racehorses and Virginia, the daughter he adored. As Mills remembered, "The Indians followed him about in bunches. He seemed to love them and prided himself in his authority over them—they were always ready to obey his commands."[32] When William A. Bell arrived at the big ranch house in August 1867, his impression was that Maxwell had completely won the confidence of the Indians; they were at ease in his presence, as he was in theirs. "They all seemed on the most familiar terms with him," Bell recalled, "talking and laughing while the children played around. These people were paying him a visit; they had just ridden in from the mountains, and had left their ponies tied under the trees."[33]

In reality, the relationship with the Natives on the ranch was more complicated. Maxwell presumably benefitted financially from the presence of the Indians, profiting from contracts for supplies issued by the Indian agency or used by soldiers detailed to the area. But there was some question as to whether Maxwell's financial business related to an Indian presence added up to an asset or amounted instead to a liability. When Maxwell began to consider a sale of the property, his attitude may have changed somewhat. Questioned in August of 1869 by a superior officer as to whether Maxwell would object to removal of Indians from his property, General George Getty replied that Maxwell had made no effort to prevent their removal and had twice expressed a wish that "these Indians could be permanently located to some other section." Concerning the profit motive, Getty reported hearing that Maxwell had lost between $10,000 and $20,000 yearly in the cost of presents for the Natives and damage to his livestock and other property.[34]

Maxwell occasionally offered his services or was called upon by the government to assist in quieting conflict involving Indians with whom he had influence, particularly the Utes. Richens Lacy "Uncle Dick" Wootton observed Maxwell at work in fall of 1866, helping settle a violent clash among a party of angry Ute warriors, area settlers, and the cavalry soldiers led by a zealous commander, Brevet Colonel A. J. Alexander. Kit Carson helped head off further hostilities in the field, near Trinidad in southern Colorado, and leaders then moved to Maxwell's ranch to discuss terms of peace. The Ute chiefs were assured that they would suffer no recriminations. According to Uncle Dick, "Maxwell made the Indians a present of a lot of ponies, and that put them again in a good humor." Wootton recalled that Maxwell had made peace in a similar manner some years earlier, when the Utes had been at war with Comanche and Kiowa Indians.[35]

Moving On

In 1867, events took a dramatic turn with the public knowledge that gold was discovered on the Maxwell grant. Maxwell professed to have known that there was gold in the hills, but he had not bestirred himself to go after it, thinking that the right time would come to do so. Perhaps he was awaiting the arrival of rail transportation in the territory, which would have simplified the shipping of heavy equipment for mining and milling, as well as transport of products and people. As it was, word of the gold strike went out and he had no choice. The miners came—prospectors, developers, laborers, and the usual assortment of craftsmen, merchants, and entrepreneurs needed wherever settlements were growing.

Maxwell moved quickly and aggressively to invest in the new industry, joining in mining ventures, building ore-crushing mills, even platting a town and offering lots in the new the town of Virginia City, which ultimately could not compete with a more lively burg, Elizabethtown. By most accounts, Maxwell was welcoming, even generous, to many immigrants who came seeking wealth or homes in the gold camps. When William Bell visited the property soon after the strike became known, he observed that, although Maxwell claimed the land on which gold was located, he did not rush to accuse the arriving prospectors of trespassing, but he instead "sent them timber from his sawmill and sheep from his flock."[36] A correspondent providing news of the West to the *Boston Herald* in 1868 reported favorably concerning the outlook for the Moreno mines, writing, "Mr. Maxwell, their owner, is spoken of as a gentleman of very affable manners, and many who are there now 'dead broke,' are being provided for by him till Spring opens and they can procure work."[37]

Such generosity did not impress all of the miners, some of whom were indignant over the modest tribute that Maxwell levied on those mining on the grant. As the owner of a property that had not yet been surveyed, Maxwell was not in the best position to assert authority over activities in marginal areas of the grant as claimed. Some of the miners insisted, erroneously, that Maxwell might own the surface rights in the mining district, but the minerals below ground were there for anyone's taking.[38] Some observers thought Maxwell's policies on mining liberal, even generous, but miners bristled at the "taxes" he imposed, one proclaiming, "The yoke is galling and must be thrown off. We are freemen, not peons."[39]

Maxwell was at ease with the indigenous people, the paisanos who had lived on the grant under Mexican rule, and non-Hispanic settlers who were intent on buying land, building homes, and establishing farms or ranches. But the mining men represented a new element. On the whole, they were more purposeful, determined, passionate, and outspoken than those he had dealt with in the past. Their presence may have triggered Maxwell's urge to divest himself of the property and the headaches that its management entailed. By E. H. Bergman's account, "The time came when Maxwell could no longer maintain the pace of a New Mexican duke. Settlers were crowding in and encroaching on the great estate."[40] Speculators were also attracted to the western territories. Some came from the eastern states, but many were from Europe. In late 1869, Jerome Chaffee of Colorado, a future U.S. senator, organized a group to essentially broker a sale of Maxwell's ambiguous claim. Attorney Stephen B. Elkins also represented Maxwell in the transaction, scored a $10,000 fee, and later said that it was, "the easiest money I ever earned."[41] The Colorado men soon turned up a willing buyer in a British syndicate, which in turn found a Dutch group with money to invest in the property.

Using $150,000 of the proceeds from the sale of the grant, Maxwell established the First National Bank of Santa Fe, the first federally chartered bank in the territory, in December 1870.[42] Maxwell's banking career was brief as, under threat of likely competition, he sold to Elkins and Thomas B. Catron in May 1871, soon after the new bank opened, keeping just ten of the original fifteen hundred shares.

Resettled at the Bosque Redondo following the abandonment of Fort Sumner as an army post and an internment site for the Navajo, Maxwell engaged in stock raising. He also kept racehorses and wagered on them in specially arranged events. Plagued by marauding Plains raiders who ran off his livestock, but unable to depend on nearby military forces as he had done in the Cimarron country, Maxwell raised his own force from among local settlers and reliable Ute and Jicarilla allies, and led them across the llano to punish the marauders and recover his animals.[43] Maxwell must have had a vision for a fine ranch on the Pecos, but a final illness intervened and he died on July 25, 1875.

If Maxwell's sale of the grant first awarded to Charles Beaubien and Guadalupe Miranda came to be experienced by him as a loss of land, status, and community, it was equally a loss for many of those left behind in the Cimarron country. The Utes, and perhaps to a lesser extent, the Jicarillas, felt most acutely the threat posed in Maxwell's departure. Tales were told of a meeting along the trail, of Maxwell and a group of Utes, at which Maxwell was threatened with his life if he should follow through on his plan for selling the grant. The response also conveyed a sense of betrayal, since many of the local Utes and Apaches considered themselves owners of the land, by whose leave Maxwell had been permitted to live there.[44]

In his time on the grant, Maxwell was viewed as something of a conciliator and a skillful peacekeeper. Concerning the import of a change in administration from Maxwell to the English company, Colonel Bergman remarked, "Very few, indeed, are the reminiscences of bloodshed about the feudal hall on the Cimarron, at least so long as its palmy days lasted. Later on there were conflicts between the purchasers and the would-be settlers on the Maxwell grant. It is said that 50 men lost their lives before the title was quieted. But the duke's reign was singularly free from homicides."[45] Maxwell's firmness in maintaining order and his generosity in dealing with Indians, servants, farmers, livestock herders, and the immigrating miners and settlers, were seen as critical elements of his success as a peacekeeper. It seems doubtful that he could have overcome the forces of change threatening his ability to dominate the estate as he had done, but as settlers reflected on Maxwell's era compared to the one that followed, they may have longed for the days when he ruled the country.

When Maxwell sold out and left in 1870, his indigenous friends received the news with a mixture of anger, anxiety, and alarm, knowing that their lives and security in a beloved homeland were changed forever. But when he died a few years later, having suffered financial setbacks and an unhappy exile at old Fort Sumner, their lasting respect and affection were plain to see. Melvin Mills owned a ranch on the Canadian River, where he grew produce in season. It was there he heard of Maxwell's desperate condition. Some older Ute men were also there to sell jerked meat and other wares, and Mills told them of Maxwell's affliction. The Ute men were visibly shaken. Cannache, or Ka-ni-ache, a chief who had many times led warriors in battle, took several others and set out on the hundred-mile trek to see his old friend. As the Utes approached on their return a few days later, Mills knew from their bearing that Maxwell had died. The men took the melons that were offered to them and sat around a bench. When asked about Maxwell, "They made no reply, but they all wept like only human mourners at a funeral can mourn, as did the rest of us."[46]

CHAPTER 3

Gold on the Maxwell Grant

Up to the end of the "war of rebellion," the conflict in the Cimarron country mainly involved the Utes and Jicarilla Apaches; Hispanic settlers; Euro-American settlers from the eastern states, Canada, and Europe; and American military forces. After 1846, the army had established a more visible and consistent presence, as compared to the Spanish or Mexican forces before them. The army built forts, helped protect travelers on the Santa Fe Trail, intervened to support local law enforcement when requested by territorial officers, and sent troops to deal with trouble between Indians and non-Indian settlers. Though people along the Rio Grande and in the upper Pecos region were disturbed by the Civil War, that traumatic collision of wills and interests had little immediate impact in the Cimarron country.

With the close of the war, change came thick and fast, bringing new competitors eager to exploit the land and its resources. Their lives disrupted by war, many discharged soldiers headed west. Some already in the borderlands courtesy of the army stayed, made families, and went into business, agriculture, or prospecting. Railroad building and development of mines and mills also accelerated, bringing more people and investment to the new American Southwest. The territory was deficient in rail transportation and commercial centers, and there was unfinished business in moving the remaining Indians to reservations. Spare though it was, in terms of "American" influence, affluence, and creature comforts, New Mexico was looked upon by many immigrants and profit seekers as a destination of opportunity.

The Slow Growth of Mining in New Mexico

Mining in New Mexico began with the indigenous people and their quest for materials of practical value: stone for building, flint and chert for weapons and tools, and clay for use in pots and other utensils. The Indians also mined turquoise, valued for ceremonial and ornamental uses. Early Spanish settlers mined copper and turquoise in southwestern New Mexico, and developed the region's first metal mine, La Mina del Tiro, near Santa Fe.[1] In the time of Mexican sovereignty, 1821 to 1846, increased prospecting yielded discoveries of gold at the "Old Placers" in the Ortiz Mountains in 1828, and at the "New Placers" near the foot of the San Pedro Mountains in 1839.[2]

Following the American occupation of New Mexico, prospectors and investors exhibited greater interest in mineral exploration and exploitation, but they were up against major obstacles, including Native resistance; lack of efficient transportation to haul equipment and supplies in and ore out; a forbidding landscape; and a climate that precluded reliance on water.[3] Just as dauntless miners and investors were getting started, war reached from Union states and rebellious states to disrupt life in the borderlands, diverting laborers to military duty and sending frontier troops off to repel an invasion of Confederate forces.

If the Civil War impacted the progress of mining negatively, it was ultimately beneficial in providing labor, experience, and talent for the resumption of a more robust mining industry in the territory. Much of that came by way of General James H. Carleton's California Column, a force of some 2,350 volunteers who marched from California but arrived after the Confederate troops threatening New Mexico had already been repulsed. The soldiers became Indian fighters for the duration of their service, and when they mustered out, more than three hundred men settled in the territory.[4] One, William Kroenig, was involved in the discovery of gold on land claimed as part of the Maxwell grant. When the discovery became well known, other former soldiers hastened to Colfax County. Several came to own mining claims or mills, and in 1870, at least seven veterans of the California Column were listed on the Colfax County census rolls as miners. Others worked in the mining camps as laborers, cooks, hired helpers, or entrepreneurs.

Once the war had ended, members of the California Column were involved in discoveries of at least five important mining locations in New Mexico: at

Elizabethtown, Pinos Altos–Silver City, Hillsboro, Magdalena, and White Oaks.[5] The railroads did not reach New Mexico for more than a decade after the end of the war, but known deposits of gold would not wait. Investors and operators, both large and small, forged ahead in developing promising mining properties.

A Man Named Kelley

Something of an origin myth has come down through the years, detailing the discovery of gold on the Maxwell grant, specifically in the Baldy Mountain region—the only part of the grant to support extensive activity in the mining of precious metals.[6] The first published account of the strike appeared in the 1870 government report, *Statistics of Mines and Mining in the States and Territories West of the Rocky Mountains*, by Rossiter W. Raymond, U.S. commissioner of mining statistics. According to Raymond's narrative, "A man by the name of Kelley discovered gold in Willow Gulch in October, 1866." The discoverers—Kelley and others—intended to keep the discovery to themselves and return to work the deposit in the spring, but, as Raymond explains, "the secret was kept pretty well during the winter, but enough leaked out to cause some excitement." When men who knew of the discovery returned to the site the following May, "they found a party of miners already at work in Michigan Gulch," near Willow Creek.[7]

The tale had been fleshed out considerably by 1904, when Fayette Alexander Jones, in a publication produced for that year's world's fair, took the story back to the appearance of a Ute Indian's display of an impressive piece of copper float at Fort Union—an event that stimulated William Kroenig to dispatch three men to perform assessment work at the apparent source of the copper-bearing rock near the top of Baldy.[8] The party included Peter Kinsinger, Larry Bronson, and Kelley, sometimes spelled as "Kelly," who had not acquired a given name and still has not, "despite persistent efforts by several historians."[9] According to the narrative set out by George B. Anderson in his 1907 *History of New Mexico*, Bronson, Kelley, and Kinsinger camped on Willow Creek one evening in October 1866. While the other men were busy building supper, this Kelley "took a gold pan and commenced washing some of the gravel along the edge of the creek." Soon Kelley was showing shiny flakes of gold to his startled companions. All immediately turned their attention to looking for more gold. Since it was late in the season, they made a landmark near the area and resolved to keep the information to themselves and return the following spring. Word of the discovery leaked and spread rapidly, so that there was plenty of traffic in the area by the time the mountains were passable in the spring of 1867.[10] In 1917, the prolific New Mexico historian Ralph Emerson Twitchell came out with a more complete history of events, naming Kroenig and William H. Moore as powers behind the discovery of gold and leaders in early efforts to develop the deposits.[11] From that time, historians have referred to the discoverer of gold on Willow Creek simply as "a man named Kelley."[12] Still less is known of the nameless Ute who led white men to the place where the discovery was made.

Word of the strike spread quickly, bringing multiple parties to the region as the snow receded from the mountains in the spring of 1867. Bronson and Kinsinger returned to the area of their earlier discoveries and were involved in separate efforts to develop mining claims. Among other early comers were partners Tim Foley and Matthew Lynch, who located claims on Willow Creek, and a group of men organized as the Michigan Company, who found gold near the town site of Elizabethtown.[13] Throughout the late spring and summer, more prospectors came to join the search for promising placer sites and ore bodies. By the first snow, most or all of the drainages leading away from Baldy Mountain had been scoured for signs of recoverable placer deposits.

One of the earliest official reports on the strike was prepared by Charles P. Clever, New Mexico's territorial delegate to Congress, based on the 1867 season's activity. Most of the efforts to that point had focused on placer deposits—massed particles of yellow metal that accumulated in streambeds with the breakdown of gold-bearing rock as it was carried down the mountainside. These deposits were easier and cheaper to find and harvest, compared to the gold-bearing quartz locked away in the mountain's interior. "Many of the lodes whence this gold has come have not been uncovered," Clever noted, "but that they exist near these fields is as certain as that a spring exists whence a rivulet flows."[14] Addressing early efforts to locate the hard rock lodes inside the mountain, John Sebrie Watts, chief justice and former delegate for the Territory of New Mexico, identified Foley and Lynch as discoverers of the Aztec Mine, which lay on the opposite slope of Baldy Mountain from their earlier placer claims.[15] The find came in June 1868; shareholders in the Aztec Mine were identified in 1870 as Lucien Maxwell, owning seven-twelfths; John Dold, who owned one-sixth; Valentine S. Shelby, one-twelfth; Matthew Lynch, one-twelfth; and the mine superintendent E. H. Bergman, one-twelfth.[16]

Developing Baldy Gold

The discoveries in the drainages of the Moreno Valley and descending from the east face of Baldy Mountain were thrilling, but capital would be needed to separate and process gold from the drainages and the rocky interior. In early exploration, "it was demonstrated beyond any doubt that gold existed in the whole Moreno valley in paying quantities," but to extract precious metals from the alluvium of several hundred creeks and gulches, "a sure and unfailing supply of water" was essential.[17] As in much of Arizona and Colorado, scarcity of water was an obstacle to placer miners. A proposed solution for the Moreno district was to construct a ditch bringing water from the Red River to the placer field. This was not the river in northern Colfax County later known as the Canadian, but one heading in the Wheeler Peak region and draining into the Rio Grande. The Moreno Water and Mining Company, jointly owned by Lucien Maxwell, William Kroenig, John Dold, W. H. Moore, Valentine Shelby, Morris Bloomfield, and Nicholas S. Davis, was organized to build and manage the waterway. Davis, formerly an officer and construction supervisor at Fort Union and a veteran of the California Column, engineered and supervised the venture, known as the Big Ditch. Bridging numerous gulches and ravines across a distance of more than forty miles, the waterway was described as "one of the most remarkable pieces of engineering in the west."[18] Hydraulic works were built at the gravel beds to be mined.

Quartz mining was impossible without investments in shafts and tunnels providing access to gold-bearing rock, and mills to crush the ore and separate the gold particles from the matrix in which they occurred. Maxwell furnished most of the capital needed for purchase and installation of stamp mills on both sides of Baldy. By the end of 1867, reports on the progress of the Moreno Mining District noted that a quartz mill and an *arrastra*, a mill usually driven by draft animals or water power, were in use.[19]

The initial excitement—doubtless amplified in the imaginations of those eager to share in the bounty of a promising but as yet unproven new strike—brought a rush of migration to Baldy Mountain and the Moreno Valley. Prospecting accelerated on both sides of the mountain—in the Moreno Valley on the west, and along Ute Creek and on the soaring slopes drained by the creek. Some locations supported paying operations employing drillers, muckers, mill workers, and other laborers directly involved in mining, while also generating business for entrepreneurs who

Hydraulic mining in the Moreno Valley, late 1870s. This method of mining was challenging in the Baldy region because of the absence of sufficient water to produce the volume and pressure needed to disaggregate the soil and gravel matrix and free the gold particles. Photo by F. C. Warnky. Courtesy Palace of the Governors Photo Archives (NMHM/DCA), neg. 014860.

made money providing food, housing, supplies, and forms of entertainment typically found in frontier mining camps. Elizabethtown crested in 1868, less than two years into the rush. Estimates of the town's population varied, ranging up to seven thousand, but the actual figure probably peaked nearer two thousand to three thousand, before falling to a number reflecting a more sustainable level of mining activity.

Among those making the trek to the new town in 1868 was a young attorney, Melvin W. Mills, who would remain a fixture in business and political activity in the region for nearly sixty years. Mills, just twenty-two years of age, was a recent graduate of the University of Michigan Law School when he landed in Elizabethtown. The timing of his arrival and his longevity in the area made him a witness to, and a participant in, events of an impressive and sometimes violent nature, not the least of which was the frenetic rush to a new gold strike, under way at the time of his coming. He later recalled how word had spread throughout the country of the "billions upon billions" in gold to be harvested in a remote mountain valley in the Territory of New Mexico. "I cannot describe these surging masses now as I saw them going up the Cimarron Canyon in lines of procession, almost tumbling over one another and as thick as bees at swarming and blackbirds in flocks, bound for this promised land," Mills recalled in the last year of his long life; "Nor can I describe the woeful disgust of these mobs of men in their disappointment after they landed where this gold was supposed to be; nor can I describe the tumult and commotion that followed."[20] The tumult and commotion that came about in the convergence of competing factions and excitement over the search for gold; the desire of settlers for land; and the desperation of Native people being driven from their homeland were real. Attorney Mills had a front-row seat, and sometimes a speaking part, in the drama that was to come.

Lucien Maxwell established a proprietary town site on Willow Creek, attempting to cash in on the sudden growth in population, but Virginia City, named for Maxwell's daughter, did not catch on in the manner of Elizabethtown, named for another daughter—that of John Moore, one of the founders of the new mining camp.[21] In 1868, a visitor reported seeing "several stores, two restaurants, and as many saloons, as also a drug store, barber shops, and gambling houses where the miner can deposit all his hard earnings of weeks in a few hours."[22] A year later the town had at least seven saloons and three dance halls, and was county seat for the newly designated Colfax County.[23]

Changing Times

By 1870 the population had receded to between three hundred and four hundred inhabitants, as estimated by a visiting reporter, but Elizabethtown had been, and remained, a remarkably unruly place, due in no small part to the nature and variety of factions represented.[24] Most of those who came to Elizabethtown seeking good fortune were from eastern and midwestern states, but there were also immigrants from Canada, England, Scotland, Wales, Italy, France, Denmark, and Hungary, and other nations on the continent of Europe. Larger numbers of immigrants from Germany and Ireland sometimes organized themselves into communities of mutual interest and protection. Many Irish residents of Elizabethtown were affiliated with the Hibernians, a mutual protection association based on their shared heritage, and were prepared at all times to seek justice or revenge for their countrymen. In the matter of gender, the town was less diverse. In the 1870 census, more than 70 percent of residents of Elizabethtown and vicinity—Colfax County Precinct 1—were recorded as male.[25]

The Mouache Utes and Jicarilla Apaches had not yet been settled on reservations as immigrants of all or nearly all origins persistently demanded. Some of the Moreno Valley miners encountered Natives who resented their presence and who doubtless were shocked by the wave of immigration and its impact on the land. It was later reported that the Indians avoided settlements out of distrust of the miners, and for fear they might carry smallpox. Even so, miners and settlers remained vulnerable to the Natives' customary practice of raiding to feed themselves and their families. Occasional thefts of livestock and other edibles continued near Maxwell's ranch and at farm and ranch houses along the Cimarron and in the Moreno Valley. In spring of 1868, an attack close to Elizabethtown was attributed to "Apaches," though there were no surviving witnesses to confirm the accusation. One "American" was left stripped and dead, and some mules and horses had been driven off by the perpetrators.[26] Speaking more generally on the subject of raiding Indians, R. H. Longwill recalled in testimony given in 1886, that in the early days of Baldy mining, raiders had killed livestock belonging to settlers, including those working mining properties.[27] At least one witness in a court proceeding claimed that some of the miners believed the Indians, being friendly with Maxwell and dominated by him, were harassing miners on his behalf. According to the witness, those who resisted paying for the right to mine and prospect for gold could expect to be raided, but those miners who recognized Maxwell's claim to ownership of the goldfield and paid his fees could work their claims in peace. The imputation was unsubstantiated but indicative of the contempt in which at least some miners held the grant's powerful claimant.[28]

People bringing other hopes and intentions were also at work in the Cimarron country of the post–Civil War era. In the tillable drainages on the eastern slope of the Cimarron Mountains, Hispanic New Mexicans and other immigrant settlers hoped to establish homes, raise crops, and run livestock on lands claimed by Maxwell but contested as to legal status. Among the ranchers and occasional outlaws and drifters who were attracted to the country were a class of visible and independent-minded men known broadly as "the Texans." Civil order, such as it was before the designation of Colfax County in 1869, was imposed mainly by Maxwell and a vigilante element that was most prominent in Elizabethtown.

By the end of 1869, a new industry of mining and milling was established in the Moreno Valley and the Baldy Mountain district. A continuing influx of new arrivals—miners and seekers of lands for farming and stock raising—reflected and buoyed hopes for future prosperity. Federal efforts to relocate the "wild tribes" on reservations continued; surely Utes and Jicarillas lingering in the country would soon be gone and railroads would cross the territory bringing long-awaited advances in immigration, commerce, and industry.

The congregation of the disparate factions in Elizabethtown and across northeastern New Mexico at the end of the 1860s made the country a veritable cauldron of aspirations—diverse in origins, cultures, and economic interests of the people, and in their visions for use of land, water, wild game, minerals, and other resources. Add a strong element of self-interest, an abundance of testosterone, an extraordinary degree of personal freedom, unrestrained by regular enforcement of the laws, and throw in a thriving liquor trade. Then consider that Maxwell, the frontiersman who had held this backwoods society together by the strength of his will and an uncanny aptitude for settling differences, was contemplating a sale of the grant. The prospective buyers were men who anticipated a quick profit from a resale of the property to foreign parties of unclear intention and doubtful competence, whose overriding interest would be to realize maximum profit on their investment. What could possibly go wrong?

CHAPTER 4

In Pain and Trouble

A native New Mexican novelist, Harvey Fergusson, had the benefit of hindsight when he wrote *Grant of Kingdom*, a historical fiction account of the Maxwell Land Grant story. As in life, Jean Ballard, the Maxwell character in Fergusson's book, does the gritty trail-breaking work of a frontiersman before giving way to a new era dominated by men who are too delicate to brave the wilderness and fight hostile Natives, but who are more shrewd in the ways of business and whose intention is to maximize profits. In death, Ballard fares somewhat better than Maxwell, staying in the country in which his best years have been lived, where his passing is mourned by admirers on a knoll overlooking the "Dark River Valley," the Cimarron country of Fergusson's story. Before an open grave, in the land in which Jean Ballard has poured out his life's most celebrated work, a speaker offers high praise for Ballard, and an ominous prophecy for those who remain. "We have all sheltered under the strength of our friend," he declares, "far more than most of us know. Now that he is gone we will learn that he was great, and some of us will learn in pain and trouble."[1] So it was for many of those who had settled on the vast claim, in the days after Maxwell's departure from the mountains and valleys of the Cimarron.

The English Company

The first half of 1870 was taken up in finalizing terms of the Maxwells' sale of the grant. Secretary of the Interior Jacob Cox threw a monkey wrench into the carefully laid plans of the men who were anxious to complete the transaction when he learned of the immense size of the tract to be submitted for official sanction and suspended the survey in process. Despite the secretary's disapproval, the

Lucien Maxwell, Charles F. Holly, and John Watts, ca. 1870. Holly and Watts were involved with Maxwell in the sale of the land grant. This image likely had more to do with an event that occurred several months later. With a portion of Maxwell's funds from the sale of the grant, they established the First National Bank of Santa Fe in December 1870. Maxwell was the bank's first president and Watts was vice president, with Holly serving as cashier. Special Collections and Center for Southwest Research, University of New Mexico Libraries, neg. 2000-13-0009.

survey was pushed to completion and was filed, without official approval, in the land office at Santa Fe. Through a group of Colorado businessmen led by Jerome Bunty Chaffee, later to serve as Colorado's delegate to Congress and still later as a U.S. senator, the grant was sold to a British syndicate headed by London capitalist John A. Collinson. The sale price to Collinson's group, organized as the Maxwell Land Grant and Railway Company, was $1,350,000. Maxwell and his wife, Luz, received between $600,000 and $750,000—various figures were reported. The initial sale was for lands totaling more-or-less two million acres, with exact boundaries pending a survey and issuance of a government patent—actions that were deferred by legal challenges. The "home ranch," including the great house on the Cimarron, was first withheld from the sale by the Maxwells, but was sold to the company a few months later in a separate transaction.[2]

The sales were consummated, and a board was organized to oversee an imminent sale of securities and arrange for administration of the property. In late July, 1870, Maxwell traveled to New York where, after a delay, he received payment for his share.[3] The mansion and the home ranch, town lots, commercial properties, mining interests, livestock, and other personal property initially reserved were sold to the new company in early September. By mid-October, Maxwell had bought the abandoned buildings at Fort Sumner to serve as headquarters for a new ranching operation. Many hired servants among the household retinue at Cimarron followed the family to the Bosque Redondo, making the overland journey and settling on the Pecos by early November, 1870.[4] The family moved into former officers' homes. Maxwell engaged in livestock production at his home on the Pecos, but never owned the grazing lands he used, and never created anything like the bustling settlement on the Cimarron. With the help of friendly Utes, Maxwell sometimes skirmished with Plains Indians who raided his herds and those of other ranchers along the Pecos, but he was soon beset with chronic kidney failure. Within a few years his fortune was exhausted, and in July 1875, the once-powerful master of the Cimarron passed.[5]

Men with a Plan

John Collinson, his associates, and fellow capitalists approached the business of making the grant pay with enthusiasm and a plan. They subscribed to premises adopted by countless architects of disaster in politics, war, and commerce since the dawn of time: (1) Shortcomings of the recent past were traceable to failings of the previous management—demonstrably inferior to the new executives, (2) The new men had a plan by which productivity would be improved to the advantage of all, especially the investors and management, and (3) It was going to be easy; those holding back their effort or resisting change would be discharged; those laboring earnestly under the previous regime would welcome the change.

The English plan, reduced to writing and published under the authorship of Collinson and W. A. Bell, fellow British subject and an accomplished author on the geography and geology of western North America, expressed serious intent on the part of the company and its principals; a larger purpose was to attract investors and capital for development, and to ensure profitability for the managers of the new venture. The report, *The Maxwell Land Grant, Situated in Colorado and New Mexico, United States of America*, supplied assurances concerning the shaky title to the vast estate, along with authoritative opinions on future prospects for stock raising, agriculture, timber production, mining, and other proposed revenue-generating activities and assets. The outlook for these endeavors was said to be bright, and the building of a railroad that would supercharge such a venture was imminent.[6] Strategies for success included shrewd leadership, expert management, and applications of superior methods in mining and agriculture. Investors were welcome.

What the report ignored entirely was the multitude of people—some three thousand just in Colfax County, New Mexico—already living on lands claimed by the company.[7] Some of the occupants, the Utes and Jicarilla Apaches primary among them, had long histories in the region, and perhaps better claims to ownership. Others had received deeds from Maxwell, varied in form and official character. A failure to account for these interests, and to make some accommodation for them in policy and management of the property, became a persistent source of conflict over the next two decades.[8] In minimizing the self-righteous indignation of these groups and their intention to resist dismissal of their claims, company managers erred grievously. Stresses that had become apparent during Maxwell's last years on the grant—as in calls for removal of indigenous people to distant reservations, miners' resistance to Maxwell's charges for lease of mining claims, and challenges from settlers engaged in farming and herding livestock on lands they believed to be on the public domain—reached a breaking point with the transition in administration from Maxwell to the new British management and allied political forces of the Santa Fe Ring.

The change from Maxwell to the English company played out over many months, starting with rumors of an impending sale of the grant in late 1869 and extending through 1871, when the region settled into a new normal that included a persistent state of conflict, both civil and violent. On April 30, 1870, Maxwell signed papers committing to terms of the sale, and by July 23, Luz had signed, and the deed was recorded in the Colfax County Court House at Elizabethtown. Signs of disquiet appeared almost immediately. On September 15, the *Santa Fe New Mexican* reported that trouble was anticipated with the Utes and Jicarilla Apaches, both of whom claimed rights of ownership established over centuries of possession and use. They were accustomed to Maxwell's ways, and to the regular disbursement of rations at his home ranch on the Cimarron. He had been regarded, the paper said, "as a sort of foster father" to the Indians. The change in ownership, with the loss of their hunting grounds, had made the Indians "troublesome and impudent, going so far on one occasion as to threaten Maxwell's life and breaking in the windows of his storerooms."[9] According to the later testimony of Dr. Robert Longwill, the Natives disputed Maxwell's right to sell their homeland, vowing to "fight anybody that came there to take it."[10] In the ensuing months, other factions would be heard from, each acting out in its own interest.

Some noticeable change was inevitable with the transition from Maxwell's autocratic but largely benevolent management style to a less personal mode of corporate administration. Agnes Morley Cleaveland, who had lived on the grant as a child, reflected, "The newcomers who had bought Maxwell out could not, like him, ride about in a buggy and tell each householder how many sheep, horses, cattle, tons of hay, pokes of gold dust he should deliver to the Maxwell corrals, granaries, and the bottom bureau drawer," the last a reference to the chest in which Maxwell had kept cash and bullion.[11]

This was but a practical reality, but some of the company's more abrasive changes resulted from unfortunate policy choices. Whereas Maxwell had welcomed immigration and allowed settlers to purchase land from him or raise crops and livestock on shares, the English company wanted to control immigration and selectively bring in workers who would implement its programs, or else purchase land outright, pay taxes, and sell their products on the open market. Mining, especially, was looked at as a proprietary activity of the company, with claims to be owned and managed by the company and not by private prospectors and entrepreneurs. This became a subject of conflict with miners who held titles from Maxwell, or who believed the company's claim to mining areas distant from Cimarron to be spurious. The company's aversion to flexible terms for immigration, prospecting, and agricultural use of lands was later criticized as a cause of the slow development of grant resources and failure to achieve promised financial success.[12]

Storm Clouds over the Sangre de Cristos

Two early flashpoints signaled trouble to come in the new era, even before the Maxwells had left Cimarron. The first involved efforts by the Maxwell Land Grant and Railway Company to press its claim to surface and mineral rights in the Moreno Valley, on Ute Creek, and in the hard rock mining areas on the slopes of Baldy Mountain. The *Colorado Transcript* of Golden, Colorado, declared on October 5, 1870, "It appears that the English Company who lately purchased the

'Maxwell Land Grant,' lying in New Mexico, and including the Moreno mines, are not to take quiet and peaceable possession of their immense purchase."[13] The paper went on to quote an article in the *Elizabethtown Railway, Press and Telegraph*, expressing the prevailing sentiment among the miners that these areas were not part of the grant and that miners would not be tenants of the company, but would "utterly disregard their demands and pretensions." Their grievance recalled the fees required of claim locators by Maxwell, who had won the goodwill of many by helping them become established and offering easy terms to leaseholders. It had been a mistake, the writer said, to accept Maxwell's demands when miners could have refused his terms and instead held out for an authoritative determination of the status of the mining lands.[14]

In the early months of the English company's administration, miners organized to oppose the company in collecting leases, abrogating deeds issued by Maxwell, or otherwise encroaching on their assumed prerogatives to engage in prospecting, and in the production of gold and other minerals. Over the months following the transfer of ownership, the miners pursued all avenues of redress—legislative, judicial, and administrative. On occasion, they resorted to civil disorder and armed confrontation.

A second flashpoint igniting the hostility of many of the miners was the special election held on October 24, 1870, to fill the locally powerful position of probate judge, recently vacated by Maxwell in anticipation of his departure from Colfax County. By this time it was becoming apparent that independent-minded citizens of the county were up against two adversaries, whose interests sometimes coincided and sometimes diverged. On one front was the English company, with its keen focus on consolidating control and maximizing profit from its new colony. On the other was an emergent and notoriously malign political combination headquartered in the capital, popularly known as the Santa Fe Ring. The Ring's presumed leaders were Stephen Elkins, who later was president of the Maxwell Company's local administration, and Thomas B. Catron, who handled legal work for the new company. Pedro Sanchez was the group's assumed agent in Taos County, and Dr. Robert Longwill was a reliable political ally in Colfax County. Attorney Melvin Mills made another strong hand for the Ring locally. When Longwill ran for probate judge, with the backing of the Maxwell Company and leaders of the reputed Ring combination, hackles were raised. Sanchez offered to campaign for Longwill, appealing especially to Hispanic residents. As election day drew near, a western paper observed, "The contest in the coming election in Colfax County, New Mexico, is narrowing down into support of, or opposition to the Maxwell Land Grant Company."[15] Longwill had an opponent in Thomas Pollock, but Longwill's friends had an ample supply of money to spread around, and the doctor won by a comfortable majority.

Perhaps thinking of the support afforded Longwill by the English company and presumed Ring members, and of likely consequences for their own interests, some of the miners were more than displeased with the result. Three nights after the election, they responded, perhaps under the influence of spirits, reportedly rioting and destroying the office of Patrick McBride, justice of the peace and presumed ally of Longwill and Elkins.[16] It is unclear how many men were involved in the incident, or how much actual "rioting" took place. The *Rocky Mountain News* referred to the event only as a "fire," but intimated that it was probably a result of arson. Officials of the English company at Cimarron wired Fort Union for assistance, and a detachment was sent to suppress the disturbance, despite the local deputy sheriff's judgment that no such help was needed.[17] McBride moved off to Trinidad, Colorado, as the turmoil in Colfax County continued.

The new company apparently had held off on some actions intended to tighten its control over the Maxwell claim, maintaining relative calm until the probate judge election had concluded as the company wished. An early provocation after the election involved the proposed eviction of Henry Osterlow, who worked a small farm on Ute Creek, below the mining and milling facilities on Baldy and the placer operations on the lower drainage.[18] Osterlow was among those known as "squatters" in the Cimarron country, because they held no title to the land that they occupied, and believed that Maxwell and the parties he had sold to had no federally certified title specifying the tract's boundaries either. According to a later telling, Elkins, then a director of the new Maxwell Company, and Longwill, managing director, devised a plan to put Osterlow off his plot by means of a lawsuit in the local justice court. They secured a judgment against Osterlow, including legal authority to evict him immediately. So armed, Longwill and a complement of law officers set off up Ute Creek to execute the judgment. Instead of a hapless farmer working his pitiable patch of ground, they found a flag flying over his cabin, and a congregation of mining men on hand, most or all of them armed. Perceiving that these friends would not tolerate having Osterlow put out of his home, the visiting party retreated.[19] According to a newspaper account, the incident occurred in December 1870, as the English company was starting to flex its muscle against local resisters.

Aggrieved miners and settlers pushed back against the Maxwell Land Grant and Railway Company and actions that were judged oppressive in view of the unsettled status of the Maxwell grant's title and boundaries. The fight continued for some two decades, carried on by those who were willing to challenge the company. In the last weeks of 1870, miners in the Moreno Valley petitioned Congress, requesting that the legislative branch withhold the coveted patent signifying federal sanction of the property's title and boundaries. The petition was signed by "257 citizens of Colfax County, New Mexico"[20] and was introduced in the Senate by Senator William M. Stewart on December 22, 1870, and in the House by Representative George W. Julian, chairman of the Committee on Public Lands, on February 20, 1871.[21]

It is not clear whether the miners' petition of 1870 elicited any favorable response from Congress. However, its stated object was satisfied, in the sense that a patent was not issued to owners of the Maxwell Land Grant until 1879, after a survey sanctioned by the Department of the Interior and a court decision that appeared to clear the way for approval of a grant larger than the Mexican limit of eleven square leagues per grantee.[22] Meanwhile, disputes regarding the rights of settlers and the rights of the Maxwell Land Grant and Railway Company continued, yielding a series of conflicts that played out in court proceedings and violent incidents.[23]

Resistance to the English Company

The management of the Maxwell Land Grant and Railway Company and local resisters—chiefly miners and farmers—entered 1871 determined to pursue and defend interests that were manifestly in conflict. On the evening of January 2, miners at Elizabethtown met and affirmed their refusal to recognize the company's right to collect lease payments on claims that many of them had held and worked since Maxwell's time.[24] A reporter for the *Cincinnati Commercial*, traveling in the Southwest during spring of 1871, had heard of Maxwell and his casual ways in dealing with settlers on the grant, and he observed,

> But a change comes o'er the spirit of their dream. As long as Maxwell owns them all goes well, but like the old slave owner of the South, Maxwell's

claim on them and their lands dies out, and they fall under the hands of new masters, who lay heavier exactions upon them, and like the Hebrew children of old, they rebel and assert their "God given rights," which in this country means what ever a person has been in peaceable possession of for twelve months.

The writer foresaw a clash of wills involving ejectment suits, retaliation, and, more likely than not, bloodshed.[25] Much that the writer foretold came true.

Meanwhile, the new company forged ahead with plans to replace low-skill or recalcitrant workers with sturdy colonists from the British Isles, and to consolidate economic activity directly under its own management. In early March, the *Monmouthshire County Observer* of the town of Usk in Wales, reported that James Temple Wightman had recently departed the Welsh village of Pontypool to manage the Maxwell Company's mining department, and that Mr. George Pritchard of White House, recently appointed as the company's farm manager, would be leaving soon with a dozen farm laborers selected from a large pool of applicants.[26]

The company's management envisioned a large migration of settlers leaving their lives in England to make new homes in the vastness of the Maxwell grant. Citing an exchange article, the *Western Home Journal* of Lawrence, Kansas, reported, in April, 1871, that preparation was being made for the transfer of some fifteen hundred colonists from England. Forty-six immigrants had already made the journey, traveling across the eastern United States to Denver by rail and to Cimarron by stagecoach.[27]

The Maxwell Company's managers—led by Collinson—approached their takeover of the vast estate with a hubris typical of men accustomed to power and privilege when contemplating a conquest in politics or business. The Englanders seemed to believe that much of their clout came from their standing as agents of a patently superior culture, placed in authority over people of an inferior society. As leaders of the new regime frequently begin by denigrating their predecessors, Collinson advised shareholders, "When we acquired the management of this property, everything was in a state of anarchy and confusion; businesslike principles were almost unknown in the dealings of its occupants." He hailed a new workforce, an improvement on the one that had made Maxwell a wealthy man and the grant a profitable enterprise, boasting, "We have now got in our service a staff of the most experienced assistants, men whose lives have been devoted to the administration of properties holding parallel positions with ours."²⁸ With application of superior methods and an infusion of capital, an 1870 prospectus declared, "This vast property must yield, ere long, returns in comparison with which its present revenues will appear insignificant."²⁹

The certainty of the new management concerning the imminent arrival of the railroad can be ascribed to the promoter's pragmatic optimism. When rails were laid to the property, investors were told, entrepreneurs would discover a fantastic array of resources, and factories would spring up on the grant. With visionary management and expertise imported from abroad, agriculture and mining would soon attain new heights of success. One report minimized the seriousness of New Mexico's most obvious resource deficiency, stating that production at the placer mines was good already, and that "obtaining a more regulated supply of water" was all that would be required to bring it up to its full potential.³⁰ This, as experience would show, was more easily said than done. Skilled, culturally compatible, compliant workers were desired. "Another very important element for the flowering of the property," the promoters stated, "is the supply of a number of immigrants from the eastern States of America and from Europe."³¹ Ute and Apache Indians would be exiled to distant reservations. Spanish-speaking farmers and immigrants suitable for low-skill labor were available in sufficient numbers already.

The grant's new owners were also willing to become more aggressive in asserting control over disputed holdings. Trouble had been brewing in the mining camps in the spring of 1871. On March 17, the Maxwell Company published a notice advising that miners could renew leases by March 25, after which no applications for renewal would be considered.³² At about this time, an Idaho paper quoted a letter from a former resident then working at Elizabethtown, reporting that miners were refusing to pay and declaring their intention to hold their claims. Maxwell Company managers were said to be hiring fighting men and supplying them with Henry rifles purchased by the company. "The miners are thoroughly organized, well armed, and are determined to fight it out, if attacked," the paper said. "The affair is expected to come to a settlement about the 25th of this month, either by one party giving way, or by a free fight."³³

The moment of confrontation approached with the arrival of a party of some twenty-three Cornish miners. Arriving with them were H. C. Clemes, "one of the most experienced consulting and mining engineers in England"; F. C. Christy, metallurgist; and Henry Jenkins, secretary and clerk.[34] Clearly the company was serious about working its assets. Of primary interest among the mining claims was the Montezuma Mine, the greater part of which had been purchased from the Maxwells. The company was, however, not the only claimant to the lode that lay within a matrix of quartz rock. John Cossairt had been working there for some time and was said to hold a deed from Maxwell to a large extension on the Montezuma. Undeterred by Cossairt's claim, Maxwell Company officials made known their intent to take over the Montezuma. Soon miners at work on Baldy Mountain and in the Ute Creek drainage were on the alert for a more aggressive attempt to seize control of the mine. Miners whose presence predated the sale of the Maxwell grant took the position that no survey had been sanctioned by the government and no patent had been issued to signify official recognition of the company's claim.

Soon after their arrival in early April, the Cornish miners were supplied with firearms and mining tools and sent up the Ute Valley to take possession of the Montezuma Mine. The Cornish workmen were reputed to be expert miners, as well as devout and courteous men of peace. They were not soldiers, however, and the clumsy attempt by the company's managers to intimidate the rugged men already working in the mountains failed. Accounts of the incident varied concerning the merits of the opposing positions of the rival parties, but they were in accord as to basic facts: the Cornish brigade, numbering in the low twenties, marched up the valley toward the mine, but the men were blocked and disarmed by a force of about half as many local miners. Informed that there was no work for them at the Montezuma, the Cornish men turned back to their camp. Their leaders advised territorial officials that the local miners were "rioting," and appealed for aid from lawmen and federal troops.[35] It was reported that the Ute Creek men had built a gallows intended for James Wightman, the English company's manager of mining operations. The gallows was not used, nor is it likely that the miners seriously meant to lynch Wightman.

Upon hearing the news from Ute Creek, the Maxwell Company management reacted with alarm, sending urgent pleas to the territorial governor, William Pile; and to the command officers at Fort Union, requesting immediate assistance with a civil disturbance. Likely participants in the calls for help were Robert Longwill and Stephen Elkins, the company's essential link to political power in Santa Fe. A military force reportedly was ordered to the area, but the soldiers kept their distance from the confrontation, ready if needed to keep the peace, but otherwise deferring to the authority of civil officers. On April 15, Governor Pile traveled to Colfax County, spoke with men on both sides of the conflict, and on April 18, issued a proclamation finding fault with both factions and calling for a peaceful resolution.[36] The governor cited the Maxwell Company's use of an armed force in an attempt to dislodge local men in possession of the Montezuma Mine as a violation of the law, and declared the confiscation of company-owned arms by the miners to be equally illegal and "in violation of the peace and dignity of the Territory of New Mexico." The governor's directive was accepted, the adversaries resolved to make use of the judicial process, and the governor returned to Santa Fe. Troops camped on Ute Creek were withdrawn to Fort Union.[37] As to Cossairt, some three years later, he was still laboring away in his portion of the Montezuma, bringing quartz out of the mountain and laying plans to run his arrastra through the coming winter to crush the ore.[38]

Pile reportedly rebuked managers of the Maxwell Company for overstating circumstances of the incident. According to an Elizabethtown paper, Pile also gave the *Santa Fe New Mexican* a "rap over the knuckles" for misleading reports on the matter.[39] A narrative of the affair published some years later in the *Cimarron News and Press* reported that Pile "took the occasion to inform the officers of the English company that they had grossly misrepresented matters to him, and that he had been entirely deceived as to the real facts."[40]

According to the *News and Press* history of the incident, Pile's actions in hearing the two sides out and responding in an ethical matter were galling to the powerful leaders of the Santa Fe Ring. The business model of Santa Fe's controlling political clique called for a dependable set of territorial officers who would carry out their directives. In the days of "Ring rule," the governor and other officials appointed by the president were expected to be pliable friends of the Ring on arrival in New Mexico, or to convert soon after.[41] Pile had been generally acceptable to the Ring, but according to the *News and Press* article, the independent streak he evinced in Colfax County was not tolerated: "For thus acting like a just and honorable executive and not as a partisan," the newspaper writer explained, "the London and Santa Fe combination made war on Pile" until his removal was achieved. From Washington, John Collinson advised his associates in the Maxwell Company that Pile's successor, though of questionable character, would be easily controlled by the company and its Santa Fe allies.[42]

By midsummer of 1871, the parties and issues of an epic confrontation were coming into focus. The object of the struggle was ownership and control of the land and resources in the vast region encompassed by the Maxwell Land Grant. Over an encounter of almost two decades, the composition of the "sides" changed somewhat, but the enduring issues were the company's effort to gain control of the property it had acquired, in the face of resistance from miners, settlers, and other claimants; and the determination of Colfax County residents to thwart the efforts of a Santa Fe power clique to dominate the county economically and politically. For the first issue, foreign investors in the Maxwell Company, interested Ring figures, and local agents of the Santa Fe men were opposed by miners, farmers, livestock grazers, and others contending that much of the area claimed by the company was or should be in the public domain. For the second controversy, the division was mainly geographic, with local people opposing rule by reputed Ring men conspiring to dominate local matters to their advantage. The Maxwell Company's foreign managers and investors exerted little influence on critical decisions concerning local governance.

Concurrent with the transition from Maxwell's hacienda to John Collinson's colony came a period of extraordinary violence—some of it related to the heated conflict between the English company and the settlers and some that may have been attributable to disintegration of order as it was maintained in Maxwell's time. While civil officers had been elected following the creation of Colfax County in 1869, order based not on the judgment of a strong patrón but on organic and statutory law was slow to take effect. Army officers had routinely dispatched troops to help curb violence involving civil disorder and Indian trouble, but they had taken their cues from Maxwell, and may have been hesitant to intervene, now that the county had its own law officers and courts. In any event, barroom gunfights, lynchings, political assassinations, grudge killings, robberies, and murders for hire were all too common in the season of intense feeling and general lawlessness that brought such pain and trouble to the people of Colfax County after those golden days, at least in memory, of "Maxwell's Ranche."

CHAPTER 5

A Brew Made for Mayhem

Writing from Elizabethtown in February 1870, a mining man offered a sunny response to a correspondent concerning the investment potential of the Moreno mines, a relatively new entry among western goldfields. He offered technical information concerning the quality and quantity of minerals produced and touted the aesthetic virtues of the country, declaring, "The climate in this elevated region is remarkably healthy. I know of but three deaths from natural causes, in two years, in a population which must have averaged about 1,500."[1] The writer, Morris Bloomfield, did not discuss the extent of deaths from "unnatural" causes, and with good reason.

In the period referenced by Bloomfield, the valley had witnessed at least two lynchings, three other murders, and allegedly, an unknown number of deaths at the hands of a serial killer.[2] These incidents, along with possible unreported killings among the Ute and Apache Indians and other residents of Colfax County, and injuries to participants in nonlethal saloon brawls, would have tempered the upbeat description of a salubrious climate in the vicinity of the Moreno mines. Truth be told, the region was racked by disorder, lawlessness, and a simmering revolt against the new Maxwell Land Grant and Railway Company.

The violence alluded to for the two-year period referred to by Bloomfield, spanning the creation of Colfax County and early steps in a transition in ownership of the large but vaguely defined parcel of land originally awarded to Beaubien and Miranda, was no aberration, but represented a new reality for Colfax County. The Cimarron country, for most of the next two decades, was to be an arena of legendary mayhem. Some, but not all, of the violence was related to a conflict between the owners and agents of the Maxwell Land Grant and Railway Company and the settlers who disputed the legitimacy of the company's claim. The mix of interests present during Maxwell's time became even more combustible with the arrival of new factions—notably, prospectors and miners, and a set of men referred to simply as "the Texans."[3]

A Lively Place

Recalling his arrival in New Mexico as a young attorney, Melvin W. Mills described the palpable excitement at Elizabethtown, his first landing place in the territory, where fabulous tales of rich gold deposits were drawing fortune seekers in droves: "Such gold-glittering reports, going over the country, did not take long to gather together not only the adventuresome gold hunters, but as well the gambler and saloon-keeper, the fugitive from justice, the dance hall speculator, and all sorts of people from all over the country, until as motley a crowd as had ever cast their fortunes together, was on the ground mingling and comingling together."[4] Citing a letter from a local resident telling of "two stage robberies, one killing, etc. in a very short space of time" in the New Mexico gold camp he had visited, an Arizona newspaperman concluded that Elizabethtown "must be a lively place."[5]

Cimarron later attained greater notoriety for its season of violent upheaval, but in Mills's opinion, "Cimarron in its palmiest days of bad men and wickedness was never in the same class with old 'E-Town' as Elizabethtown was known."[6] E-Town's fame has been moderated because of its relatively short duration as a place of importance; following a brief gold rush and a fleeting business boom, the town's population declined. Elizabethtown was designated the county seat of Colfax in 1869, but that honor soon passed to Cimarron. Elizabethtown had at least one weekly newspaper most of the time from 1868 until 1874, but only about a dozen issues survive, three of those being copies of the *Thunderbolt*, an entertaining but uninformative journal of satire ginned up by a few creative miners. The chaos at Cimarron drew national attention, eventually bringing political reform, but the pot that boiled over at Cimarron had started to simmer at Elizabethtown, and in the Moreno goldfield.

Elizabethtown, between 1868 and 1875, was exemplary of common notions of "frontier justice," a term implying that, out West, they didn't have just plain justice, but a special kind of justice. Theirs was a form of justice that claimed waivers on the usual protocols of due process, on account of weak provisions for law

Elizabethtown, New Mexico, 1868. Elizabethtown is seen here near its peak population, in the first years following the discovery of gold in the Moreno Valley and on Baldy Mountain. With several saloons and dance halls, it was little wonder that "E-Town" became a hotbed of frontier violence. Maxwell Land Grant Co. Photo Collection, Special Collections and Center for Southwest Research, University of New Mexico Libraries, neg. 000-147-0076.

enforcement, inefficient judicial processes, and the long distances between towns and infrequent visits of courts to outlying precincts. To the extent that homemade or summary justice flourished in the days of Lucien Maxwell, it mostly ran through Maxwell. Following his departure, the advent of more volatile factions and a slow transition to conventional legal order meant that a high proportion of disputes continued to be settled outside the law.

Mills and his contemporaries in Elizabethtown referred to the prevailing system as "six shooter law." Those who subscribed to this notion were not strictly opposed to due process, but neither did they feel compelled to wait on the slow slog of legal process when circumstances of an incident were clear enough to those present. Mills described the workings of Elizabethtown's vigilance committee, the group that met in secret to deal with disturbers of the peace—or of the prevailing order. "This band of resolute and determined men would meet in a dark room," Mills said,

> sending for young Mills to come to their place of meeting and pass a cigar box containing black and white gamblers' chips around, and by this means

decide the fate of some desperado and also decide who should put him away; and in the next day or so, the fate of the condemned was known to everybody. It was not long after a few of the bad men had met this kind of fate, that this class of men who boasted of having "got their man" began to disappear.[7]

The vigilantism Mills describes apparently amounted to assassination. Whatever occurred along these lines in the boom days of Elizabethtown, little was left in the way of a paper trail, but closely related is the phenomenon of "murder for hire." While no evidence of an occurrence was offered, a contemporary testified that Maxwell was not above eliminating an adversary, allowing that, if any man had attempted to steal any part of the grant, "he would either have run him off or killed him or had him killed."[8] Other, more detailed intimations of assassination for money came to light in later years.

Another form of vigilantism, often more spontaneous, was lynching, or extralegal killing of an accused party by a group or mob. Definitions of lynching allow for a variety of methods, but in territorial New Mexico, it was usually taken to mean execution by hanging. Elizabethtown saw at least one lynching a year from 1869 to 1871. In late summer 1869, counsel for an unnamed "Mexican" male on trial for murder at Elizabethtown requested and was granted a change of venue to Taos. Thinking the move would lead to an acquittal, friends of the murder victim, or of "justice," took the man from the makeshift jail and hanged him before courts and lawyers could secure a decision contrary to their conclusion that the accused was guilty and deserving of swift, sure, and severe punishment. According to an account of the affair, affixed to the man's clothing was a card that read, "So much for change of *Venue*."[9]

Charles Kennedy was the subject of a lynching in fall 1870. Kennedy was a mysterious man who lived at the fork of trails that diverged from the southern end of the Moreno Valley, the left fork leading to Mora, the right fork following the road to Taos up a steep pass and over into the canyon of the Rio Fernando de Taos. While Kennedy lived in his cabin at the base of Palo Flechado Pass, rumors began to circulate, concerning travelers who had apparently disappeared after stopping at Kennedy's place; by some, Kennedy was suspected of murdering the visitors. According to a popular but unsubstantiated narrative, Kennedy's nimble wife climbed up the cabin's chimney one dark night and crossed the Moreno

Valley to alert men at Elizabethtown to her husband's savagery in killing multiple visitors. In response to her account, men rode from Elizabethtown to investigate. On the basis of their findings, legal proceedings were started, but before they could conclude, Kennedy was taken from the makeshift jail at Elizabethtown and hanged at the local slaughterhouse. In later years, the story of his demise took on sensational features that made it legendary in the lore of northeastern New Mexico. A cherished coda to the story of the serial murders holds that some men in the lynch mob, led by Clay Allison, took Kennedy's severed head to Cimarron, where it was hoisted on a stake outside Henri Lambert's saloon to remain as an object lesson for potential malefactors.

These lurid details have been widely disseminated and are integral to the enduring story of Charlie Kennedy, but some parts are unsubstantiated, if not patently untrue. Estimates of the number of people killed by Kennedy vary wildly, one source reckoning as many as a hundred. According to Joseph Kinsinger, recalling the affair in 1885, an inquiry found that Kennedy had murdered at least nine persons, and a witness said that Kennedy had confessed to killing twenty-one people.[10] Melvin Mills, attorney for Kennedy at his impromptu hearing at Elizabethtown, insisted based on his conversation with the accused that he had killed only one man.[11] Mills did not mention Clay Allison or the posting of Kennedy's head for display near Lambert's Saloon. Mills stated instead that the skeleton had been sent to the Smithsonian Institution, on account of the unusual shape of Kennedy's head. No contemporaneous news account implicated Allison, who later gave 1871 as the year of his arrival in Colfax County. As to the tale involving a public display of Kennedy's head, Henri Lambert did not have a saloon at Cimarron before 1872, and no such detail was reported at the time of the lynching.

The *Elizabethtown Press and Telegraph* had nothing good to say of Kennedy, but deplored the impromptu execution, observing, "The time has passed when it was necessary for the people of this community to take the punishment of offenders into their own hands. We have laws that will give justice to all, and we have faithful and efficient officers to execute them, and it is time the citizens of this place should realize that vengeance is not justice—nor a midnight mob the proper guardian of public safety."[12]

Fighting the Maxwell Company

Some of the violence was directly related to the larger conflict over ownership and use of land, between the English company and its Santa Fe allies and the miners and settlers of Colfax County who disputed the company's claim. Rumors persisted to the effect that the shooting death of John Glass in 1871 resulted from a falling out between the company and two formerly reliable agents at Elizabethtown, Glass and Patrick McBride.

At least seven other violent deaths in 1871 and 1872 emanated from disputes involving Maxwell Company interests. The English company and its friends in Santa Fe can hardly be held responsible for the senseless spree of outlawry attributed to James Buckley (or "Coal Oil Jimmy") and Thomas Taylor, but their discharge as employees apparently ignited their enmity against the company and launched a sequence of road agent robberies. Having announced their intention to "rob and steal from the company," they reportedly ran off several fine horses from the company site at the Montezuma mills and, on October 9, 1871, held up the stagecoach between Cimarron and Elizabethtown.[13] They robbed another coach in the Vermejo drainage and reportedly held up other travelers in the region. When ranchman Jack Booth extended hospitality to them, the men made no secret of their deeds, recalled Booth, but "swore fearful oaths to him that they would take the life of every Englishman in the Cimarron colony they could catch, stigmatizing them by a name excluded from polite vocabularies." The outlaws were especially bitter toward J. Langham Reed, vice president of the Maxwell Company, and James Wightman, the company's supervisor of mining operations, and "cursed themselves by everything holy and foul if they did not have their blood."[14] The lives of Coal Oil Jimmy and Tom Taylor ended shortly when they were tricked by two bounty hunters. The robbers were trailed to the Turkey Mountains near Las Vegas and killed there, returning to Cimarron as corpses grotesquely arrayed in the wagon driven by their killers.[15] Bounties, six hundred dollars per highwayman, were provided by the English company.

A third incident leading to multiple violent deaths and growing out of the clash between the Maxwell Company and persons claiming conflicting rights, began with the shooting death of John Fisher, a Moreno miner whose self-professed legal claims were denied by the company, in November 1871. Outraged, Fisher traveled to Cimarron to confront Reed, the young Englishman serving as vice president and on-site manager of the company.[16] Under the influence of liquor, Fisher used hard language and may have threatened Reed and others. Fisher left Reed, but later reportedly challenged him to fight. A few days later, Fisher's lifeless body was found on the road between Cimarron and the Ponil Creek with a bullet in his head. As reported by the *New Mexican*, "Fisher was a desperado, and had threatened the lives of several persons," but some of the locals saw the killing as an assassination carried out in the interest of the Maxwell Company. Hearsay reported years later in the *Cimarron News and Press* alleged that the company had aided the escape of some of Fisher's killers.[17] Charles Morris, a sometime tool of the English company, was among those suspected to have been complicit in Fisher's murder. A man believed to have witnessed Fisher's death reportedly was killed in a barroom fight not long after the incident.[18]

In late February 1872, Morris undertook another mission on behalf of the Maxwell Land Grant and Railway Company, leading a party in pursuit of men who had entered the home of the company's mining manager, Mr. Wightman, near the Montezuma Mine on Baldy Mountain, and had taken provisions, pistols, and ammunition, as well as two mules and a horse to facilitate their flight. The men, known only as "Smith and Graham," were accused of committing outrages in the area, and later claimed to have been persecuted by the English company and threatened with "lynch law," causing them to flee in fear for their lives. The pursuing force located the missing animals and the thieves who had taken them, but in a shoot-out at the cabin where the fugitives sheltered, two men of Morris's party, both teamsters for the Maxwell Company, were killed. The rustlers escaped capture, but wrote to the *Trinidad Enterprise*, stating their case.[19] They had been heard to express interest in exploring the inside of the Maxwell Company safe in Cimarron.[20]

On July 27, 1872, Charles Morris was shot and killed in Cimarron. The killing may have been related to Morris's alleged role in the murder of John Fisher and the widely held view that the Maxwell Company had arranged for Fisher's death. Morris's identity as a company enforcer suggests the plausibility of such a connection.[21] Denver newspapers reported Morris's death and the shooting and pummeling of a German man by three Irish drinking companions the same day, the *Denver Times* remarking, "A sweet place—that Cimarron."[22]

Lively and sweet—that was Colfax County in the 1870s, as the days of Lucien Maxwell's backwoods barony faded and lines among the warring factions hardened. A monstrous storm was brewing, as divisions among economic, political, and cultural groups widened; public authorities that might have provided legal certainty dithered; and the English company bungled management of its claim in every possible way. The directors worked to enrich themselves while fleecing their Dutch financial backers and dismissing the interests of those who had been working the land and developing minerals and other natural wealth of the property long before them. Management that was aggressive, arrogant, and ham-handed exacerbated differences and helped create a society of allies and enemies, winners and losers.

The Texans

With a decline in mining activity and population in the Moreno Valley and an expanding cattle industry in the grasslands between the Cimarron Mountains and the Colorado border, the locus of violence in Colfax County moved north to an area including the village of Cimarron, the Clifton House hotel and stage station, and the valleys of the Red River, later called the Canadian; the Vermejo; and Ponil Creek. By the early 1870s, a new faction had joined the combustible mix of economic interests and cultural groups represented in the county of Colfax.

The word "Texan" had taken on a meaning in New Mexico beyond geography through experiences dating from the ambitious but ill-fated Texan–Santa Fe Expedition of 1841, similarly unsuccessful incursions that followed, and the 1862 invasion of Confederate forces raised wholly in Texas and widely identified with the ambitions of expansion-minded Texas leaders. Following the Civil War's end, Texas cattlemen began driving their herds through New Mexico and seeking pasture in the grasslands just over the Texas–New Mexico boundary, as established in the Compromise of 1850. "Texans," as a class, were regarded with suspicion by many New Mexicans, particularly those in regions of contact on the Llano Estacado, in the Rio Grande Valley, and among Hispanic farmers, herdsmen, and villagers on the eastern slope of the Sangre de Cristo Mountains near Las Vegas. Not all Texans were from Texas. Those so identified may have been coming from Texas, but many were born in older southern states. Some were looking for opportunity and a fresh start. Some brought the emotional baggage of defeat, loss, and grievance with Reconstruction regimes.

The Texan immigration to Colfax County began as early as 1867, when Thomas Stockton of Stephens County, Texas, settled south of Raton Pass and, at a site near the Red River, built the Clifton House hotel and stage station.[23] The way station was on the mountain branch of the Santa Fe Trail, the main path of commerce and immigration from the states before the railroad came in the early months of 1879. The migration of Texas cattlemen to the region picked up after John B. Dawson's purchase of land in the Vermejo and Ponil drainages in 1868, on behalf of a group that included several neighbors and relatives from Stephens County, Texas.

Some of the men became long-term residents and good and valued citizens, but many did not.[24] Recalled merchant Henry Porter, thinking of some of the men called Texans, "The younger set of the Vermejo crowd would frequently come into Cimarron, get full, and, as they called it, shoot up the town; that is, shoot at men, chickens, dogs and pigs, and at the pictures on the walls of the barrooms, make men they did not fancy dance at the point of their guns and cut all kinds of capers for their amusement." "During these escapades," Porter added, "the stores and houses would be closed and the streets deserted."[25]

Most aggressive were some of those coming from the cattle-rich Brazos country in north-central Texas as employees of three prominent cattlemen: L. G. Coleman, I. W. Lacy, and Hiram Washington Cox, of Erath County, Texas. Few of the men were native Texans, but Coleman and Lacy had been in partnership for years, and many of their men had known each other and worked together. Among the malevolent actors in this cluster were brothers Porter and Isaac Stockton—"Port" and "Ike"—who may also have been related to another pair of Stockton brothers in Colfax County, Thomas and Mathias or "Thike" Stockton.[26] Robert Clay Allison, a noted stockman in the Erath County group, would have a large role in future struggles in New Mexico. Two others associated with the Coleman and Lacy brand, David Crockett, a relative of the legendary hero of the Alamo, and Augustus "Gus" Heffron, would also contribute to the coming disorder.

The Hittson Cattle Raid

The most notable episode of aggression on the part of Texas cattle owners and herders in the post–Civil War period occurred with the "great New Mexico cattle raid" of 1872, organized by John Hittson. Colfax County was peripherally involved—principally as a staging area for the raiders.[27] The expedition was organized and carried off in response to the stealing of Texas cattle and other livestock by *Comancheros*—Hispanic New Mexicans who carried on a lucrative trade with their Comanche trading partners, exchanging goods for cattle stolen from Texas herds. New Mexican ranchers allegedly enabled the thievery by buying livestock with little regard for brand. The practice had been going on for decades, to the detriment of Texas ranchers. Hittson, a known figure in the cattle trade in Texas and Colorado, was determined to do something about it. Armed with powers of attorney from other owners who had lost livestock to Comanche raiders, he raised a force estimated at 60 to 240 men—armed and organized into three crews for the purpose of scouring areas of Comanchero activity in New Mexico, confiscating cattle belonging to ranchers represented by Hittson, and driving them home.[28]

Colfax County was not a primary objective of Hittson's raid, but Tom Stockton's Clifton House provided a convenient staging place. Hittson and Tom Stockton had known one another in Texas. Cowboys hired for the crews met there and rode out to look for stolen animals in assigned areas. While the primary objects of attention were the ranches and rural villages of Mora and San Miguel Counties, some animals may have been confiscated in Colfax County. In the March 1873 session of the district court in Colfax County, Hittson, Thomas Stockton, and others were charged with "cattle stealing" and "carrying arms." For unknown reasons, the charges of cattle theft were not prosecuted.[29]

Miguel Antonio Otero, a governor in the late territorial period, remembered the raid in a memoir written decades later. His father, a prominent businessman and politico known as "Don Miguel," was asked to appeal to the Texas men on behalf of besieged villagers and agreed to do so. Allowed to go with their father to the Texans' camp near Las Vegas, Otero's sons witnessed a memorable encounter. The reply to Don Miguel's entreaty was that "God damn greasers" had been stealing Texas livestock for fifty years, and that the men meant to find stolen animals and drive them home. Otero recalled, "I have never forgotten the episode, for it revealed the hostile and vengeful feeling displayed by the Texans which produced acts of lawlessness calculated to make the name 'Tejano' a hated word among the New Mexicans."[30]

Hittson's campaign was only partly successful, resulting in recovery of an estimated five thousand to six thousand animals—a number sufficient to cover costs but, according to Hittson, probably no more than that.[31] New Mexico officials for whom the Comanchero trade was an embarrassment of long standing were sympathetic to Hittson's cause, but the raid left bitter memories in villages visited by Hittson's men, and it ended as an episode in which old grievances were reinforced and prejudices on both sides were confirmed.[32]

The Texans of Colfax County were by no means the first or only group in New Mexico to exhibit racial prejudice. They provided an easy example, however, many of them hailing from southern states in which resentment toward legally free Black persons ran high in the years after the Civil War. Having spent time in Texas, where bitter memories of atrocities committed by the Mexican army during the Texas Revolution lingered, some of the men called Texans also carried grudges against Hispanic people.

"Mexicans," the few who may have been Mexican citizens and the many who were more likely Mexican Americans by birth or by virtue of U.S. citizenship conferred under the Treaty of Guadalupe Hidalgo, were frequent victims of prejudice. A verse in John A. Lomax's *Songs of the Cattle Trail and Cow Camp*, quoted in Michael Maddox's discussion of unruly Texans in Colfax County, suggests the nature of prejudice that some men likely brought to New Mexico from Palo Pinto County in the Texas cattle country, where brown-skinned people lived in jeopardy because of "a powerful feelin' of hatred ag'in the whole Greaser race."[33]

White Man Trouble

The alarm that spread among the Natives of Colfax County—Mouache Utes and Jicarilla Apaches—over the news that Lucien Maxwell would sell the grant and move elsewhere proved justified as the Maxwell Land Grant and Railway Company's plans for managing the estate took shape. Instead of being ruled by a man the tribal leaders knew and respected, one for whom the presence of Indians was a familiar and agreeable circumstance, the property had passed into the hands of British speculators and the Santa Fe politicians with whom they had become associated for business reasons. For this combination, every resource—land, water, timber, mineral, forage, and game—was of interest as a commodity. The company made little or no effort to engage with Native people, instead agitating for their early removal to reservations.

Increased hostility toward the Natives of the Cimarron country could be traced to violent resistance of other tribes across the West and mounting impatience with the pace of federal effort to move the local tribes to reservations. Indians of the Cimarron region were relatively peaceful, with common transgressions consisting of drunkenness on the part of a few, a tendency to raid settler crops and herds when other means of subsistence failed, and conflicts within and among the local tribes. Frustrations of the settlers were expressed in calloused and hostile attitudes, as reflected in comments in the regional press.

An attack on Colfax County settlers in July 1874 was surprising in extent and shocking in its ferocity. The raiders were not the local Ute and Jicarilla Indians who, in fact, helped repel the Plains Indian warriors. The hostiles were variously reported as Apaches, Comanches, Cheyennes, Arapahos, and Kiowas, with evidence favoring the latter two groups, who could easily travel from reservations in the Indian Territory.[34] An account of the event originating in Cimarron, probably expressing a common view among non-Indians, held that raiding parties were allowed by federal authorities to prey on settlers in adjacent parts of the Southwest, driving stolen cattle, sheep, and horses ahead of them as they returned home. At least twenty-six herders and other settlers were reported to have been killed, with some victims scalped and otherwise mutilated.[35]

The attack drew angry responses. A letter to the *Daily Inter-Ocean* of Chicago, regarding reports from Colfax County and other places in which attacks had occurred, suggested that local militias "wage a war of extermination against all hostile tribes and their allies, the Quaker agents and Commissioners." Militias were urged to pursue the Indians relentlessly and "follow them to their agencies, shoot them down on the steps of their sanctuaries," and then "hang their thieving agents." "If this policy is pursued for six short months," the writer declared, "an Indian will be as seldom seen in New Mexico as in New York."[36]

In Colfax County, the anger level was decidedly lower, but a change of tone in references to the local Utes and Jicarillas in the post-Maxwell era had been evident for some time. In May 1874, it was reported, possibly in jest, that a local official of Cimarron, "while out gunning last week, killed two ducks and three Indians."[37] The Natives' resistance to conquest and eviction was increasingly resented, as evident in the complaint of 203 petitioners identified as citizens of Colfax County, who addressed the secretary of the interior in December 1874, to complain about damage to crops, theft of animals, menacing behavior, men fired on while trying to protect their property, and other evidence of "serious inconvenience and annoyance" justifying removal of the tribes to reservations.[38]

Lucien Maxwell's death on the Pecos in 1875 may have moved his Native friends to tears, but there was, by the beginning of the year, no love lost between Indians of the Cimarron country and settlers on the Maxwell grant, be they European or American; English or Texan; partisans of the Union or of the Confederacy; Black, white, or Brown. Ute and Apache people would continue in Colfax County for a time in an uneasy state of limbo, before trekking west toward a future that was uncertain, but that could hardly be less satisfactory than the circumstances experienced daily in their lost homeland.

The Territory of New Mexico in 1875 was far from being "tamed" with respect to outbreaks of violence, and far from resolving its issues concerning land grants and Native populations. Despite its fervent aspirations for statehood, especially among those who expected to profit financially or win more powerful political offices, the territory remained a far piece from that cherished goal.

CHAPTER 6

Unsettled

Maxwell's sale of the former Beaubien and Miranda Land Grant was at least partially in response to pressures falling on him as owner and manager, on account of increasing settlement, the discovery of gold, and an intensifying quandary over what to do with an Indian presence that had no place in the designs of any non-Indian group desiring to develop the region economically. Four years after Maxwell's departure, the assortment of factions competing for resources, and for economic and political dominance, had grown, as had stress and unrest in the region.

The Cimarron country had never known sustained calm—certainly not since the coming of conquerors, claimants, and settlers of European origin, nor over the centuries of tribal warfare that preceded the intrusions of non-Natives. But after Maxwell's departure, factions multiplied and conflicts had intensified, leaving Colfax County a powder keg in search of a match. The long anticipated railroad would exert an organizing influence on the territory, but as 1875 rolled in, its arrival was still years away. Meanwhile, the West was wild, and matters formally assigned to law and judicial processes were often decided by the strongest and boldest, with a gun or a rope.

Across a majestic landscape of soaring mountains, deep canyons, and the wide-extended grassland was a country of limitless beauty, but with a good deal of grievance and impatience as well. Ute and Jicarilla Apache Indians were aggrieved about the forcible taking of lands that had belonged to their people for an age, and about rations that were unreliable and frequently of poor quality, especially in the years after Maxwell, when there was no patron to make up deficiencies.

The people had tired of being made unwelcome in their homeland, sent away, or threatened with removal to a reservation. Plans and treaties had been made and failed, but a relocation that would last was yet to be devised. Meanwhile, white settlers besieged by recurring mischief, much of which reflected a desperate effort by Native people to sustain themselves in the absence of traditional sources of food and shelter, were impatient for the Indians' removal. For the time being, conflict between Natives and settlers was practically inevitable.

The other cloud over Colfax County concerned the uncertain status of the Maxwell Land Grant claim. The right of the Maxwell Company to the expansive tract defined in its own survey maps was treated by the company as a fait accompli. Ejectment actions proceeded against settlers without written titles, while miners were pressed to pay a heftier tribute to the company or forfeit their claims. To recalcitrant miners and settlers, issues concerning the size and status of the grant were far from settled, and they would not be settled legally for years to come. For the time being, the conflict played out in quarrels between company agents and settlers, in miners' and squatters' meetings, in petitions to political authorities, and in court decisions. The controversy did not lend itself to rational compromise; parties on all sides were armed and determined to fight rather than settle. Peace was not at hand, and would not be for decades.

An Inept Owner and a Willing Proxy

The English company never really had a clear head or a steady hand concerning its New Mexico investment. The investors could not know exactly what they had purchased; the Maxwell Land Grant remained a contested possession, with boundaries that were ill-defined and disputed throughout the years of British administration. John Collinson had led in organizing the Maxwell Land Grant and Railway Company, concluding the purchase and securing new investors. He had headed the enterprise from its inception and would do so until 1878, when it entered receivership to emerge two years later reorganized and under new management. During his time as president, and as essentially a managing partner thereafter, Collinson was often out of the country trying to sell the company's securities. He managed well in his own interest, not so well in the interests of others who had invested, including the Dutch bondholders who had supplied most of the needed capital. Having surveyed the situation following his arrival in February 1873, Frank Springer, the company's new attorney, vented to his father

Cimarron, New Mexico, ca. 1872. This image reflects evidence of the new Maxwell Land Grant and Railway Company's impact on the town of Cimarron. To the buildings that remained from Maxwell's ranch—notably the Maxwell home, two long buildings connected by an enclosed courtyard; the four-level gristmill; and the large barn at center right—the company has added several new structures, including houses for company managers and employees. New Mexico State University Library, Archives and Special Collections, Cleaveland Collection.

in Iowa, writing, "Over a half-million dollars have been squandered here, prior to the incoming of the present management, with practically nothing to show for it."[1]

Some of the money actually had been spent in furtherance of the announced intention of colonizing the land and modernizing operations. A neat town plat had been laid out, showing the divergence of railroads in four directions, with town lots and city blocks divided by straight-line streets with familiar names of prominent founders: Collinson, Elkins, and Longwill; and a square named in honor of company director and western railroad builder William J. Palmer, in the fond hope that one or more of the projected lines would materialize.[2] A visitor in February 1873 made a cheerful report, praising Cimarron for presenting "the neatest and most inhabitable appearance of any town in New Mexico." In apparent contrast to other New Mexico settlements, he found it remarkable that the town was laid out in city blocks, with streets that crossed at right angles. The English company had erected many new houses, "built in the American style, mostly of adobe," with shingle roofs and handsome cornices, all finished with a light gray plaster.³ Two years later, the bloom was off the rose, as another newspaper writer reported that the English had indeed put up many houses, but he noted that "on account of the bad manner in which they were plastered," and because of the rains that had fallen that summer, they were looking "a little dilapidated."⁴ In the five years of English management, British miners and farmers had been imported to work the mines and till the soil, but not enough to fully exploit the grant's resources or supplant the unruly Euro-American squatters.

Provisions were made for on-site management, first through English-born administrators who knew less about managing in the unique circumstance of Maxwell's vast estate than he had known, and later through the employment of Americans who were more thoroughly acquainted with the country, the issues, and the structures and influential figures of the government. But the company floundered, not so much for want of capital as for its lack of workable strategies, clear direction, and honest, competent administration.

In need of a local face for the company, local management, and political connections, the English company walked into the welcoming embrace of an emerging and, so far, highly potent territorial ring. From the beginning, Collinson and his associates had aligned themselves with the power elite as found in territorial New Mexico, including its members as incorporators, directors, and intermediaries. The alliance was more firmly clinched when Stephen Elkins, the generally acknowledged leader of the Santa Fe Ring, was appointed president of the Maxwell Company in 1872.⁵ When elected New Mexico's delegate to Congress the following year, Elkins acquired the capacity to represent not only the territory's interests, but his personal interests and those of his friends and allies as well, including the interests of the Maxwell Company. Ethical aspects aside, he did not fail to look well to the company's interests, including the advancement of processes to secure favorable treatment of the Maxwell Land Grant claim. In fact, before acquiring the title of president, Elkins had already exerted considerable influence over management of the company's business, and on local Colfax County affairs. This had come about through the stratagem familiar to successful bosses, later given the benign and cheery title of "networking."

Elkins's network was the Santa Fe Ring, an informal but potent combination that he built, along with his Missouri friend and business associate, Thomas Catron.

There was nothing formal about the association. Its existence was denied by most of those named as members, but it was, by reputation, a strong and potentially dominant scrum of business and political interests with involvements in land speculation, government contracts, mining, and other enterprises. The Ring worked its will through creative use of the territorial and federal political and judicial systems.[6]

Comprised primarily of attorneys, businessmen, and speculators, the coalition was mostly Republican in party affiliation, but like-minded men of other persuasions were not excluded, and provided some insurance against the possibility of a shift in party control at higher levels. At the pinnacle of its influence, between 1872 and 1884, bosses of the combination could depend on an array of territorial officials: judges, legislative leaders, the governor, surveyor general, territorial secretary, attorney general, U.S. attorney, and others, for sympathetic response and, often, direct complicity. Appointment of right-minded or pliable officials could be secured through the U.S. president with the help of his cabinet ministers, or an official already appointed could be brought into the fold by an inducement, such as an invitation to invest with influential local leaders in a promising business venture. Election of helpful legislators was a recurring concern, entirely manageable for the Ring's political machine, when the machine was operating as intended. The Ring worked informally and was not visible as an organized entity. Individuals named as Ring members generally denied the existence of any such association, but it remained a real and formidable presence for rival factions through the last decades of the nineteenth century and until patterns of governance changed with New Mexico's attainment of statehood.

This powerful coalition, having financial and political interests that extended across the territory, was able to exert influence through the agency of its allies in principal towns, and in nearly every county. In Colfax County, the Ring's most conspicuous associate was Dr. Robert Longwill, who had come to the Southwest as an army physician and stayed because he could see opportunity. A secondary ally in the county was lawyer Melvin Mills, who had migrated from Wisconsin in 1868, and who had become a reliable campaigner for Ring-backed candidates in Colfax County.

There was much about the Maxwell Land Grant to attract ambitious men like those of the Elkins-Catron alliance. There were many ways to make money off such a resource-rich property. As Elkins's involvement with the company increased to include ongoing legal representation and the exercise of executive authority, aspirations grew and other presumed Ring figures were taken into the Maxwell Company's orbit.[7] With the English principals giving only divided attention to their American property, and with fervent confidence in their partners' expertise in U.S. law and governance, Elkins and his associates were well positioned to pursue their own interests.

In the effort to gain effective control over the Maxwell grant and its resources, the Santa Fe combination and its local allies were not unopposed. A viable opposition emerged, led by two energetic young men from Iowa: William R. Morley, a railroad construction engineer idled by a global financial panic; and Frank Springer, an attorney and Morley's classmate at the University of Iowa. To avoid potential legal troubles, the Maxwell Company had been organized under laws of the Territory of New Mexico, governed by American trustees who would manage the property on behalf of the English and Dutch investors, in accordance with a trust deed executed by the investors.[8]

One of the directors, William J. Palmer, was Morley's associate in railroad construction. Elected president of the Maxwell Company board, Palmer had employed Morley as engineer and surveyor for the company, and Morley soon became vice president and executive officer. When Stephen Elkins succeeded to the presidency, bringing Catron along as the company's attorney, Morley sensed a difference between his ethical sensibilities and vision for the company and those of the Santa Fe men; his response was to fortify his position, inducing Springer, then an attorney in Burlington, Iowa, to join him in New Mexico.[9] Springer arrived in February 1873. Later that year, Elkins was reelected president of the Maxwell Land Grant and Railway Company board.

The group led by Springer and Morley became an effective counterforce to the Santa Fe combination, framing the developing conflict as one between local control and dictation of local matters from Santa Fe. But with the company's British and Dutch investors increasingly isolated by virtue of their delegation of administrative functions to an American board, it was also about direction and control of the vast Maxwell property. Increasingly distrustful of Elkins and Catron, Morley arranged for Springer to take over the company's routine legal work. Much of it involved the filing of ejectment suits on behalf of the Maxwell Company, a role that made for a precarious balance between Springer's fidelity to the owners of the grant and his advocacy of local interests in league with settlers whose claims he might be called on to contest.

Figures in a Landscape

In *Figures in a Landscape*, a panoramic narrative of the Southwest and the diverse people who met there, Paul Horgan directs attention to a triad of cultural forces, a cherished ideal in the story of New Mexico—Native Americans; Spanish-Mexican colonists and their descendants; and westering Euro-Americans.[10] The distinctions were significant in relation to the Colfax County turmoil of the mid-1870s, but other group identities were also notable in the clash of factions that set off the violence. The Jicarilla Apaches and Mouache Utes, awaiting relocation to reservations, had no direct role in the struggle for economic and political dominance of Colfax County and the Maxwell grant, but they carried on a concurrent fight for survival.

Miners in the Moreno Valley and on Baldy Mountain, home seekers, and cowmen strewn across the northeastern portion of Colfax County stood ready to challenge the Maxwell Company in its plans to consolidate control and monopolize resources of the land that it claimed. By 1875, most of the individuals who would figure prominently in the violent conflicts that would erupt in the coming months were present in the county.

Although Elkins was company president when events most directly associated with the Colfax County War started, and New Mexico's delegate to Congress from 1873 to 1877, he might best be described as an absent but interested spectator to the chaos. By 1875, his attention had shifted to matters in the eastern United States, and to the national political arena, and he was seldom present in the territory. He had also married Hallie Davis, daughter of West Virginia industrialist and senator Henry G. Davis. Although Elkins accepted a final term as territorial delegate in 1875 and had investments and political alliances in New Mexico to the end of his life, his involvement in the territory was greatly diminished. In November 1875, perhaps in part because of the violent events that had erupted in Colfax County, he resigned as president of the Maxwell Company, and presumably gave up any designs he had fostered of winning control of the grant.[11]

Morley and Springer were relative newcomers but were united in opposition to the Santa Fe Ring and in alliance with residents who did not want to see the Maxwell Land Grant or local political matters dominated by the Ring. Morley and Springer were still in their twenties, well educated, in the classical sense and vocationally. Morley was a civil engineer who had come west to build railroads,

Springer an attorney by day and a serious paleontologist as time allowed. They were politically astute, ambitious, and unafraid to join in public debate. They jointly edited the *Cimarron News*, later the *News and Press*. After turning over the editorial duties, temporarily in 1874 and 1875, then permanently in 1877, they continued to express themselves in newspaper articles locally, and perhaps nationally.

In spring, 1875, Morley and his wife, Ada, received an extended visit from her widowed mother, Mary Tibbles McPherson of Iowa. The family visit to see a new grandchild was of little seeming consequence at the time, but McPherson was interested, articulate, and inclined to enter into debate and action on political and social matters. Through William Morley's involvement in issues involving the Ring and the Maxwell Company, Ada Morley and her mother also became embroiled in the struggle. Ada Morley, McPherson, and Emma Hunt, a friend and teacher living with her family in northern Colfax County, were among the few women actively involved in issues related to the 1875 upheaval and its aftermath.[12]

Elections held in September 1875 produced a slate of officials who would be involved in investigation, enforcement, and judicial action arising out of turmoil to come. Among candidates on the ballot were two men of special interest to the Santa Fe political faction—probate judge Robert Longwill, who had attained an enviable status as a Maxwell Company director and interim manager, and lawyer Melvin Mills. Mills was seeking a seat in the territorial House, and was opposed by the emerging Ring nemesis, Frank Springer. Elkins, Longwill, and Mills comprised what critics referred to as the Ring "slate" in Colfax County.

While 1870 census data did not designate Hispanic or Latino identity, a plurality of those counted in Colfax County had Spanish surnames.[13] Despite their inferior numbers, non-Hispanic newcomers dominated in politics and business affairs. Selected Hispanic leaders were cultivated by political party organizers for help in gaining the votes of Spanish-Mexican citizens. Francisco "Pancho" Griego was an associate of presumed Ring figures in Colfax County and a hard man to turn down. With his help, Elkins, Longwill, and Mills prevailed in the fall election. Cruz Vega, a relative of Griego, was elected constable for Precinct 3, including Cimarron, the principal town and county seat. Also elected was a new Precinct 3 justice of the peace, Samuel S. Trauer.

At least three officials who figured prominently in the turbulence to come were appointed by the president in accordance with laws providing for administration of U.S. territories. Samuel B. Axtell had been appointed governor for New Mexico by

Francisco "Pancho" Griego. Griego came to Colfax County in the early 1870s and was an influential supporter for political men and groups seeking to collect votes among the county's Hispanic residents. His extended family lived in or near Santa Fe. Denver Public Library, Western History Collection.

President Ulysses S. Grant, following his ouster from the same office in Utah. If not the first choice of leading Ring figures, Axtell was soon seen as a valuable ally or, as detractors preferred, "tool" of the Ring. After Elkins's election as territorial delegate in 1873, Catron had been appointed to succeed Elkins as U.S. attorney for New Mexico. Throughout his half century in New Mexico politics, Catron repeatedly plunged or stumbled headlong into controversy and would do so in Colfax County as the conflict grew more heated. As chief justice for New Mexico, appointed by Grant in 1869, Joseph G. Palen served as district judge for the First Judicial District, including Colfax County. As resistance to the Santa Fe Ring became more general, Palen was increasingly seen by adversaries as a "Ring judge" and an instrument of corruption.[14] Others defended him as a competent and fair judge.[15]

Also taking a large interest and an active part in local matters was Robert Clay Allison, a native of Tennessee, but a "Texan" in local parlance, because he had come from the north-central Texas cattle country. Allison was a rare bird in the lore of the Old West—a real gunfighter and a real cowman. He came with a reputation as a fighting man, and added to it during his time in northern New Mexico.

Two others who came on the scene were unlikely candidates for leading roles in a violent clash on the Southwest frontier. They were Methodist preachers.

Rev. Franklin J. Tolby was a native of Indiana. Born in September 1841, he was listed in the 1860 census as a "school teacher." Tolby was ordained in the Methodist Episcopal Church in 1863 and was a member of the Northwest Indiana Conference—an annual meeting as well as a unit of church governance from which preachers were assigned to local pastorates or other work. In 1873, he was assigned to the church's mission work in New Mexico, and ventured forth with his wife of three years, Mary, and their two young daughters. He was to have a two-point charge, living and preaching at Cimarron, and riding horseback along Cimarron Canyon and into the Moreno Valley to preach and teach at Elizabethtown on alternate Sundays.[16]

The assignment to a parish so remote and so lacking in resources for ministry would have discouraged many a young preacher, but Tolby embraced the work of preaching and building up the churches, while interesting himself in local affairs such as the welfare of the Indians. He kept up a steady correspondence with family and friends, and sent reports to the *Chicago Daily Inter-Ocean* when Plains Indians attacked nearby settlers in summer of 1874.[17] To a niece, he verbally doted on his young daughters, Rachel and Grace, and reported on Rachie's reminding him at bedtime to bring the weapon he kept near the bed for defense, cautioning, "Papa, if you do not bring in your 'volver, the first thing you know you will see that some big Indian will get your girls."[18] They were living the frontier life.

The other preacher who would go from obscurity to notoriety was Oscar P. McMains, an Ohio native, late of Colorado, where he had worn out his welcome—as usual, through vociferous advocacy of his opinions. In Colorado, the trouble had started with McMains's defense of "parlor dancing," as a harmless and sin-free activity. After knocking around southern Colorado for a few months, McMains headed south and, in June 1875, made his way to Cimarron, where he assisted in Tolby's ministry on a part-time basis. To support himself, he worked as a printer for the *News and Press*, and like Tolby, he took an interest in local affairs—in the uncertain future of the local Indians and the difficulties of settlers concerning the legal status of the Maxwell Land Grant and the demands of the English company.[19]

An Anxious New Year

Writing about outbreaks of fistfighting that occurred often in the fictional town of Hi-Lo, Max Evans said the fights were explained by gales that came howling across the plain, such that the people were always on edge "from bucking this infernal wind."[20] The region of which Evans wrote, the northeastern corner of New Mexico, was part of Colfax County when it was created in 1869, and until the beginning of 1894.

The wind that blew in Colfax County at the outset of 1875 was likely neither as forceful nor as dust-laden as those seen in Evans's Hi Lo country, but it was certainly an infernal wind, and people living in and around the Maxwell grant were very much on edge. Natives were edgy about bad rations and an impending eviction from their homeland. Others were tense about the Indians and the government's interminable delays in locating them elsewhere. Many settlers and miners were edgy about the status of titles, boundaries, and ownership of lands in which they had invested money and effort, and about the Maxwell Company's aggressive posture in seeking to enforce its claim in the absence of a legal determination by federal authorities. Factions in the gathering struggle between local residents and overbearing powers in Santa Fe were ready to do battle in political, judicial, and administrative arenas, and if necessary, on the ground. The Dutch bondholders, heavily vested financially, but excluded from management, were stressed about the way their money was being used and the prospects for a reasonable return. Little wonder that the Cimarron country should feel so unsettled heading into a new year.

On a Saturday afternoon in January, a fracas broke out when four men associated with the large contingent of Texas livestock grazers in the Red River country hit Cimarron in a hellraising mood. As to the motive, they were reportedly inebriated, and were in Cimarron to "run the town" and annoy Sheriff John Turner, with whom the leader of the party had a grudge to settle.[21] They rode the streets, brandishing firearms and sounding off in a belligerent manner. When confronted by the sheriff, they responded with threats, but when he returned with a posse, they took cover in Maurice Trauer's general store, where they knocked out the window glass and prepared to shoot. A "Mexican" man was conscripted to hold their horses for a speedy getaway, but their plan went awry, and they fled in disarray. The day ended with one herder lying on the floor of the Saint James Hotel, riddled with bullets and buckshot. Another man was hit in the wrist, but still escaped. Two others, James Spiller and George Morrison, leader of the band, apparently got away unharmed.[22]

Fearing that a larger force of Texans would return to avenge Morrison's men, citizens of Cimarron organized a fearsome defense, headed by the sheriff and aided by miners who heard of the trouble and came to help. No assault ensued, but aroused residents met in mass and adopted resolutions pledging support to the sheriff and vowing their determination to maintain order and protect the safety of the citizens. In response, L. G. Coleman, I. W. Lacy, and other Texas cattlemen moved to quash the possibility of a pending range war. To head off trouble, the Texas bosses resolved to make some of their "toughest and clearest thinking men" available to fill jobs in law enforcement as elective and appointive vacancies occurred.[23] In this and other incidents, however, the herders working the Vermejo and Red River country north of Cimarron revealed their band to be a "wild card" in the tangled web of alliances in Colfax County, including men who, drunk or sober, were willing to plunge into disputes that engaged their sensibilities and prejudices. The *Denver Mirror* was incredulous that, in spite of the reported arrests of horse thieves and "drunken rowdies" in their midst, the *News and Press* could still claim, "The Cimarron folks continue at peace with their surrounding neighbors."[24]

Two developments in the spring of 1875 reinforced the instability of the Maxwell Land Grant claim, and of new investments lying within its disputed boundaries—investments of the English company and its Dutch partners, and those of the settlers whose land and improvements might be swallowed up in a resolution favoring company investors. First, a representative of the Dutch bondholders was said to be traveling to New Mexico to look into Maxwell Company affairs and act in the interest of the bondholders. This would not be the first or last time that the Dutch would find it necessary to intervene in defense of their interest as investors, to limit their losses in a venture that had been questionable for them from the start.[25]

Of more immediate import to those living on or invested in the Maxwell Land Grant was the news that the commissioner of the U.S. General Land Office had initiated a survey of lands claimed by the company.[26] This development signaled intent on the part of the Department of the Interior to open the almost two million acre tract to settlement as public domain, exclusive of the twenty-two-square-league tract that the department believed the claimant was entitled to possess by virtue of treaty provisions and legal interpretation. By July, Lewis Kingman had been retained by the government to complete the survey.[27]

The *Cimarron News and Press* soon carried a long and detailed article explaining why the law was apt to favor the Maxwell Company claim.[28] It was signed "LEX," but reflected the style and official view of Frank Springer, attorney for the Maxwell Company, whose position differed from that of many settlers on the issue, though he was aligned with most residents, including the settlers, in appealing for removal of the Indians and resisting Ring domination of Colfax County. The *Las Vegas Gazette* was betting on the company, advising, "The best class of settlers will not pre-empt land and expend their money upon it in improvements, when the courts may declare title in somebody else, and they may have no recourse upon the government, except for the entry price."[29] The *Gazette* echoed common sentiment among American newcomers and speculators in declaring that the territory would have been better off without any land grants and that both sides would be best served by a speedy resolution permitting greater certainty in land transactions. For the time being, citizens could only wait while the dispute was heard and resolved in federal court and in the administrative agencies at Washington.

The late spring and summer of 1875 brought more violence. On May 31, James Grover, "managing the floor" at a dance hall in Elizabethtown, reportedly ordered two boisterous men to leave the hall. When he stepped out the door a short time later, Grover was cut down by a pistol shot, believed to have come from Emanuel Garcia, a man Grover had ejected. No motive beyond revenge was noted for the killing.[30] The night was a busy one. Down Cimarron Canyon at the Saint James Hotel bar, Pancho Griego, the monte dealer that night, tangled with three privates—companions with common Irish roots, soldiers in a Sixth Cavalry detachment deployed from Fort Union. Griego shot Private Benjamin Sheahan dead and seriously wounded the other men.

A warrant was issued for Griego's arrest, but he walked free in exchange, some said, for promising to work in the interest of Ring candidates in the forthcoming election.[31] Neither of the incidents appeared to have been connected to the larger disputes in Colfax County, but they may have been exemplary of two conditions that exacerbated other clashes. These were first, the readiness of more than a few county residents to resort to gun violence as a response to a grudge, dispute, or issue of any kind; and second, the widespread use or abuse of alcohol, which seemed to be so common in violent incidents.

With warm weather came recurring worries of possible trouble between Indians and non-Indian residents of Colfax County. The deadly attack of Plains Indians on rural settlers the previous summer was fresh in local memory. An exchange between the Indian agent at Cimarron and the commander at Fort Union reflected the state of "high alert" concerning possible hostilities. Agent Alexander G. Irvine reported by telegram on May 10 that Utes and Apaches within the agency's purview planned to go "out on the plains in a day or two," but noted that he had refused passes to them.[32] Lieutenant Colonel Thomas G. Devlin replied on May 11 that he had no concern with Indian affairs other than in case of hostilities, but that those proposing to leave the area should know that any killing or stealing of the livestock of settlers would result in his sending troops to "kill every one I catch off their reservation."[33] The agency was not a reservation, but the commander's meaning was clear enough.

In anticipation of possible hostilities, a company of armed non-Indian residents of Colfax County was organized in early summer 1875, under the captaincy of Clay Allison; recruits were told to "keep constantly on hand a hundred rounds of ammunition and five days rations and meet for duty at the captain's house at a moment's warning."[34] A correspondent traveling through the country with the Wheeler Expedition in mid-July found worries about possible attacks by hostile Natives to be much on the minds of white residents. He told readers, "The people in this county have organized themselves into a company to protect their property, and I am informed by one of the members that as soon as the Apaches or Utes commit another depredation they will not ask for assistance from the government, which would, as usual, take the part of the red men, but will hunt down the offenders until every one of them is killed."[35] Despite such anxieties, the summer proved to be a mild one for trouble between Native and non-Native people of the Cimarron country.

Personal and Political Fractures

In July 1875, Ada McPherson Morley, wife of William Morley, was federally indicted for theft of the U.S. mail. Her indiscretion was slight by Colfax County standards. She had taken a letter dropped in the outgoing mail receptacle at the Cimarron post office. The letter, written by a family member, supposedly carried allegations of corruption in the territorial administration and was addressed to officials in Washington—thus Ada's urgency to retrieve it and mitigate conflict between her husband and the Santa Fe powers.[36] On its face, the matter was of minor import, but it had the potential to hurt the family by furnishing an issue that could be used to their detriment, as U.S. Attorney Catron apparently intended to do.

By August, residents were turning their attention the upcoming election of territorial and county officials on September 6. A visiting correspondent for the *Leader* of Las Animas, Colorado, passed through the country and reported, on August 24, that there seemed to be little excitement in Cimarron except for politics, observing that "to a stranger it seemed as if every other person in the place was a candidate for some office."[37] The writer's impression was reasonable in light of a report describing Colfax County politics as "decidedly interesting," with "three full tickets in the field, and more promised," a wealth of entrants for a county of fewer than two thousand voters.[38]

As a new resident of Colfax County, Reverend Tolby took a large interest in political matters. He had struck up a conversational relationship with the territorial chief justice, Joseph Palen, who came to town a few times a year to preside over sessions of the district court. They were of different political and party affinities but could otherwise enjoy each other's company. During the first week of September, when Judge Palen was in Cimarron to hold court and he and Tolby were discussing current affairs, the conversation took an acrimonious turn, with Tolby threatening to write the judge up for corruption, "so that 200,000 readers should see his record."[39] Based in part on this conversation, men connected to the alleged Santa Fe Ring may have suspected Tolby, and perhaps Morley, as the authors of an accusatorial article published in the *New York Sun* under the heading, "The Territory of Elkins: The Petty Despotism that is Called New Mexico."[40] The piece was unsigned, but reflected the writer's close observation of political life in the territory, and of leading figures involved. This was a period in which newspapers were explicit in their political allegiances and frank in expressing them. Tolby had been advised, somewhat bluntly, to "Go on saving souls and let the courts alone," moving Clay Allison to whisper to the preacher, "Parson, if you ever need a friend, call on me."[41]

Tolby was also said to be engaged in efforts to help the local Utes and Jicarillas that, if successful, would have displeased many residents. He apparently planned to establish a reserve that would keep the Natives in their homeland and had worked with a fellow Indianan to bring the idea to fruition.[42] Having been only a few months in the territory, Tolby had won numerous friends, but between his criticism of powerful Ring men and an effort to accommodate the local tribes, he was also accumulating adversaries, some of whom were not gentle souls.

Autumn came early to the mountains, and to the high plain stretching north and east from Cimarron, parts of which were above six thousand feet. By September 1875, fall was in the air. Pine, fir, and spruce were little changed to the eye. In the high forest, aspens would soon shimmer brightly and fleetingly, leaves glinting golden with splashes of red and orange. In lower elevations, nature would put on a final show before winter, in the changing of the broadleaf trees: mountain maple, cottonwood, Gambel oak, and boxelder. Hastened by cooler nights and short days, leaves would surrender their summer green, turning briefly to a palette of bright and subtle shades, then swoon to earth in hues of mousy brown, golden corn and pumpkin, old straw, and dry blood.[43]

CHAPTER 7

The Tolby Murder and Its Aftermath

The fall elections were over. Some aspirants and many voters were gratified; others were sore. In the only territory-wide election, that of the territorial delegate to Congress, there was the usual controversy. Two years before, in 1873, there had been claims of voter fraud in the race, officially won by Stephen Elkins. In 1875, it was again charged that friends and allies of Elkins had engaged in fraudulent activity, including ballot tampering in Colfax County.[1] Totals trickled in to Santa Fe, and the *New Mexican* updated returns on several days following the September 6 election. Frank Springer was among the sore, having been thrashed in his contest for a legislative seat by Melvin Mills, whose candidacy had the blessing of official Santa Fe. Dr. Robert Longwill, favored candidate of the Santa Fe political machine, won reelection as probate judge, but remained deeply unpopular with those who opposed Ring domination of local affairs.

Those unhappy with the election aired or nursed their complaints but resumed their usual routines. Deep political, cultural, and social fractures had long been evident in the county. The stresses they generated were palpable, but people of varied identities and affinities were shocked to learn of the brutal murder of Rev. Franklin J. Tolby on the homeward horseback ride from his biweekly journey to preach and advance the work of the church at Elizabethtown. He had ridden across the northeastern margin of the Moreno Valley and over the rim that defined the high vega, into the canyon of the Cimarron. He was riding down a shady streambed beneath steep, timbered slopes broken by spectacular outcrops. The road along the meandering streambed was a track of pristine beauty, but on this day, a place of ambush and death. Tolby's body was found by passersby on Thursday, September 16, but from its deteriorated condition, he likely had died on the day he left Elizabethtown, on Tuesday the fourteenth.[2] Newspapers reported only that he had been felled by two gunshots, but an account published nine years after the fact described a gruesome scene, perhaps based on the coroner's examination, stating that the body had been found "pierced with shot and stab wounds and with the skull shattered in with stones."[3] An examination of the body resulted in a difference of opinion as to whether Tolby had been shot twice by a single assassin or, as at least one examiner surmised, brought down by two shots coming from different angles.

Curiously, Tolby's horse was found nearby and his belongings had not been taken. This, along with Tolby's recent and well-publicized conflict with Judge Palen and other officials, led to speculation that the murder had been politically motivated, but there were then no suspects to be pursued or questioned. There was, however, outrage on the part of Tolby's friends, and a few theories of the killing were circulating.

Tolby's remains were returned to Cimarron and he was buried in the hilltop cemetery just south of town, with honors befitting his service as senior deacon of the local Masonic Lodge.[4] Rev. Thomas Harwood, superintendent for Methodist missions in New Mexico, was traveling at the time of Tolby's death. The news found him in Chicago, and he hurried back to the territory to find the country "in great excitement" and Tolby's young family crushed under the weight of the shock and grief.[5] Jane Crocker took the suddenly widowed Mary Tolby and the two girls in at the Crocker home, pending settlement of their affairs and a return to her parents' home in Indiana.[6]

While staying with the Crockers, Mary Tolby received word that Clay Allison had asked to call on her. Reticent about meeting with the famed cowman and gunman alone, she asked that Mrs. Crocker join them. Jane Crocker recalled Allison's manner as gentlemanly and kind. Clay inquired whether he might help financially, gave the young widow a roll of bills, and stated that she need not hesitate to call on him for assistance.[7]

On Thursday, October 28, Mary Tolby and her daughters took leave of Cimarron for her parents' home in Brookston, Indiana, with additional help from Reverend Harwood and the Methodist mission churches, and the Masonic order.[8] By November 14, Mrs. Tolby and her daughters were back home in Indiana.[9]

Franklin J. Tolby, an ordained minister of the Methodist Episcopal Church, came from Indiana with his family to build up the mission churches at Cimarron and Elizabethtown. He became well acquainted with local men of all stripes and took an active interest in social and political matters, including the condition of the Indians in Colfax County. Courtesy private collection of Quentin Robinson.

Surely some solace and comfort could be found among family, after the hardships of overland travel and a frontier adventure that had ended so horribly. What the future held for Mary Tolby, and for Rachel and Grace, no one could have said.[10] When the next session of the Northwest Indiana Conference of the Methodist Episcopal Church convened, Reverend Tolby was memorialized as one of three ministers who had been "transferred from circuit work on earth to a station in the grand tabernacle on high."[11]

Inquiry and Retribution

In Cimarron, the unfinished matter of justice for Tolby's killer or killers festered through the weeks immediately following the murder. Those officially empowered to investigate, identify suspects, and prosecute offenses seemed to do little or nothing to advance the cause of justice. At the same time, theories of motive and method, and identity of possible suspects, made the rounds in loose conversation. The common theory among Tolby's friends and allies was that the murder had been perpetrated—or at least hired—by agents of powerful officials in Santa Fe, who wished to silence opposition and dominate affairs in Colfax County. A competing rationale centered on an altercation that Tolby had witnessed a few days before his demise, in which Francisco Griego, familiarly known as "Pancho," had assaulted a man, nearly killing him before Tolby intervened, taking the victim to the parson's home to aid in his recovery.[12] Tolby had threatened to report the matter to authorities. Since Tolby was the only "outside" witness, it was supposed he might have been murdered to prevent his testifying in the event of a trial. More far-fetched were a notion that O. P. McMains, an ordained minister partially employed as Tolby's assistant, had killed Tolby in hopes of securing his position; and a theory speculating that a man from Indiana had traveled to Cimarron to murder the preacher for the yearly stipend he was to have received.[13]

Colfax County residents, alarmed by the brutal murder of Tolby, clamored for territorial and local officials to take positive action to apprehend and punish those responsible. To this end, some fifty-four persons identified as "citizens of Colfax County, New Mexico," signed a petition requesting that the governor authorize a reward on behalf of the territory. Governor Axtell responded, issuing a proclamation on October 7, 1875, offering a reward of five hundred dollars "for the apprehension and conviction of the perpetrators of this dreadful crime."[14]

Having waited—patiently, he thought—for the law to take its course, McMains gave up on that hope and undertook an investigation of the murder on his own initiative. He had taken on at least some of Tolby's former responsibilities, and as he traveled the country, he multitasked, seeking leads on the murder case. Attention fell upon two men: Cruz Vega, the recently elected constable for Precinct 3 of Colfax County; and Manuel Cardenas, about whom rumors circulated, and whose criminal past recommended him as a suspect. According to ranchman John H. "Jack" Culley, who was not on hand for the events but got his information from people who were there, McMains took the scuttlebutt he had gathered and rode around the country seeking support for a citizens' investigation. One of the men he talked with was Clay Allison, who was interested, and who took part in the episodes that were to follow.[15]

Through weeks of mourning and waiting for the legal processes to kick in, the people of Colfax County had not forgotten the heinous crime that had taken a respected preacher, leaving his two children fatherless and their mother widowed. Frank Springer recalled, "The county was intensely excited over the murder, and the people generally were fiercely indignant, and determined to punish the guilty if they could find them."[16] McMains, lacking any official power or authority to enforce the law, was determined to press the case, and he was willing to act.

Based on the persistent suspicions concerning Vega and Cardenas, McMains arranged to "interview" Vega—not in the sheriff's office or in a court of law, but in a dark cornfield, with the aid of some of the more prejudiced and uninhibited men he could have asked for help. McMains first approached Isaiah Rinehart, a private citizen who later served as sheriff of Colfax County, for help in arranging an interrogation of Vega. Finding him unenthusiastic, McMains sought and received help from William Low, who worked farmland in the lower Ponil drainage. Low agreed to have Vega stand night watch over his corn on three nights in late October 1875.[17] McMains also arranged for a party of men to provide an intimidating presence, and sufficient muscle in the event that force was needed to secure Vega's cooperation, or, presumably, to repel any party that might show in his defense. It was not McMains's intention to harm Vega, but McMains seemed not to mind threatening or scaring the detainee, if that would produce the information he sought.

McMains wanted to bring a murderer to justice, but at this night rendezvous on the Ponil, he mainly wanted information. From multiple sources, he had ample reason to believe that Vega, who had carried the mail from Elizabethtown to Cimarron on the fateful day, had at least been in the area when the killing occurred and knew what had happened, and may have been involved in the murder. McMains did not imagine that, in setting a trap to obtain Vega's account, he was not advancing the cause of justice, but setting off a series of events that would compound, rather than resolve, the tragedy and treachery that had already rocked Colfax County.

Vega's first night on the job, Friday, October 29, was uneventful. But on the second night, his employer joined him in the field and built a small fire, supposedly to provide warmth and a cheering presence on a cool fall evening. At some point, both Vega and Low slept, and woke to find that a small group of men had come to their fire, one of whom dropped a lariat over Vega's head and directed him to "come on." The men walked their prisoner several hundred yards along a road and into a stand of timber, following the telegraph line to a point at which other men were waiting—perhaps forty or fifty, by Low's estimate.[18] The men handling Vega were described by Low as "disguised"; the near-universal sense of persons familiar with the incident was that those directly involved were cowmen and herders of the Vermejo and Red River regions—popularly if not precisely known as Texans or *Tejanos*.

Vega and the small group that had escorted him to the place stood next to a pole, while McMains stood several paces away, directing his questions through the handlers. Vega's early reticence may have prompted the leaders of the interrogation to direct the youngest man in the crowd, seventeen-year-old Zenas Curtis, to climb the pole and put the loose end of the lead rope over the cleat or crossarm, so that Vega could be lifted off the ground. Curtis later professed that he thought the men were bluffing and said that he might have refused had he known what was to come, but as a youth in the presence of older men emboldened in the moment, he likely had little choice in the matter.[19] Vega was briefly lifted off the ground, then set back down. Apparently he gave the information that McMains wanted, telling the men that he had seen Manuel Cardenas kill Tolby in Cimarron Canyon.

At this point, McMains was becoming alarmed at the severity of the interrogation and the apparent intent of the interrogators to continue with the punishment of Vega. Evidently there had been no plan for turning him over to the sheriff or any other duly constituted authority; there may have been a sense that those officials were actively disinterested in pursuing an investigation that might lead to more prominent enablers behind the assassination of Tolby. In any event, McMains had lost control of the situation. He later told cattleman Irvin W. Lacy of his attempt to have men in the crowd of bystanders intervene to keep Vega from being killed, but they were too much in liquor to hear or heed.[20]

McMains apparently panicked and quit the scene, leaving Vega at the mercy of an unruly mob.[21] McMains walked back to the nearby house of Erastus Welding, where he and Low were staying. In a while he heard gunshots and felt certain that Vega had died violently at the hands of the mob. The following morning, Low woke about sunrise to find McMains distraught, crying in dread that his presentiment of Vega's death was realized. Low at first thought he would return to the site of the previous night's interrogation in search of the body, but he decided instead to go to town and report the matter to authorities.[22]

Francisco Gonzales, deputy sheriff, led a coroner's jury to the scene of Vega's lynching, where the evidence told of a horrifying death. Ground disturbed by the digging of boots showed a struggle had taken place; a handful of Vega's hair lay nearby. He had been hanged, shot in the back, and bludgeoned, and his body had apparently been dragged through the range brush. None of this comported with the intent of McMains, whose remorse over the debacle was more for the loss of Vega's testimony than for the man.[23] McMains's prior assurances that Vega was not to be harmed may have been genuine, but his zeal to obtain an incriminating statement had overcome his judgment. Witting or not, he had placed Vega in the hands of a haphazardly assembled mob, a collection of undisciplined men, many single and away from home on a Saturday night, in the presence of alcohol, adrenaline, and rage.

The *Las Animas Leader* in southern Colorado reported that the incident was the work of a "vigilance committee" and identified its subject as "a Mexican named Cruz Vega." Other papers referred to the crowd as a "lynch mob." The *Leader* also alleged that "a Mexican named Griego" had accused Allison of taking part in the hanging.[24] The elements of racial conflict and prejudice inherent in the treatment of Vega, and in some reports of the affair, were immediately apparent to wide-awake residents of Colfax County and New Mexico. The *New Mexican* newspaper declared the affair "a disgrace to our people" and commented further, "It is feared that more bloodshed is likely to occur between bad Mexicans and equally bad Americans."[25]

There seem to be few instances in the history of lynchings and assassinations, in Colfax County or elsewhere, in which the instigators have been held accountable. Most often, they were never identified, except through the rumor mill. In some cases, bonds of mutual silence have held firm; in other instances, there seems to have been little appetite for investigating or prosecuting the perpetrators. McMains and fourteen other men were charged in Cruz Vega's death, but only McMains was ultimately prosecuted. His sorrow the morning after Vega's gruesome death gave way to worries about his own fate, particularly after he was arrested, charged, and lodged in the Cimarron jail to await trial. Lawyers of the anti–Santa Fe Ring faction put on a defense, arguing that McMains was not involved in the actions leading to Vega's death, was absent when the acts occurred, and despite apparent lapses in judgment, he had not intended to take Vega's life.

Apprehensions regarding possible retribution for Vega's death were justified. Francisco Griego, an influential man among Hispanic residents, was a relative of Vega, thought by some to be the dead man's uncle.[26] According the *Las Animas*

Leader report, Griego had openly blamed Allison for Vega's death, and had threatened to kill him.[27] Allison's manner in public places was nearly always guarded, likely more so when he came face to face with Griego in Cimarron on the first day of November, following Vega's death.

Robert Clay Allison: Cowman and Gunman

Historians of New Mexico have found it interesting to compare the two best known range wars of territorial times, centered in Colfax County and Lincoln County. They were fierce fights for political and economic domination, contested by rival factions in each region, with territorial officials allied with one side or the other in each place. In each of these conflicts, the outrageous killing of a respected and largely benign figure—Reverend Tolby in Colfax County and John Tunstall in Lincoln, provided a flashpoint for violence. The powerful clique known as the Santa Fe Ring was a shadowy force in both struggles, and federal troops were involved in both places—reluctantly in Colfax County, but with too much enthusiasm in Lincoln.

The Lincoln County War has enjoyed much greater notoriety in comparison to the Colfax County War, as evidenced by the countless appearances of the Lincoln County story in works of fiction, movies, and other objects of popular culture. The discrepancy is owed principally to high audience fascination with an enigmatic character in Lincoln County, in the man known as Henry Antrim or William Bonney—"Billy the Kid." The Colfax County War had no Billy the Kid. The nearest Colfax County could come to such an alluring figure was Clay Allison, a flawed version, who was older and more sullen, and whose violent acts were more calculated, having much to do with his ideas of honor and justice. A maxim applied to Allison by cattleman John Culley, based on Culley's impression of the esteem for Allison among his friends and neighbors, might just as easily have described Billy's reputation with friends; in both cases, admirers were "to his faults a little blind, and to his virtues very kind."[28]

Billy made no pretense to power but appeared to have an easy rapport with the Spanish-speaking people of the rural villages. Allison was, by some reports, serious, intense, and perhaps too ready to intervene boldly in issues on which he held a strong opinion. Southwestern historian and folklorist J. Frank Dobie, informed by the accounts of old-timers who had seen Allison in action or heard of his exploits, noted that the famed gunman "was quixotic in standing up for his rights," which were determined by his own sensibilities, which were subject to his current frame of mind. "The more whiskey he drank, the more rights he possessed," Dobie wrote.[29]

Alcohol, in fact, seems to have been a critical determinant in Allison's behavior. Several personal reminiscences have referred to Allison as a gentleman, a man of principle, a man of his word, an honorable man. But all of that changed when he was drinking, and by most accounts, he drank often and to excess. Said former territorial governor Miguel Otero, recalling chaotic times, "When sober, Clay Allison was well mannered and extremely likable, but under the influence of liquor he was a terror to the whole neighborhood and a good man to avoid."[30] As a soldier in the army of the Confederacy, Allison had been judged unfit for service, because of mental instability brought on by a head injury.[31] This was another object of curiosity for those trying to make sense of Allison's recurring violent episodes and the self-justification that usually accompanied them.

Clay Allison carried on an ambiguous relationship with the law. He was not an outlaw in the usual sense, and doubtless thought of himself as a respectable citizen. In the memoir of Frank Clifford, a teenage youth living in the area during and after his father's time as mining manager for the Maxwell Company between 1871 and 1874, Allison was recalled as "by common consent the leader of the 'Law and Order League.'"[32] In several instances when accused of offenses, Allison submitted to judicial processes. But his predictable inclination was to engage in or invite confrontation, as opposed to defusing it or referring a matter to the local authorities. In recorded cases in which Allison was formally accused of murder, he was not indicted, or was acquitted on grounds of self-defense. In some instances, he paid for property he had damaged or destroyed—most often in a dance hall or barroom fracas.[33] Allison sometimes exempted himself from laws, especially those requiring him to disarm in designated places. His refusal to surrender his weapons in a saloon, or within the limits of a town having a no-carry law, seems to have been related to almost constant fear for his personal safety, which came with his growing reputation as a gunfighter and man-killer.[34]

Defenders of Allison's reputation pointed to numerous dismissals, no bills, and findings of self-defense in charges brought against him and subscribed to the popular notion that he had "never killed a man that did not need killing," a slogan immortalized on his gravestone. This tribute was intended to justify, and even confer approval on, the widely publicized killings for which he had been responsible. It might be noted that this notion—that Allison never killed a man who didn't need killing—constitutes a case statement for assassination and lynching and does very little to justify spontaneous execution in a society in which determination of guilt and administration of justice are reserved to the law, the judicial system, and elected or appointed agents of the law. In a partial defense of lynching and vigilantism, feud scholar C. L. Sonnichsen pointed out that such actions were not always regarded as lawless but were sometimes intended to ensure justice when legal authority failed or was nonexistent in the circumstance.[35]

Allison is worth knowing, because his involvement in the most violent phase of the Colfax County War was extensive. Among the varied contemporary and historical accounts, he has been assigned a leading role in virtually every event that has been considered integral to the history of the conflict, including the killings of Cruz Vega and Pancho Griego, the arrest and assassination of Manuel Cardenas, the pursuit of Dr. Robert Longwill, and the attempt to silence the *Cimarron News and Press* for publishing content not to Allison's liking.

In some of these episodes Allison's involvement is well established; in some it is strongly indicated. In other instances, he is named with little evidence, in the manner of a "usual suspect." Determination of Allison's culpability for acts attributed to him but not confirmed is complicated by the seeming reluctance of acquaintances to talk about matters that may have been offensive or damaging to him. George W. Coe, whose family raised livestock in the Sugarite area of northern Colfax County, arrived in August 1874, in time to witness the peak turmoil of the Colfax County War. The family departed in early 1876 for Lincoln County, where they experienced the equally disastrous Lincoln County War. Of the notorious affair of Allison's killing of Chunk Colbert at Clifton House, Coe recalled, "This, in common with many other such incidents, was regarded as nobody's business."[36] Reviewing Allison's reputation in the Cimarron country, one writer noted, "Most Colfax County citizens feared Allison and deplored his maniacal rages, but Clay was a desperate man and few desired to confront him."[37]

Even a friendly word might not be well received. George Coe recalled looking on with pleasure as Allison confronted Finis Ernest, a fellow cattleman, about grievances of farmers who had been forced to leave their crops and families for days, because of lawsuits filed against them by Ernest concerning a grazing lease. Allison talked plain language and gave Ernest a "tap on the head-piece" for emphasis, admonishing Ernest to get on with his lawsuits or dismiss them and let the farmers go home. Coe appreciated the performance and started to let out a shout of approval, but thought again and concluded, "There are indeed times when silence is golden, and I decided this was one of them."[38] In Allison, neighbors knew a man who, despite acknowledged virtues, drank too much too often and liked to "run the town" with companions when drunk. Also, he was usually armed and ready to kill on short notice, and he might be a little crazy. The prudent among them found it best to stay indoors, and to see, hear, and say little when he was around.

The Killing of Pancho Griego

On Allison's arrival in Cimarron on Monday, November 1, following the Saturday night death of Vega, he was warned of high feeling running against him on the part of "Mexicans" led by Pancho Griego. Allison was advised that his life had been threatened, and that he should leave town at once, ahead of any possible trouble.[39] Allison replied that he had some business to attend to in town and believed he would stay and attend to it. His business may have been taking on the issue he knew was brewing with Griego.

Having driven to Cimarron from his ranch, Allison put up his wagon and team and started down a street and met up with Griego, who was walking toward him in company with other men. Allison refused a handshake, declaring that he did not trust Griego and had heard that Griego had threatened his life, and Griego stated that Allison had accused him of complicity in the murder of Tolby. Allison replied that "he thought circumstances pointed very strongly in that direction."[40]

Allison and Pancho agreed to part ways, but in the evening, Allison was with a friend at Lambert's saloon when Pancho came in with two companions. Griego went toward the back end of the hall and asked that Allison join him for conversation. Cautious of the men with Griego and noticing that one of them had placed a pistol beneath a shawl on the table in front of him, Allison kept his hand near his own weapon and his eyes on Griego and his friends. Allison's glance away from Pancho and toward one of the friends prompted Griego to draw a pistol from under his coat, but when he pulled the weapon, the lock reportedly snagged on a button hole. In an instant, Clay Allison drew his weapon and fired the shots that settled his trouble with Griego. The dead man's friends fled, and the place was immediately emptied, darkened, and closed for business. Griego's body was found there the next morning. As with other instances of gunplay in which

Allison was involved, there was some ambiguity concerning the extent to which he was acting in self-defense or instigating the violence. He was ordered to appear before a justice of the peace for a hearing to determine whether he should stand trial in district court on charges related to the Griego's death.

The Mysterious Dr. Longwill

Tolby's avengers continued to pursue leads to the identities of other possible participants in the plot to murder the parson. There lingered speculation that the order to kill Tolby had come from men of higher rank and station, compared to those accused of pulling the trigger. Suspicion fell heavily on Dr. Robert Longwill, who had come to Colfax County in the late 1860s and had since become a private citizen and resident of the county, and a highly unpopular figure. He left several years later with life and limb intact, but with a reputation that was badly tarnished.

Longwill had enlisted in the Union army as a medical cadet following graduation from medical school in 1863 and mustered out as a captain at the end of the Civil War in 1865. Between 1865 and 1870, he was employed by the army as a contract physician, with the modest title of acting assistant surgeon. He was assigned to the Department of New Mexico and was stationed at Fort Wingate and Fort Union, with duty at other posts as required.[41] He was often sent to Cimarron, or "Maxwell's ranch," when hostilities or overt disorder required a military presence.

Dr. Longwill was not popular with the army officers, whom he antagonized with occasional recalcitrance in reporting to remote assignments. He developed an affinity for Cimarron and the Moreno Valley, where the discovery of gold had generated considerable excitement. Longwill's interest in local affairs and an increasing disinterest in the army's business may have been noted when, in March 1870, he was evasive regarding orders to go with a cavalry unit to Fort Wingate. A telegram requesting an explanation elicited the information that he had been ill and might not report as requested. Piqued at Longwill's attitude, General William Grier passed the response to his superior, adding, "If the Actg. Asst. Surgeons are so unfortunate as to be sick whenever required for any special and important duty, would it not be for the best interests of the service, that their contracts be annulled."[42]

By fall of 1870, Longwill was a shareholder in the new Maxwell Land Grant and Railway Company, had resigned from the army, and was running for the

Robert Hamilton Longwill was a former U.S. Army contract physician posted in New Mexico, who found opportunity in Colfax County. He separated from the army, settled in the county, and won election as probate judge. Longwill was also involved in management of the Maxwell Land Grant and Railway Company, before fleeing the county when accused of complicity in the murder of Franklin Tolby. Photo from Ralph Emerson Twitchell, *Leading Facts of New Mexican History*, vol. 2.

office of probate judge in Colfax County.[43] He won by a margin of 315 votes out of 639 cast.[44] His victory was impressive, but all was not well in the beautiful Moreno Valley. The officer in charge of an army detail at Cimarron was obliged to tell his superiors at Fort Union, "I was called upon last evening by the English Company here, to send a detachment from the troop to Elizabethtown for the purpose of quelling a disturbance among the Citizens of that place, in consequence of the election of Dr. Longwill to the office of Probate Judge."[45] Agitated by the company's efforts to drive them from their claims or charge additional fees, miners had acted to express displeasure with the company and with the men who had supported Longwill's election.[46]

The probate judge and sheriff were the most powerful elected county officials. In an 1878 article, the *Cimarron News and Press* declared, with reference to

Longwill, that the probate judge occupied a position "pretty near equal to king."[47] Probate judges had some judicial functions, but they also wielded administrative powers normally associated with the office of county supervisor or county judge: hiring teachers and overseeing schools, managing money and supervising public works, compiling jury pools and administering elections, for example.[48]

A common supposition in the county was that Stephen Elkins and others associated with the Santa Fe Ring were strongly vested in Longwill's effort to win the office of probate judge.[49] But Longwill carried a larger portfolio, starting with his designation as "managing director" of the Maxwell Company during the company's early months of operation. He was also in charge of the Indian agency at Cimarron twice between October 1872 and early 1875.[50] When Elkins and Tom Catron acquired control of the First National Bank of Santa Fe, they brought Longwill in as an investor and director. As evidence of Longwill's devotion to his sponsor in politics and business, his eldest son, born in 1874, was given the name of Stephen Benton Elkins Longwill.[51]

An old-timer talking to the *New York Sun* about the Tolby murder in 1894 said, "In those desperate times assassination was a trade, and men's lives were a matter of barter and sale."[52] He must have been thinking of the shooting deaths of John Fisher and John Glass, both in 1871, rumored to have been ordered up by officials of the Maxwell Company with ties to the territorial ring in Santa Fe. Longwill had been linked to the Glass killing, though not charged or convicted.

According to a *News and Press* account published well after the fact, in June 1878, Glass and Elizabethtown Justice of the Peace Patrick McBride had been tools in service of the Maxwell Company until, with the benefit of confidential information, "they ceased to work well in harness and became refractory" and were viewed as "traitors and breeders of treason."[53] The company's response, according to the article, had been to have them killed, paying assassins and furnishing means for their escape. On the night of May 8, 1871, Glass was killed in Elizabethtown. Perhaps guessing that he might be next, McBride fled to Trinidad, Colorado.

The murder of Glass was never officially resolved, but two witness accounts persisted in the area, both identifying Longwill as the individual who had arranged for the killing. William Morley recalled an incident that had taken place in the company store at Cimarron. He had heard of the killing of Glass, and that Lemuel Jones and W. B. Hogan might have been involved. Jones entered the store in an excited state and asked where Longwill was. Jones had come for horses on which to ride out, explaining that Elizabethtown had become "too hot" for Jones and Hogan. It seemed that some around town suspected that they had done the killing. Soon the doctor came in. After a private talk with Longwill, Jones left to get the horses, and rode out toward Trinidad with Hogan and other companions. Longwill later commented, in Morley's presence, that "he had the juries fixed and could indict and convict who he damned pleased," and said that "the right way to run a country was to get somebody to shoot the sons of bitches who opposed you."[54]

The other anecdote came from James Wightman, administrator of the Maxwell Company when Glass was killed, as retold by O. P. McMains in an 1885 newspaper interview. Questioned by a sheriff's deputy concerning the matter, Wightman had recalled talking with Longwill in the company offices when two rough-looking men entered and told the doctor, in apparent reference to John Glass, "We put a hole in him and we want the fixings."[55] More evidence later surfaced in correspondence between Longwill and the assassins and between Longwill and Elkins, reflecting Longwill's role in the killing and Elkins's knowledge of the incident. The letters may have been recovered in Longwill's office following his frantic flight to Santa Fe in November 1875.[56]

When Dr. Longwill's name came up in connection with the Tolby murder in fall of 1875, in a context that brought to mind the killing of John Glass and the rumors respecting the doctor's possible involvement in that incident, it was not hard for fellow citizens, many of whom already had a poor opinion of him, to think there could be something to it. By the time the charges came up for a courtroom hearing in Cimarron, Longwill had already made himself scarce. Even so, he was the most talked-about man in town.

CHAPTER 8

A Town in Turmoil

The eight-week interval since Franklin J. Tolby's death had done nothing to relieve the outrage in Colfax County by the second week of November. If anything, the lynching of Cruz Vega and the killing of Pancho Griego gave citizens a sense that the case was finally moving and inspired a renewed interest in the pursuit of other suspects. By Monday, November 8, interested residents were arriving in Cimarron, the county seat, on the news of the arrest of Manuel Cardenas, and in anticipation of further arrests and pending court appearances.

The gathering had been peaceful, but in Santa Fe, the *New Mexican* told a different story, informing readers, "For the past week Cimarron has been more or less in a complete state of anarchy."[1] The paper decried a "spirit of lawlessness" said to have been raging in Colfax County. The local reaction to Tolby's death was denounced as "only a pretext for this armed band to visit their violence upon the peaceable citizens of Cimarron."[2] A detachment of soldiers had been sent from Fort Union to keep order at the request of territorial officials.

Justice or Vengeance?

Following Pancho Griego's death, the attention of those still on the trail of Tolby's killers turned to Manuel Cardenas, named by Cruz Vega as the triggerman. Cardenas and Vega were suspected as assassins or accessories; higher-ups were believed to have paid them to kill Tolby. Cardenas was "interviewed" at Elizabethtown by Joseph Herberger, a private citizen of uncertain character, and a sometime participant in local "vigilance committee" actions. On November 5, Cardenas related his story in a sworn statement before Elizabethtown justice of the peace

Dallas Cummings.[3] The statement was sensational, in that it named notable local men as sponsors of the killing, consistent with theories that the murder was politically motivated. Cardenas swore that Vega had been paid five hundred dollars to shoot Tolby, from funds provided by Robert Longwill, Melvin Mills, Florencio Donoghue, and Pancho Griego. Donoghue allegedly collected and held the money on behalf of the group, but according to Cardenas, the person who had spoken directly with him to solicit the murder was Longwill.[4]

Cardenas's statement was carried down the canyon from Elizabethtown to Cimarron, the county seat, on Saturday, November 6. Word of Cardenas's dramatic disclosures spread quickly and was especially alarming to Dr. Longwill. Having learned of fates that had been dealt to Vega and Griego, and now finding himself publicly accused, Longwill made a speedy departure for Fort Union. Meanwhile, learning of the accusations against those who were supposed to have ordered Tolby's murder, people began to gather in anticipation of further developments. Among those crowding the streets and saloons of Cimarron were many of the men called Texans.

On the basis of Cardenas's statement, Samuel S. Trauer, justice of the peace for Precinct 3 in northern Colfax County, issued warrants for the arrest of Florencio Donoghue, Melvin Mills, and the absent Dr. Longwill. On Sunday, November 7, Cardenas was brought down to Cimarron from Elizabethtown and, according to the *News and Press*, Donoghue and Mills were taken into custody pending a hearing to determine whether they should be tried in the district court.[5] Clay and John Allison and Pete Burleson rode to Fort Union in pursuit of Longwill, but found that he had been given protection by officers at the fort; he had since fled south to Santa Fe. Longwill had intended to return to Cimarron with soldiers sent to keep order, but reconsidered. According to Lieutenant George A. Cornish, he "refused to come to Cimarron saying they would hang him."[6] In his report to his superior officer, Cornish added, "A large number of Texans present all armed."

Mills learned of the accusations against him in Trinidad, Colorado, where he had gone on legal business. He received telegrams telling him of the charges and warning of the reception that he might face if he returned to Cimarron. In spite of the warnings, Mills later recalled, "It seemed so absurd and ridiculous to me that I took my team and buggy and started to go back to Cimarron, running my horses over thirty miles until they were exhausted to overtake the coach and go on to Cimarron."[7] Mills was greeted by an angry mob. He feared for his life, but then was placed in custody of a guard consisting of twelve of his own friends and twelve seekers of justice for Tolby. When Lieutenant Cornish's detachment arrived from Fort Union, Mills was handed over to be detained by the soldiers until the hearing.

Henry Waldo, a Santa Fe lawyer and sometime associate of the Ring, had been sent from Santa Fe to defend those men accused of procuring Tolby's killing—Donoghue, Longwill, and Mills. He carried writs of habeas corpus demanding that the defendants be given up for transfer to Santa Fe County. The writs were to be enforced by Lieutenant Cornish and his men from Fort Union. Seeing the popular outrage that prevailed among many of the men gathered in Cimarron, Cornish expressed doubt that he could execute a peaceful transfer of the accused men, advising a superior officer on November 9 that he thought he might have to use force to carry out the order. "The Texans might put seventy five men under arms to resist," he wrote, "but I think I'll get the men before they know it."[8] Waldo decided to forego the writs and allow Donoghue and Mills to face the hearing in Cimarron.[9] Longwill, meanwhile, had already transferred himself to Santa Fe.

The Brothers Trauer

Albert and Kate Trauer came from Bohemia in eastern Europe to settle in Saint Louis in the mid-1850s. They had at least five sons and three daughters, all but the two youngest having been born in the old country. They were of Jewish faith and heritage, a family of merchants—mostly clothing and dry goods. Albert had established a business in Saint Louis, in which he was joined at various times and for various intervals by four of his five sons, the fifth having died in his youth.

The four Trauer sons who survived to maturity, each in his turn, trekked to New Mexico, the older two making their lives in the Southwest, the two youngest reverting to Saint Louis after a period of years. The eldest, Maurice Trauer, was in New Mexico as early as 1862, drumming up business for the family firm at frontier forts.[10] In the early 1870s, Trauer was associated with the Spiegelberg brothers in Santa Fe; they backed him with a stock of merchandise when he opened a retail establishment in Cimarron in August 1873. Maurice learned about the local penchant for forcible settlement of differences when, in November 1874, he was threatened with lynching in a dispute concerning ownership of a quantity of grain. The lesson was reinforced in January 1875, when his store was the refuge of four well-lubricated cowboys who wanted to "run the town."[11]

The Trauer brothers mostly went separate ways in the Southwest, each getting a start in the mercantile business and falling back on that familiar occupation as needed, but only Maurice made it his career. Louis Trauer became a successful sheep and wool trader, and Sigmund a cigar maker. The brothers worked together only once, perhaps intermittently, in the store that Maurice had established in Cimarron, in a period that happened to coincide with the central conflict of the Colfax County trouble. Three of the four brothers signed the petition asking Governor Axtell to issue a reward for information leading to the arrest and punishment of the killer of Reverend Tolby.[12]

Samuel Trauer, or "Sam," was something of a free spirit, but seemingly popular wherever he went in his sojourn of about a decade in the territory. In addition to Cimarron, he lived in Las Vegas, Santa Fe, Socorro, and Albuquerque, and worked as a store clerk and window decorator, a wool dealer, and a dance instructor, and managed a mining and real estate office and an auction store. He was, at leisure, a baseball umpire, thespian, bugler for the Albuquerque Guard, and minstrel performer. His large feet attracted notice and invited some friendly razzing. In Cimarron, he won a hundred-yard foot race and "came near blowing his head into a million of atoms" fooling with a Spencer rifle.[13] Somehow, during a brief residency in Cimarron, Sam was elected justice of the peace for Colfax County Precinct 3 and found himself presiding over some of the more gripping courtroom proceedings of the Colfax County War.

A Day in Court

It was the duty of the justice of the peace court in each county to conduct a preliminary examination of persons accused of serious offenses and determine whether grounds were evident to warrant their being referred to the district court for review by the grand jury. On Wednesday, November 10, 1875, four such cases came for hearing before the Precinct 3 justice of the peace court in Cimarron, with Hon. Samuel S. Trauer presiding. Dallas Cummings, the justice of the peace for Precinct 1—Elizabethtown, the Moreno Valley, and vicinity—sat with Trauer for the hearing.

In the morning, the court held an inquiry into the shooting death of Francisco "Pancho" Griego by Clay Allison. That Allison had shot and killed Griego was not disputed. The hearing, as depicted in the *News and Press*, may seem somewhat friendly to Allison, in that, as reported, "No witnesses appeared for the prosecution."[14] This, despite the presence at the shooting of two men who accompanied Griego, but who may, for their own reasons, have preferred not to testify. Referring to the night of the shooting, defense witnesses, perhaps including the defendant, made statements to persuade the court that "the action of some Mexicans nearby were so suspicious as to lead Allison to believe that an attack on him was imminent and the danger great." The killing was ruled "justifiable," and Allison was discharged to face no further jeopardy on this charge.[15]

Despite the finding, circumstances of the shooting remained clouded, and there lingered some doubt that the threat to Allison was as dire as claimed. Cimarron resident George Crocker, nine years old at the time, perhaps informed more by hearsay than by personal observation, was persuaded that Allison had shot Chunk Colbert and Griego, "not in self defense, but because he was afraid of them."[16] No report was made of attendance at the hearing, but given descriptions of the crowd gathered in Cimarron—messages sent by Lieutenant Cornish to his superior officers at the fort refer to the prevalence of "Texans" in town—it seems probable that the court's decision, whether or not it was just, was popular and perhaps prudent.[17]

In the afternoon following the Allison hearing, charges against Manuel Cardenas, Melvin Mills, and Florencio Donoghue were taken up jointly. Some testimony was also heard in relation to the charges against Robert Longwill, but no finding was rendered relative to him, since he had not been arrested and was not present. Over several hours, the court heard from some thirty-two witnesses, including Mills and Donoghue. O. P. McMains read the statement given to the coroner's jury by William Low concerning the death of Cruz Vega, as well as the statement given at Elizabethtown by Cardenas. Of the thirty-two witnesses who spoke, all except one were men. None of the men had usual Spanish-language surnames, even though an estimated three-fourths of the residents of Cimarron were known as "Mexicans."[18] Antonia Luna, the only woman, told the court that she had known Cardenas from childhood, that he had killed a woman in Taos some years ago, that he was a bad man, and that it was his habit to carry weapons, as he did around the time of the September 6 election.[19]

Based on his testimony and Cruz Vega's story, Cardenas may have been presumed to be sufficiently implicated as a perpetrator or accomplice in Tolby's murder to warrant referral of the charges for grand jury consideration. Perhaps more intriguing to spectators was a statement made earlier by Cardenas regarding the men named as having paid for Tolby's assassination. Cardenas named

Donoghue, Longwill, and Mills, along with the departed Francisco Griego, as having paid a total of five hundred dollars to have Tolby killed. Cardenas had also said at Elizabethtown that Longwill had talked with him about the need for someone to eliminate Tolby, naming Donoghue, Griego, and Mills as other contributors of funds with which to hire an assassin. Cardenas said that he had turned down the proposition but was told that Vega had agreed to do the job.

Most vexing in the testimony was the revelation that, since transport from Elizabethtown to Cimarron, Cardenas had recanted the testimony given earlier, including his implication of the four men accused of paying for the assassination, saying it was all false and forced from him at gunpoint. This important revision came from witnesses who had gone to see Cardenas at the jail in Cimarron prior to the hearing. According to men who had attended the informal proceeding at Elizabethtown, the sworn statement that Cardenas gave there was not made under duress. Joseph Herberger testified that in his preliminary interview with the accused, Cardenas had been assured that he would not be hurt; however, the assurance is somewhat ambiguous, in that Herberger also stated that he had laid his gun on the table before Cardenas prior to the interview.

Most problematic for Cardenas, in trying to avoid conviction and hanging, was testimony to the effect that he had told people in Taos about Tolby's demise before news of the murder had reached Cimarron. This led to questions about Cardenas's whereabouts on the day of the ambush and at other days and times as they related to the discovery of Tolby's body and the reporting of the murder. Cardenas could not give answers sufficient to disqualify himself as a suspect.

Donoghue had some explaining to do when at least two witnesses testified to hearing him express intent to do away with Tolby by means of a "blue pill," or bullet. One witness related an incident in which Donoghue, obviously drunk, had accosted the preacher on a street in Cimarron, prompting Tolby to call for help in getting Donoghue away from him. Donoghue could not recall such expressions of hostility toward Tolby, but admitted that he might not remember what he had said under the influence. Other witnesses stated that they had never heard Donoghue offer threats against Tolby. Donoghue insisted that, despite arguments and "warm words" that had passed between them, he had never wanted to hurt the preacher.[20]

Though absent from the hearing, Longwill was the subject of damaging testimony—some recalling his rumored involvement in the murder of John Glass several years earlier. One witness described an excited manner when Longwill was speaking about particulars of the Tolby murder; another recalled his hoping for an early end to the inquiry. Alexander Dull who, with Cummings, had brought Cardenas's statement to Cimarron, talked of Longwill's observable anxiety in seeing them, and noted that Longwill had returned to his office and left town about fifteen minutes later. According to a source recalling the events in 1895, Longwill owned a fine horse with "speed and bottom." Seemingly in a panic, he had hitched up and "started his buggy for Santa Fe, driving for his life."[21]

Longwill drove toward Fort Union. He reportedly intended to return to Cimarron with the soldiers who had been requested by territorial officials, but he changed his mind for fear of being hanged.[22] Instead, he hurried to Santa Fe and the protection of powerful men with whom he was aligned in business and politics: Samuel Axtell, the governor; Thomas Catron, the U.S. attorney; William Breeden, the attorney general; John Pratt, U.S. marshal; and, of course, Stephen Elkins, the territorial delegate to Congress, president of the First National Bank of Santa Fe, and former president of the Maxwell Company.[23] Pursued by Clay Allison and other men of Colfax County, he welcomed the intervention of officers at Fort Union who prevented his arrest, then hightailed it to Santa Fe.

Following the airing of witness testimony over a period of several hours, Justices Trauer and Cummings took a recess and returned with a decision signed by Trauer and "concurred in" by Cummings. Cardenas was found "guilty of the murder of Rev. F. J. Tolby"—strong language, it seems, for a proceeding the purpose of which was limited to determining whether the evidence was sufficient to justify referring the case to a grand jury. Donoghue was judged an accessory to the killing. Cardenas and Donoghue were ordered returned to jail to await the action of the grand jury, and Donoghue was allowed to give bail in the amount of twenty thousand dollars. Insufficient evidence was found to justify referring Mills to the grand jury, and his charges were dismissed. The court made no official decision as to the culpability of Longwill.[24]

The Death of Manuel Cardenas

A witness account given to the *New York Sun* nearly two decades after the fact revealed that the hearing for Cardenas, Donoghue, and Mills concluded "on the edge of evening."[25] It was dark enough that a party of cowboys standing "in the deepest shadow" beyond the corner of the stone jail could not be distinguished

Stone jail, Cimarron, ca. 1910. The jail was built in 1872, when Cimarron became the county seat, before yielding that distinction to Springer in 1879. A high wall surrounded the jail and reportedly shielded the men who, in November 1875, waited there to ambush Manuel Cardenas, a prisoner charged with killing Franklin Tolby. Photo by Edward Troutman. Denver Public Library, Western History Collection.

one from another by a passerby, as two law officers walked up, one on either side of Manuel Cardenas as he was being returned to his jail cell. Cardenas was having a cigarette as they walked. As Cardenas and the guards drew near to the jail, "a tall figure stepped forth to meet them, leveling a pistol as he did so." The two officers, presumably startled, but perhaps not, fell away on each side of the prisoner, and the tall cowboy, "sighting by the light of the cigarette, shot Cardenas square through the forehead," bringing his case and his life to a shocking and sudden end.[26]

Functional pandemonium ensued, as the cowboys dispersed, running, riding, shouting—vanishing into the night to leave the jail site deserted and quiet within a short minute, and no clue as to who had fired the fatal round. The commander of the soldiers sent from Fort Union to keep order, perhaps feeling egg on his face, wired the district command in Santa Fe to explain, "I was on the ground in 5 minutes but everybody had disappeared."[27]

It seems inconceivable that the "fifteen to twenty" men reported by Cornish to have been in wait to ambush the prisoner did not know who killed Cardenas, or did not reveal it, ever. The *Sun* informant hinted at the obvious, commenting, "When the street got quiet again no one not in the secret could have told who among the crowd of wild drinkers at Lambert's bar was the man who fired the shot."[28] Surely most or all of the men waiting for Cardenas must have been "in the secret," but no one claiming to have been in the scrum at the jail, even from the relative safety of old age or long distance, gave a definitive answer as to who had shot Cardenas. Those mentioned as likely candidates were Joseph Herberger, saloon owner and vigilante from Elizabethtown; and Clay Allison.[29] The idea of Herberger as the shooter squares with the reports of Lieutenant Cornish, who understood that the men around the jail may have been from Elizabethtown.[30] The *Sun* informant referred to them as "cowboys," pointing to the more frequently named suspect, Clay Allison, as the shooter.[31]

A practical consequence of the killings of Vega and Cardenas, common in such instances of mob violence and spontaneous pronouncement of guilt, was the loss of information that could potentially have convicted or exonerated those accused of arranging and paying for the murder. Of O. P. McMains's clumsy and deadly attempt to find the killers and bring them to justice, his superior in the Methodist Church, Rev. Thomas Harwood, lamented the interference, observing, "If there were others mixed up in the case other than the three who lost their lives as heretofore given, I have always thought the unwise methods of McMains helped to cover up the tracks of evidence and they have never been found."[32]

There remained deep suspicions concerning the possible involvement of Robert Longwill and Florencio Donoghue, but there also remained two competing theories of the assassination of Tolby—one concerning the desire of Pancho Griego to avoid conviction for a violent altercation witnessed by Tolby; and the other alleging a conspiracy on the part of allies of the Santa Fe Ring to eliminate a vocal and articulate critic.

As if a full day of hearings and the assassination of one of the suspects accused of killing Tolby were not enough for a day's work, a "Citizens' Meeting" was convened for the purpose of "deliberating upon the facts connected with the murder of the Rev. F. J. Tolby" and allegations related to the crime. McMains was elected president. Men from diverse parts of the county were designated as vice presidents, and Frank Springer served as secretary. The most urgent issue was the adoption of a resolution stating the common view that Tolby had been killed for political reasons rather than plunder, and that Vega and Cardenas had been the "duped and hired tools" of other men whose actions were more egregious. The object was to express to all the determination of Colfax County citizens to see the investigation through and ensure that the guilty parties were subjected to "the extreme penalty of the law."[33]

As indicated, attorney Henry L. Waldo was in Cimarron during the week of the hearings and served as defense counsel for the men accused of having Tolby killed. At the conclusion of the citizens' meeting, he was called upon for remarks. Setting aside the unfortunate assassination of Cardenas, Waldo complimented citizens on the orderly proceedings and the state of civil order in Colfax County.[34] His remarks were repeated in the *New Mexican* upon his return to Santa Fe.

On Thursday, November 11, Lieutenant Cornish reported to his superior officers that most of the Texans had left town, apparently satisfied.[35] Others had also dispersed to their homes and labors, leaving Cimarron quiet, at least for the moment.

A War of Words

In the subregion of northern New Mexico and southern Colorado, the *New Mexican* of Santa Fe, the *Colorado Chieftain* of Pueblo, and several Denver papers covered matters of broad interest and generated stories that were picked up on "exchange" by newspapers in distant cities. The *Cimarron News and Press* produced a thoughtful and provocative paper under the editorship of Morley and Springer in the mid-1870s, going toe to toe with the *New Mexican*. The newspaper broke stride for several weeks in late December 1875 and early 1876, over editorial disharmony between Morley and Springer, as publishers of the paper, and Will Dawson, who had contracted to edit content and manage production when the *Cimarron News* merged with the *Elizabethtown Railway, Press and Telegraph*. Dawson seemed to line up with the miners, settlers, and locals in opposing domination by the Santa Fe politicians, but an abrupt move favoring Ring positions and candidates amid the stresses of 1875 troubled some local readers, including Morley and Springer. Order was restored with Dawson's departure and the old team's resumption of editorial duties.

A propaganda war broke out as factional interests emerged, each with its prized facts and interpretations. The *New Mexican* and the *News and Press* tried to get their divergent versions of events to a national readership, the *New Mexican* depicting Colfax County as a place in rebellion, requiring supervision from Santa Fe and Fort Union, the *News and Press* of Morley and Springer disparaging a corrupt ring in Santa Fe with its hand in the till and its foot on the necks of citizens across the territory. Each of the regional papers hoped others across the country would adopt and disseminate its version of the facts.

Regardless the position taken, the unfavorable publicity concerning political violence and allegations of public corruption could not have helped New Mexico's effort to be promoted from territorial status to statehood, but the struggle between the Santa Fe and Colfax County factions would continue for some time, before the grievances of the anti-Ring residents of Cimarron were satisfactorily resolved. In the meantime, the quest for favorable public opinion continued. Some newspapers across the country lined up with one of the sides, while others were more reserved in judging. The *Western Christian Advocate* of Cincinnati, an official news organ of the Methodist Church, lined up with neither side, but commented, "Whether Cimarron is a more desirable place for a preacher of the Gospel than among the cannibals who are said to love missionary soup, is a question; but there can be no doubt that they are in as great need for the Gospel of Peace."[36]

CHAPTER 9
Rumors of an Indian War

There was palpable relief when, after a full day of testimony, justice court decisions, and the assassination of Manuel Cardenas, the throng that had descended on Cimarron dispersed. The men—presumably they were mostly men—vacated town streets and drinking establishments and returned to their places of work and residence. On November 11, 1875, Lieutenant George Cornish was able to notify superior officers at Fort Union and at the district headquarters in Santa Fe that the "Texans," identified as a major source of potential and actual violence, were leaving, apparently satisfied with the current state of affairs. They were satisfied, seemingly, with the referral of two men accused in connection with Tolby's murder to the grand jury; with continued determination to hold Robert Longwill accountable for possible involvement in the plot; and with the murder of Cardenas—an act that, in spite of the usual finger wagging of newspapers decrying "lynch law," was surely regarded by some as a righteous and conclusive imposition of justice. In response to the news of progress in restoring peace to Colfax County, Lieutenant Thomas Blair, on behalf of the commanding officer in Santa Fe, wired Cornish, "Return at once to your proper station," meaning Fort Union.[1] The soldiers decamped and rode back to their post.

The Indian Agent
The post of Indian agent was coveted, but relatively few appointees found it a satisfying career. The job placed its holder in the impossible position of trying to satisfy multiple factions, most of them implacable and widely divergent in their wants of the government and its appointed representative. Whether competent and

engaged, or incompetent, lazy, and corrupt, agents stood a good chance of seeing their reputations damaged or destroyed. If the agent was well meaning and competent, he was apt to see his work undercut or overruled through the effort of political actors, administrators, land-seeking settlers, contractors, missionary agencies, or the Indians themselves. During the years in which Cimarron was the location for a designated Indian agency or as a place from which provisions and "presents" were distributed on a temporary basis, agents were usually short term, and varied considerably as to their interest, ability, and orientation toward the people for whom they were at least nominally responsible as both caretaker and regulator.

Alexander Irvine and his immediate superior, Indian Commissioner Edward P. Smith, were among the many short-timers who passed through the Interior Department's Indian service. They were competent men of principle, Smith a Congregational Church minister who devoted much of his life to missionary activities. Irvine was a true disciple of the commissioner's policy of firmness in dealing with the nomadic tribes classed as "wild" Indians, embracing the principle that "All outrages or depredations should be followed up promptly, and punished at all hazards and at any cost."[2] Military men with experience fighting Indians did not always see it this way.

An Angry Revolt of Original Americans

The army's time of standing down in Colfax County was brief. In the midst of the trouble precipitated by the Tolby assassination and the larger struggle between the Santa Fe powers and local citizens over control of Colfax County and the Maxwell grant, the gravest threat to peace among local Natives and non-Indian residents in more than twenty years erupted over the issue of substandard rations distributed at the Indian agency at Cimarron. The Utes and Jicarillas, plainly unwanted in their homeland, were living in the limbo of an uncertain future, on the grudging and unreliable support of the federal government. This episode can be viewed as an isolated incident but underlying the responses of the Native men at Cimarron were the larger issues of invasions by foreign powers and the forcible taking of Indian land.[3]

The Indian agent, Alexander G. Irvine, had been appointed to the agency at Cimarron in early 1875. His relationship with the Jicarillas and the Mouache Utes had not gone well, perhaps owing to the hardline stance he assumed in dealing with the Indians, including incidents like one that occurred in February 1875, when one

Issue day at Maxwell's ranch, 1870s. On issue days, Ute and Jicarilla people of the region came to Cimarron to draw rations provided by the federal government. Maxwell's whitewashed home, two long buildings with a courtyard between, is seen in the distance. At the far right edge of the photo is the end of a building that appears to be the county courthouse. New Mexico State University Library, Archives and Special Collections.

of the Indians was jailed for drunkenness, "there to be starved into a confession as to where he got his liquor."[4] Such tactics apparently didn't work, but some local citizens applauded Irvine's effort to curb illegal sale of liquor to Native men.[5]

Tension had been mounting since Irvine's coming, but some grievances were beyond his control. These included legal and illegal trespassing by settlers on the Natives' homeland; conflict over alleged theft of settlers' livestock by Indians on land that the indigenous people regarded as their own; and government-issued supplies that were frequently overdue, inadequate, and of poor quality.[6] Failures of the government to meet the subsistence needs of Native residents whose food supply had been destroyed were sometimes due to lapses in political or administrative processes. Often they were attributed to corruption among agents and contractors.[7] In this instance, Irvine's integrity was not in question, but it was his responsibility to address the issue of deficient rations and deal with the angry responses of those dependent on agency services.

The crisis erupted on Tuesday, November 16, when the band of Jicarilla Apaches led by Juan Julian came to draw rations at the Cimarron Agency. According to the reports published in Santa Fe, several of the men were intoxicated, and one became agitated at the poor condition of the meat issued for their use, throwing it in the face of the agent. According to early reports from Cimarron, Agent Irvine heaved it back.[8]

Irvine and several of the Indians drew weapons and fired, two of Irvine's shots wounding Jicarilla men, one in the shoulder, the other in the wrist. One of his own hands was damaged by a gunshot fired by one of the Apaches. After some time—Irvine estimated about fifteen minutes—local citizens came to the aid of the agent and his staff, and the confrontation subsided. One man involved in the altercation, Juan Barela, was arrested and lodged in the Cimarron jail. Two other Jicarilla men, Juan Julian and Chino, went back to their camp.[9]

A fragmentary version of the story, preserved in Jicarilla tradition, was collected in 1909 by Pliny Earle Goddard, a linguist and ethnologist who worked among the Indians of the West. According to Goddard's interview transcript and his translation, the episode occurred as follows:

> After that, rations were issued again and the meat was being given out. He gave the bones to two men. One of them struck the Agent with the bone. They shot him through the flesh of the arm. They shot there inside. Then the Agent ran into his house. After a while, the Agent came out; he had been shot in his hand. They ran toward us and we started toward them. We were going to shoot but they did not attack us.[10]

This account made no mention of intoxication among the Jicarilla men. According to Goddard or his informant, Juan Julian had thrown the bony meat at Irvine.

The day after the confrontation at the agency, Irvine telegraphed Colonel Gordon Granger, commanding officer for the District of New Mexico in Santa Fe, to report the incident, advising him, "Troops will be absolutely necessary as the Indians have threatened to burn the town."[11] Irvine's dispatch may have been the product of rational assessment or the scream of an alarmist moved by his fears and prejudices, but similar appeals were not uncommon as settlers and local officeholders sought to enlist the help of military forces and newspaper publicity in support of their own closely held judgments and interests.

At Granger's direction, Lieutenant John Lafferty was ordered to Cimarron with a detail of horse soldiers, arriving at midday on Thursday, November 18. The following morning, he rode out to the Jicarilla camps, attempting to comply with Agent Irvine's request that two Jicarilla men who were involved in the incident and were still at large be arrested. The men were not arrested. As a result of his venture into the Indian camps, Lafferty was obliged to report to the Santa Fe district headquarters, "Things are red hot here," the town of Cimarron "alive with armed Indians."[12] For two more days, Lafferty attempted to arrest the Jicarilla men. Faced with continued defiance, he advised the district command that more troops might be required if an outbreak of hostilities occurred. In the hotbed of turmoil that was Colfax County, a new front had been opened—one involving issues and alliances that were distinct from, but not entirely unrelated to, the chaos set in motion by Tolby's death, regarding ownership and use of Maxwell grant resources and control of local political and legal affairs.

On November 20, Agent Irvine advised military authorities in Santa Fe that he considered current forces sufficient to repel an attack on the town of Cimarron, but not sufficient to enforce his demand that the Jicarillas surrender the tribesmen accused of attacking him. Underscoring his determination to follow through, the agent said that a larger force would be needed to pursue the Indians for the purpose of making arrests. He asked that "all the available men in [Fort] Union be put in readiness," and that the post commander be instructed to honor his request, should a larger force be needed.[13] By November 21, Captain William McCleave was on site with a troop of cavalry soldiers and Lieutenant Cornish had arrived with an infantry detachment, making for a force of about forty-five men, including Lafferty's cavalrymen.[14] McCleave assumed command of the full contingent and continued efforts to accommodate the agent's insistence that the army pursue and arrest Indians involved in the commissary incident of November 16.

On Monday, November 22, a new incident further provoked the Indians and escalated tensions in the region. The guard in charge of the Cimarron jail, a small stone building with five cells and the jailer's quarters, requested soldiers' assistance in moving his prisoner, Juan Barela, from one cell to another. In the process, Barela reportedly produced a large knife and lunged at one of the soldiers. Two others drew weapons and fired, killing Barela. A hearing before Justice of the Peace Sam Trauer cleared the soldiers of criminal culpability, but that mattered not to the Jicarillas, who appeared to be preparing for war, sending women and children to the nearby hills for safety. Sources in Cimarron estimated that as many as 250 Jicarilla men might soon be joined by a smaller force of Ute warriors.[15] The report, appearing in the *Santa Fe Weekly New Mexican*, was likely to generate outrage and alarm well beyond Colfax County, but the Indians' own views on the situation remained opaque, and indeed irrelevant, to most readers of the account.

In its weekly issue of November 27, following the killing of Juan Barela, the *Gazette* of Las Vegas, neighbor and sometime rival to Cimarron, ventured a cheery observation: "Cimarron is quiet. Nobody killed for at least three days." The remark was rich in sarcasm, but it underscored the unhappy reality that violence had become a routine feature of life in Colfax County.

Meanwhile, issue of rations to the Natives was suspended, pending arrest of the Jicarillas accused in the incident of November 16. On the evening of Barela's death, San Pablo, a chief of the Jicarillas, discussed matters with Agent Irvine, Captain McCleave, Lieutenant Lafferty, and Lieutenant Cornish. The chief expressed his desire for peace, but disclaimed any power to turn over the accused, so the standoff continued, as did preparations for imminent hostilities.[16] W. R. Morley, vice president and executive officer for the Maxwell Company, had raised a party of volunteers. He requested and received arms and ammunition from Fort Union. From Cimarron came the startling and possibly questionable report that "Capt. Allison's company of volunteers and perhaps 200 to 300 citizens" would respond to an attack by the Natives.[17] Reports traveled across the country, describing the state of excitement and advising readers, "A general outbreak of all of the Apache Indians in Eastern New Mexico is feared."[18]

Since the beginning of the crisis, the threat of force, in the form of troop deployments and citizen militias, had been increased several times on request of the Indian agent, but the Jicarillas, angry and pushed to the wall, did not scare easily. Having forced the issue with success in raising the threat of an Indian war, but with no success in getting the men he wanted arrested, Irvine sent an urgent telegram to superiors at the Interior Department at Washington, asking that the military be placed in charge of affairs at Cimarron.[19] By December 2, the request had been approved, and Alexander Irvine and his wife were on a coach heading west to Fort Defiance, Arizona, where he was to assume a promotion as Indian agent for the Navajos.[20]

An urgent message from General John Pope, the departmental commander at Fort Leavenworth, Kansas, instructed Colonel Gordon Granger to "proceed in person to Cimarron and settle this Indian trouble." Pope's telegram, dispatched on November 27, elicited the somewhat overdue news that the colonel had suffered a stroke on November 19 and was unable to comply. As an afterthought, before learning of Granger's condition, and without the knowledge that Irvine had left his post as Indian agent, Pope sent a second telegram, advising that responsibility for Indian matters at Cimarron had been turned over to the army. Pope further stipulated that Granger was to apply his own judgment, "without regard to the opinion of the Indian Agent."[21] This instruction may have reflected underlying disapproval of Irvine's approach on the parts of army officers who had gone to some lengths to accommodate the agent's insistence that the insubordinate Indians be arrested, a demand that may have obstructed the ultimate goal of resolving substantive issues and moving the Native people toward relocation to a mutually acceptable reservation home.

The *News and Press* was moved to reflect broadly on the "Indian Question" that had long vexed Colfax County residents—those who had come within the past twenty years and who were not Indians. The paper recited a familiar litany of complaints that included pilferage of crops and livestock, grazing of horses in cultivated fields, and drunkenness abetted by weak provisions for regulation of illicit liquor sales; and pronounced the people "an undoubted pest and nuisance." The native languages of the indigenous tribes likely included words to describe their experiences of subjugation and destruction of traditional means of subsistence, but they were of no interest to the advancing Euro-Americans or their journalists. The remedy called for by the *News and Press* was confinement of the tribes to reservations, but the writer hailed as a promising sign the recent transfer of authority for Indian affairs to the War Department. "The experience of the past, in Indian affairs, makes us naturally put little faith in promises of firm, decisive action," the writer stated, "but we are satisfied that if the matter is *left* in the hands of the military we may justly expect the best results."[22] The article reflected a glaring change in the Indians' status, as between Maxwell's benevolent autocracy and the governance of corporate and territorial institutions. It was a change from personal to impersonal, in which Natives were viewed solely as an obstacle to development, devoid of personhood. The writer named multiple individuals associated with the military and in federal administration of Indian affairs but referred to none of the indigenous leaders by name or tribal affiliation.

Colonel Miles Calms the Waters

Frustrated, no doubt, with the failure of previous measures to resolve the difficulty with the Jicarillas, General Pope, commander of the Department of the

Missouri at Fort Leavenworth, played the strongest card he had, detailing Colonel Nelson A. Miles, a Civil War general and veteran of Indian wars, to assume command at Cimarron and settle the matter conclusively.[23] A peaceful resolution was preferred, but instructions to district headquarters at Santa Fe concerning Miles's appointment included the information that Fort Union would send, to Cimarron, ten days' rations for 100 men; and would obtain forage for 150 horses. Clearly, military force was an option. The *Las Vegas Gazette*, attuned to military matters on account of the town's proximity to Fort Union, reported that three companies of cavalry would be dispatched from Fort Leavenworth to Cimarron, and opined with apparent disapproval, that the affair was "liable to be the cause of three million dollars cost to the government."[24]

By December 10, Miles was on the ground in Cimarron and in discussions with a chief of the Jicarillas—possibly San Pablo. Miles apparently ignored the allegations of Indian misconduct and the issue of pending arrests. He instead gave the Jicarillas a chance to tell their story before considering punitive hostilities. The chief told Miles that his people wanted peace, but stated that assurances concerning provisions for their subsistence had been made and broken repeatedly. Promised beef and flour, they had instead been given "shorts," or ground husks, for flour; and the meat they were given was all "skin, bones, hides, hoofs and horns." Miles recalled, "I found the Indians very poor, and among what little stores they had, they showed me the supplies that had been given to them as food, and I found the statements made to me by the chief to be only too fully corroborated."[25]

By his own recollection, Miles put an officer in charge of rations in place of the departed Irvine—Lieutenant Cornish had already been so appointed by his own command—and insisted that good beef be furnished by purveyors who "were receiving ample compensation from the government." Confident that the Jicarillas would honor their bargain, Miles returned to his duty station at Fort Leavenworth. "It is much better, if possible," he declared, recalling the experience, "to avoid an Indian war, and much easier than to end one after hostilities have once been fully entered on."[26]

Miles may have been a bit self-congratulatory in his assessment, and he viewed the result as one who would not be living with the situation daily. In its Christmas Day issue, the *Las Vegas Gazette* expressed a cynical view, not uncommon among the dominant non-Native immigrants in Indian country. "As we predicted," the *Gazette* writer noted, "the Indians in and about Cimarron have quietly settled down to draw their rations and enjoy themselves in a peaceable manner during the winter. It would pay the territory of New Mexico to provide for the board of these two bands of beggarly poor Indians at some hotel in the east rather than to allow them to remain longer in New Mexico." Disparaging to the last, the writer stated, "They constitute but a handful of poorly clothed, dirty, disgusting men, women and children and could be transferred to some mountain cañon where they would never be heard of again in the world."[27]

As usual, frontier newspapers, instruments of a booster mentality among the immigrant developers of western lands, were quick to blame the Natives—for resisting taking of their land and destruction of staples of their subsistence; for objecting to the substandard quality of rations issued them in place of meat that they had themselves supplied before the slaughter of the great buffalo herds; and for taking up space and causing disorder in an otherwise unoccupied land that was rich in resources but underutilized due to the backwardness of Native inhabitants.

As to the military presence, many fair and competent officers passed through the western country during the time of the "Indian wars," most probably following orders to the best of their ability and working to fulfill assigned missions, including protection of travelers, maintenance of peaceful relations, and from time to time, enforcement of government orders to move indigenous people to reservations. Leaders among the military men were people and were subject to notable variation in their views and approaches. Some were summarily harsh in judgments and proposed solutions regarding the Indians, some more sympathetic to the Native side of the story. Few were so fair minded as Colonel Miles in his willingness to listen and work to find peaceful and reasonable resolutions to Indian-settler conflicts, but politics and popular sentiment of the times were bigger than Nelson Miles and a few like-minded military officers and civilian administrators. The result was a military presence in the West that supported and enforced the taking of Indian land and the separation of indigenous people from their way of life in favor of concentration on reservations, often with disastrous results. Concurrently, the contracting system, through which military posts and reservations were supplied, produced a class of motivated stakeholders with vested interests in perpetuating the presence of troops and forts in the western territories and sustaining demand for the goods by which they profited. The contracting system and laws providing for government payment for settler losses to alleged depredation were highly susceptible to fraud, and a good deal of fraud was found to have occurred.[28]

Back at Fort Leavenworth, Miles was questioned by a local newspaper writer concerning his latest assignment. In the interview, Colonel Miles expressed the opinion "in very positive terms," that the Indians at Cimarron had long been victims of mismanagement, and of the unscrupulous greed of contractors. Further, he offered a critique of U.S. Indian policy, arguing, "One branch of government is continually arming the Indians, while another branch is fighting them."[29] John E. Pyle of Helena, Montana, was appointed as the new Indian agent at Cimarron. Upon his arrival at the agency in late January 1876, Lieutenant Cornish was released to resume his regular assignment, and the desire expressed earlier in the *News and Press*, that the military would continue in control of Indian matters, was not realized.[30]

Earlier in the affair, Alexander Irvine had urged immediate removal of the Natives from the Cimarron area. Such changes were more easily measured in decades than in days, but official Washington apparently agreed that it was time to move forward with relocation. Captain McCleave had, therefore, been tasked with estimating the cost of moving the Jicarillas from Cimarron to the Mescalero Apache Agency at Fort Stanton.[31] Such an estimate was prepared and submitted, along with the suggestion that any effort to move the band be deferred until spring of 1876. Disinclined to the idea, the Jicarillas managed to resist the planned move until the summer of 1878, when the Cimarron Agency was closed permanently. In the move that finally got under way, only thirty-two Jicarillas completed the journey to Mescalero, with others dropping off to stay near Abiquiu. The long-awaited move turned out to be a temporary one, pending a trickling, unauthorized migration back to the home country, and further efforts to achieve a permanent relocation of the tribe.[32]

By the summer of 1879, a good many of the Jicarillas and a smaller number of Utes were back in the Cimarron country, living off settlers' beef in the absence of regular rations. The affair of late 1875 and early 1876, then, was just part of a futile, cyclical effort to resettle the Jicarillas in an area that was acceptable to them, and that could be held against the encroachments of land-hungry settlers. The peace brokered by Colonel Miles did, however, avert what appeared to many to be a likely outbreak of hostilities between the settlers and Natives in the Cimarron country. Miles would later have occasion to assist the Jicarillas again in their quest for a suitable reservation on which they might make a new tribal home.

CHAPTER 10

The Whirlwind

On December 22, 1875, Judge Joseph Palen, with whom the late Reverend Tolby had heatedly argued over political differences, died at the age of sixty in Santa Fe, attended in his last hours by Dr. Robert Longwill, a new resident of the city. Because Palen's acrimonious exchange with Franklin Tolby was thought by some to have set off the eruption of violence in Colfax County, the judge's decease might have marked a fitting end to a dark season. But such was not to be, for the infernal wind that had carried Tolby off had loosed a foul whirlwind.

A glowing tribute in the *Cimarron News and Press* did not begin to express the reactions of many Colfax County residents who believed that Palen had corrupted the judicial process to serve his own political and personal interests, and those of the territorial ring. The obituary was, instead, a reflection of a growing strain between the owners of the paper, William Morley and Frank Springer; and Will Dawson, the managing editor and former editor of the Elizabethtown paper.[1] The *News and Press* was supposed to be neutral in politics, but in reality, it never was; and Dawson had lately shown an affinity for his new friends of the Santa Fe political clique.

Ring men promptly pressed for the appointment of Henry Waldo, a boyhood friend of Stephen Elkins, to succeed Palen as chief justice and judge for the first judicial district. As New Mexico's delegate to Congress, Elkins was well positioned to help secure Waldo's confirmation, but the upheaval was not over, and recent bloodshed bred more turmoil in the beautiful, troubled Sangre de Cristo Mountains, and in the valleys of the Ponil, the Vermejo, the Red River, and the Cimarron.

Press Freedom and Its Limits

Newspapers helped keep the conflict between the Santa Fe power structure and its Colfax County critics simmering. A piece published in the *New York Sun* on December 16, 1875, "The Territory of Elkins," helped stir the pot in New Mexico. The article was not signed, but a dateline identified Santa Fe as the origin, and the writer was apparently well informed concerning leading figures and issues of the controversy. The article referred to a "political revolution" under way in the territory, pitting the Ring against a strong and vocal resistance in Colfax County. The writer reviewed the Tolby assassination and related events, including the hearings and citizens' meeting in Cimarron on November 10. The writer implied that the Ring's most visible leader, Elkins, had suffered major damage to his reputation in the affair, declaring, "If a new election for Delegate to Congress could be held tomorrow, Elkins would be defeated by such a tremendous majority that even the tools of the Santa Fé Ring would not dare attempt the job of counting him in."[2]

In the *Cimarron News and Press* of December 31, Will Dawson, a convert to the Santa Fe perspective, condemned the *Sun* article and chastised the Ring's Colfax County critics. The piece attracted substantial attention, much of it negative, among county residents, and it set off a ripple of consequences. Dawson's abrupt change in editorial bearing prompted Morley and Springer to declare in the edition of January 7, 1876, that "on account of disagreement as to the management, political and otherwise," they would no longer be associated with the paper in an editorial capacity.

The Texas cowboy faction led by Clay Allison had once supported the Santa Fe political leaders, but apparently swung to support the local resistance following the murder of Tolby. On Thursday, January 20, 1876, people in New Mexico and southern Colorado were startled to find that, on the previous night, "a mob" had vandalized the *News and Press*, throwing press and type into the Cimarron River.[3] The conventional explanation in Colfax County was that Allison and a number of followers had done the deed to dramatize their anger with the editor, and with any and all persons believed to be responsible for killing Tolby. The Santa Fe perspective was different, a dispatch declaring that the rioters consisted of "outlaws and fugitives from justice," men provoked to violence by "evil-disposed persons" dissatisfied with Elkins's reelection as the territory's delegate to Congress. These were the agitators who, in the Santa Fe writer's view, had stirred up hostility toward Mills and Longwill following the assassination of Tolby; the supposed intent was to drive all agents of Santa Fe interests out of Colfax county.[4] It was not clear in early reports that Allison was behind the raid, but local citizens must have known of his involvement.

The tale of Allison and friends' dumping of the press and type in the river in a nighttime raid has been the material of legend, with retellings varying in their details. Henry Porter, partner with Asa Middaugh in a store at Cimarron, recalled Allison's scooping up partially printed sheets for the forthcoming edition and selling them around town at twenty-five cents each, for the pages printed on one side. Porter presumed that "most people bought one to avoid further argument."[5] Some accounts added that the night raiders scrawled the words "Clay Allison's Edition" on the unfinished papers they offered for sale.[6]

Another incident, credibly substantiated, occurred the morning following Allison's spree. An account of his effort to make amends with Ada Morley was in print no later than 1916, when a writer familiar with the matter recalled that William Morley and his teary wife were surveying the damage when Allison came up "mild as a spring lamb on toast." Ada was afraid that Allison had come to do them further harm, but he approached with gestures of truce, saying he had come to apologize and pay for the damage. With that he produced a roll of bills and gave Ada Morley the sum of two hundred dollars, to the startled satisfaction of the Morleys. Their daughter, Agnes, would write her account of the incident years later, presumably from family tradition. Though present in the home when Allison wrecked the *News and Press*, she was less than two years old at the time. By the time she grew up and became a published writer, Allison had become a hero in her mother's eyes. "Are you Mrs. Morley?" a contrite and sober offender inquired in Agnes's version. "Well, go buy yourself another printing press," he said, shoving a roll of bills into her hand and saying, "I don't fight women."[7]

It was in character for Allison to pay for the damage from his drunken spree. In a lifetime of hellraising, he extricated himself time and again, relying upon three lines of defense. First, his killings were justified by the crimes of the victims. Second, he only killed in self-defense. Third, he generally paid for what he broke in nonlethal incidents resulting in damage to property.

By mutual consent, Will Dawson yielded the editorship of the *News and Press*. As others had done when local sentiment turned against them, he soon relocated to the relative security of Santa Fe. He later moved west to California, where he disappeared into obscurity.[8] Using a small press, Morley and Springer resumed control of the paper and restored its former editorial policy, and were out with a four-page, letter-size issue on January 28, declaring the return of the former editorial team with the heading "Richard Is Himself Again." The reference was to a phrase often quoted, but incorrectly attributed to Shakespeare; its meaning in this context was simply that the paper had returned to its true character.

Morley and Springer were remarkably unperturbed about the wrecking of the newspaper office, explaining in the next edition of the *News and Press* that the bedlam, including unlawful entry, destruction of property, and disorderly conduct, was the result of "an excessive overflow of public sentiment." The *New Mexican* took exception, opining, "There is a richness about 'excessive overflow of public sentiment,' which we do not think was ever equaled." Morley and Springer were criticized for excusing criminal behavior by refusing to sue for damages or press for criminal prosecution, a position that the *New Mexican* judged improper for an organ proposing to serve the public interest.[9] No mention was made in either paper about the involvement of Allison, a fact most likely known to all. Where he was concerned, discretion was seemingly advisable, even among rival newspapers.

The continuing effort to expose corruption in the dominant political faction known as the Santa Fe Ring was renewed when Morley and Springer published a letter that had been sent to former editor Dawson, requesting that Dawson reprint the original *Sun* article "The Territory of Elkins," alongside his criticism of it, "that all may see and know where the right is."[10] This letter, signed by 153 "citizens of Colfax County," was published by Morley and Springer with the *Sun* article and Dawson's earlier comments, in the *News and Press* of February 18, 1876.

The Santa Fe Alliance Asserts Itself

Santa Fe had become a gathering place for refugees from the mayhem in Colfax County, particularly for those considered to be allies of the Santa Fe Ring. Dr. Longwill had taken refuge there before the November 10 hearings in Cimarron, the better to escape possible violence to his person. Melvin Mills, against whom no evidence had been found to warrant referral for grand jury review, was nevertheless relieved to be on a coach to Santa Fe before daybreak just after the hearing in Cimarron.[11] His going was for the purpose of taking part in the pending session of the territorial legislature, to which he had recently been elected. His being in the capital for the session would at least give time for the local outrage to subside. Will Dawson left Cimarron for Santa Fe soon after his ouster as *News and Press* editor, and Florencio Donoghue, still in the Cimarron jail pending grand jury action on charges in connection with Tolby's death, was removed to Santa Fe on a writ of habeas corpus on January 16, 1876.

Longwill and Donoghue made permanent homes in Santa Fe, but Mills returned to Colfax County after the legislative session and carried on an active career in law and business until his death in 1925. Probably not related to the other relocations were the departures of the four Trauer brothers—Maurice, Louis, Samuel, and Sigmund—from Cimarron in spring, 1876. Having been threatened with lynching, and having another time had his business visited by outlaws on the run, Maurice had likely seen enough of life in Colfax County, so he moved his enterprises—store and cigar factory—to Santa Fe. After his short but eventful tenure as justice of the peace, Sam Trauer resigned his office and relocated to Santa Fe.[12]

The destruction of the *News and Press* bolstered the accusations of Santa Fe officials that anarchy and chaos were rampant in Colfax County. Depending on one's perspective, the premise either compelled the territorial government to intervene in local affairs, or alternatively, provided a pretext for doing so. Just two days after the raid, Orson K. Chittenden, elected sheriff of Colfax County in September 1875, wired the governor to plead, "It is impossible for me to enforce civil law." Governor Axtell's response was blunt and succinct: "Will accept your resignation forwarded by mail."[13] Chittenden's likely intent in contacting Axtell was to request his help in gaining military support for enforcement of the law. Axtell requested aid from Fort Union on January 24 but was advised that any approval would have to come from the district commander, who sent the request to the departmental command at Fort Leavenworth, Kansas. The issue dragged along until March 13, when troops were dispatched to Cimarron.[14]

Saying that Orson Chittenden had resigned, Axtell appointed Isaiah Rinehart, a man more to the liking of the Santa Fe political bosses, as sheriff of Colfax County, but controversy ensued as to whether Chittenden had, in fact, "resigned." Axtell insisted that he had, but Chittenden held proof of his "removal from the office of Sheriff of Colfax County."[15] The removal of an elected local official, and his replacement with a political ally, was one of several actions taken by Axtell and the legislature in spring of 1876 in which Colfax County dissidents perceived a plot to usurp local control and impose the will of the Santa Fe bosses. Colfax County citizens, Frank Springer in particular, were taking names and keeping score.

The resisters to Ring rule in Colfax County were already annoyed at Governor Axtell and the legislature, which had seen fit, in the last days of the legislative session, to suspend sessions of the district court at Cimarron and attach Colfax to Taos County "for judicial purposes." The bill was passed on January 14.[16] The action was obnoxious—first, because it represented a rebuke to the people of Colfax County; second, because of the practical inconvenience to Colfax residents in having to travel over a high pass to attend court sessions in Taos; and third, it meant that juries hearing Colfax County cases would most likely be Taos County residents selected for jury service through the influence of Pedro Sanchez, a territorial legislator and supposed Ring friend. As the local legislative delegate, Melvin Mills took up for Colfax County, opposing the bill when it went before the House in Santa Fe.

Before his departure as editor, Dawson wired the governor to request a meeting on behalf of Colfax County citizens who hoped that Axtell could be persuaded to withhold his approval of the bill. The entreaty brought a fast response: "Bill signed. S. B. Axtell."[17] Morley, Henry Porter, and W. O. Cunningham sent telegrams on January 19 and 20. Springer met with Axtell in Santa Fe in early February, hoping to change his mind, but the governor would not be moved.

Since the complaint against Colfax County alleged widespread lawlessness and disorder, Springer, via the *News and Press*, attempted to disprove the notion. This was no easy task, but for the issue of February 4, he compiled a chronology of violent events in New Mexico to show that mob activity, riots, and shooting deaths were common all over, and were no more prevalent in Colfax than in other counties. The next week he concentrated on Doña Ana County, reciting numerous violent crimes there, with no arrests made. All the *News and Press* could reasonably assert was a rough parity, concluding, "We don't claim Colfax to be any more orderly than is customary with frontier counties, but it will compare favorably with most of them."[18]

"Saturday's Coach" and the Arrest of Clay Allison

After the failure of multiple attempts to speak directly to the governor, several citizens of Colfax County made a final effort, preparing a written invitation asking

Governor Axtell to "visit the county and see for himself the true condition of affairs." The letter inviting Axtell was signed by "some twelve or fifteen citizens," including Springer, Morley, and Henry Porter. The governor did not immediately respond, but later used the invitation for his own purpose.[19]

Clay Allison had come to Axtell's attention as a deadly gunman and frequent disturber of the peace. The governor was determined to corral Allison and, if possible, to convict and punish him or run him out of the territory. Where others shrunk from the challenge, Axtell could muster the courage to challenge Allison from the relative safety of Santa Fe, and with the backing of the U.S. Army. It was in his determination to curb Allison that Axtell stumbled into one of the more damaging blunders of his tenure as governor.

With Benjamin Stevens, district attorney in New Mexico's second judicial district, Axtell made a plan for arresting Allison. It failed but ignited a controversy that would ultimately bring down the governor and his administration. Frank Springer was not a disinterested observer but witnessed much of the affair at close range and later conveyed his account in documents offered as evidence of Axtell's unfitness for the office of governor. Springer's first notice of the scheme came in a brief encounter with Ben Stevens at Las Vegas in early March. Stevens was on his way to Cimarron, and Springer had just left home on law business of several days' duration.[20] Stevens mentioned that he was interested in possibly moving to Cimarron, and was going to look the area over and talk with people there, and see for himself whether things written and said about the late disorders were true or whether, as he was inclined to believe, the situation had been exaggerated.

Upon Springer's return to Cimarron two weeks later, he found Stevens there, seemingly acting in an official capacity, along with a company of soldiers from Fort Union. Evidently these were the troops that were finally sent in response to Axtell's much earlier request of January 24, 1876.[21] Springer soon became aware of Axtell's planned visit to Cimarron to meet with citizens who had recently invited the governor to come and listen to their concerns. Springer later learned that one of the local men—Clay Allison—was to have been arrested, and that soldiers had been instructed to "fire upon and kill the whole party" of those objecting on Allison's behalf in case of any show of resistance to the arrest. The word from Stevens was that certain of the men who had signed the invitation should be present to meet the governor's coach on Saturday evening, March 18, when Axtell would stop and speak with them.[22] Springer would later see a missive to Stevens detailing the governor's plan, but there were already enough oddities in the invitation to make curious men suspicious. For this reason, the men of Colfax County did not show for the proposed meeting, nor did the governor.

Axtell remained determined to see Allison arrested, and if possible, punished, for alleged crimes and disorders for which he was deemed responsible. According to Springer's affidavit of June 1878, Ben Stevens and the soldiers from Fort Union stayed in the area for about two weeks following the governor's non-visit to Cimarron. Their most notable activity in an otherwise quiet expedition was to "march out into the country and arrest Mr. R. C. Allison, who came in quietly with the officers, and after being detained about two hours was set at liberty" to await the coming session of the district court grand jury.[23] The arrest occurred on March 20, 1876.

For Frank Springer, whose anger had been building in response to Santa Fe's paternalistic acts toward Colfax County, the latest outrage, a plot to arrest Allison through a ruse while killing Springer and others if they resisted, was a summons to action. Whatever Axtell's intent, Springer dismissed any notion of working with him and began to anticipate the governor's early departure from office. Axtell became the singular object of Springer's ire, as Clay Allison was the focus of Axtell's prescription for restoring peace and order in Colfax County.

The Carnage Continues

The long time of trouble in Colfax County had its full share of deadly violence, much of it hideous and appalling. But this was also a war fought in the press, in political jousting, and in the courts. Angry threats flew and there was howling and gnashing of teeth, but through January and most of February 1876, there had been little or no serious violence since the death of Juan Barela in December.

The respite ended with the strange murder of Martin Baird by his herder, Juan Trujillo, at Baird's home on the Dry Cimarron, near Colorado, on February 27. The incident had nothing to do with the greater turmoil wracking Colfax County. According to Trujillo, the men were talking casually about ranch matters following Baird's return to the place, when Baird turned his head to one side. Trujillo drew a revolver, put it to Baird's head and fired. Trujillo's motive was baffling, but not complicated: he just wanted to kill somebody. An early dispatch indicated that the herder was arrested and "remanded to jail in Cimarron," but a subsequent report from Trinidad said that Trujillo had been taken out and hanged from a cottonwood tree by neighbors in the area, proving that lynching was still an option in the minds of some residents.[24]

An incident of more general interest because it reinforced the notion popular in Santa Fe, of Colfax County as a hotbed of disorder and violence, was the killing of three of the soldiers on the night of March 24. The men had been sent to Cimarron to assist in the arrest of Clay Allison, and to help local officials maintain order. The troops sent from Fort Union were of Company L, Ninth U.S. Cavalry: Black soldiers serving under white officers.[25] Considering the contingent of aggressively white Texans working livestock in northern Colfax County and spending too much money and time at Lambert's saloon, the presence of buffalo soldiers in roles of authority made for a volatile situation. The soldiers who went into Lambert's were young men away from home and away from their post at Fort Union. They had reportedly been ordered to avoid the bars, but went anyway.[26] Referring to the incident some months later, Frank Springer characterized it as a "mere drinking affray." But military dispatches between Cimarron and Fort Union referred to the "murders" of the three soldiers and made inquiries concerning arrest of the shooters.[27] According to one account, the incident was set off by an encounter at the front door. One of the soldiers was just entering as David Crockett, Gus Heffron, and Henry Goodman were leaving. Flummoxed by the doorknob, perhaps also annoyed by the color of the soldiers, Crockett reacted, "pouring lead" into the soldiers.[28] From "conflicting reports," the *Las Vegas Gazette* gave readers a summary of the affair. According to this account, "some twenty shots were fired," with nine finding their way into the bodies of the three cavalrymen.[29] Killed were Privates John Hanson, Anthony Harvey, and George Small.

Henry Goodman managed to vanish from the scene and was not mentioned in newspaper accounts of the incident. He later told George Crocker of making a quick exit and hiding behind a woodpile at Crocker's home.[30] That decision probably helped preserve Goodman's chances for a better future. After working in the San Juan country of southwestern Colorado and northwestern New Mexico, Goodman married, raised a family, and spent his last forty years or so raising cattle near Moab, Utah, an admired citizen of his community and state.[31]

Crockett and Heffron were not immediately apprehended, but by August 1876, they had been formally accused. Their charges came up for consideration in the justice court at Cimarron. Regarding the murder charge, the *News and Press* told readers, "The evidence failed to show any reason for holding them, and they were

David Crockett, Gus Heffron, and Henry Goodman, photographed in Trinidad, Colorado. Crockett, a relative of the Alamo hero, and his companion Heffron were involved in violent and deadly events in Cimarron in 1876. Goodman parted ways with the other men and became a respected cowman and citizen in eastern Utah. Courtesy Chuck and V. J. Hornung New Mexico History Collection.

accordingly discharged."[32] Crockett, however, was found guilty of "carrying arms," and was assessed a fine of fifty dollars.[33]

At least one critic believed that Crockett and Heffron got off too easy because of "a weak Justice of the Peace"—to their own detriment, since the lenient verdict seemed to embolden them to further excess, finally resulting in a violent death for Crockett, and the scare of a lifetime for Heffron.[34] Less than two months after the finding in the justice court, they tried to "run the town" one time too many, charging through the streets of Cimarron, yelling and firing their pistols, and "endangering the lives of all, without regard to sex or age." But on that day, September 30, 1876, Crockett and Heffron found that the law was ready for them. Sheriff Rinehart, backed by a posse, told them to "throw up their arms and surrender." When they refused, the sheriff ordered his men to fire, and the offenders were put to flight, running their horses across the creek, where Crockett was killed by gunfire. When a physician was called to attend to his wounds, Heffron "begged Dr. Michaels for heavens sake not to allow anyone to kill him."[35]

Roots of Frontier Violence

Despite the attempts of the *News and Press* to depict Cimarron as a typical frontier town, there was no denying that violence had been rampant in the area since the gold-mining boom and the departure of Lucien Maxwell in 1870. As to the causes of an epidemic of rage and bloodshed, they were not so different in Colfax County as those seen elsewhere in the West in the early days of white settlement. Robert M. Utley, a longtime student of the frontier West and its borderlands, named four elements common to most violent acts. These included the influence of alcohol, easy availability of firearms, greed for money and power, and a cause that he found most compelling: the code of the West, requiring that men avenge any actual or imagined wrong and retreat before no aggressor.[36] In the cases of Crockett and Heffron, all but one of these causes was apparent. Their antisocial acts were not visibly motivated by pursuit of money or power.

The circumstances named by Utley were discernibly common triggers to violent incidents in the late nineteenth-century American West, at least one such condition being present in almost every instance of lethal violence arising outside the realms of military action or law enforcement. Beyond these immediate stimuli, however, there were often broader issues underlying the present moment and contributing to outbreaks of violence.

A common cause of violence in the Southwest borderlands, as apparent in Colfax County in the 1870s, was racial prejudice. Monroe Lee Billington devoted extensive study to the exploits and experiences of Black soldiers in New Mexico and the West. Regarding the episode involving Crockett, Heffron, and the soldiers, he wrote, "The deaths of the three troopers were seemingly unrelated to the political troubles in Colfax County." This was true, laying aside the fact that they were in Colfax County because of disorders growing out of the political troubles. As to one other likely cause of the violence that took the soldiers' lives, Billington remarked, "Because Crockett had earlier expressed his dislike of the presence of black soldiers in Cimarron, the incident was more likely related to racial prejudice than to politics."[37]

Prejudice may also have contributed to failed or apathetic investigations and prosecution in cases of lynching or assassination of persons accused and awaiting trial in Colfax County. O. P. McMains, who instigated the "interrogation" leading to the lynching of Cruz Vega, was charged in connection with Vega's death, as were Clay Allison and several others. Chief Justice Waldo was resting on the law when, in April 1876, he told the pool of grand jurors assembled in Taos that each man taking part in the lynching of Vega or the shooting of Manuel Cardenas was guilty of murder, but such lawbreakers were seldom pursued, much less convicted. This seems to have been especially the case when the victim of a lynching, assassination, or other questionable killing was Black, Hispanic, or Indian; and those wielding the machinery of justice were mostly non-Hispanic white Euro-Americans.[38] In Indian country across the West, the "otherness" of the indigenous people and a constant apprehension concerning the possibility of attack gave rise to a rational impulse for people to be well armed and watchful; readiness and ability to fight Natives presumably carried over to increase the likelihood of violent conflict with other people who were different in culture or color, and with competing factions regardless of race or ethnicity.[39]

A circumstance conducive to violence in Colfax County was the ongoing, self-interested, passionate pursuit of property or possession—of land, minerals, water, grazing land, or anything potentially contributing to the prosperity or wealth of those willing to fight for it. Indecision and inconsistency of policy and enforcement on the part of the federal government likely impeded the establishment of legal structures for avoidance and settlement of disputes, leaving competitors on the ground to settle their own differences. In Colfax County of the 1870s, the deficit in social order was exaggerated with the transition in administration from Maxwell to the English company, and with the arrival of new competing factions.

By late March 1876, the docket for the April session of the district court, held in Taos but combining the caseloads of Taos and Colfax Counties, was filling up. In addition to charges to be considered in the killing of Vega, the court would also examine accusations against Clay Allison, regarding the disappearance and alleged killing of Charles Cooper, witness to Allison's notorious and deadly shoot-out with Chunk Colbert at Clifton House. Charges against Longwill and Donoghue in connection with their alleged involvement in arranging and paying for the murder of Reverend Tolby were also pending.[40] It was going to be a busy term, one not without conflict as to the procedures followed and allegations of bias in jury selection, and regarding the territory's handling of cases against several of the accused.

The field of conflict was shifting from the streets and saloons of Cimarron, and the open country of northern New Mexico, to the courtroom. The cast of prominent characters would also change, from gunmen, lawmen, and soldiers to the orbit of lawyers and public figures said to be aligned with the Santa Fe Ring. These included the territorial chief justice, who also presided as judge for the first judicial district; the politically powerful attorney general; and a member of the territorial legislature from Taos who also functioned as a campaign organizer for the Republican Party and—allegedly—a part-time jury fixer.

CHAPTER II

The Coming of the Law

The change from Spanish to Mexican administration occurring in 1821 had produced little disruption in the remote province of New Mexico. But with the occupying American authorities came a more disruptive shift in administrative and judicial practices, involving an abrupt change from the Spanish-Mexican system to a new regime based on Anglo-American civil and common law and the adoption of English as the primary language of law and courts in New Mexico. Despite its virtues in the eyes of proponents, the law imposed under U.S. authority also supplied the means by which designing men could and would dispossess indigenous Americans and some land grant claimants, taking the ground on which they and their forebears had lived and worked.[1]

Through nearly two and a half centuries in which the governments of Spain and Mexico claimed sovereignty over New Mexico preceding the occupation by U.S. forces in 1846, some framework for government and civil law had been present in the vast region adjacent to the Rio Grande north of El Paso del Norte. A governor was set over the province, sometimes exercising strong influence over legislative and judicial as well as executive functions; an alcalde or other entity carried out governmental functions in communities.[2] Disputes were settled under Spanish-Mexican civil law, heavily influenced by custom.[3] In addition to the jurisdiction vested in local officials for settlement of local issues, special jurisdictions, or *fueros*, were constituted for the purpose of adjudicating specialized matters involving ecclesiastical and military affairs.[4]

A common thread among the three governing regimes—Spanish, Mexican, and American or U.S.—was the difficulty that central governments faced in imposing systems of governance, law, and justice in a remote jurisdiction, much of which was highly rural and broadly dispersed, and in which resources for administration were scant. The farther settlements lay from the center of the provincial government, the more people relied on surrogates to fill the functions of public officials and institutions—*patrónes* who both used and sustained peasant laborers, the *Penitente* brotherhood, and in the early phase of the American era, vigilance committees or mobs. The new American regime may have seen itself as the bringer of law, but it was also responsible for many of the conflicts that generated increased need for order and legal protection.

In a novel exploring the transition of a frontier society from lawlessness to one of orderly conduct, amity, and justice, a southern New Mexico judge explains the untidy process of change, relying on remembered truths from his father, a judge of earlier times. Judge Charles Vaught, the son, remembered his father's words: "First you must have order. You get it however you can, usually with a gun and a rope. Then you need law. You write that and try to live by it. Order and law—these come first, even among animals. When you have them, you can take time to think about wallpaper and a choir for the church and sunsets and indoor privies. Oh yes, and justice."[5]

In the 1870s, immigrants and investors in Colfax County and other places in the territory were struggling to build societies worthy of migration and investment, and ultimately, statehood. Order was approximate and enforcement frequently ad hoc. Despite the lofty ideals of American democracy, rural New Mexico was a work in progress, concerning its transformation to a society in which crimes were punished and disputes settled based on written laws and judicial processes. The structure for organized society was defined, but some aspects of the frontier order, including lynching and assassinations and shoot-outs between aggrieved parties, were still common. In the deaths of Cruz Vega and Manuel Cardenas, the events in Colfax County affirmed the persistence of "lynch law" and "six-shooter law."

When the spring term of the First Judicial District Court opened in Taos on Monday, April 3, 1876, months of criminal violence and accusations had produced a heavy load of cases, many of them from Colfax County, some provoking strong personal and political biases. The notoriety surrounding some of the defendants, the political odor associated with some official participants, and the open resentment of Colfax County residents at having their cases decided by Taos juries virtually assured that the court's decisions would not satisfy everyone.

The Traveling Bench and Bar

From the U.S. occupation in 1846 and extending to 1887, New Mexico had the simplest model of judicial apparatus prescribed in the organic acts under which western territories were created. Regardless of geographic size or population, each territory was to have a judicial system composed of three judicial districts, each one presided over by a federally appointed judge who held court in the district, usually twice each year. The same three judges, at least annually, sat as a territorial supreme court, one having been designated by appointment as the chief justice.[6]

At first, the only prosecutors for New Mexico were the attorney general, handling matters subject to territorial laws, and the U.S. attorney, dealing with cases arising under federal law. By 1876, district attorneys had been appointed for the Second and Third Judicial Districts, but the attorney general continued to represent the territory as prosecutor for the First District. When the court for Colfax and Taos Counties met in April 1876, there was a new chief justice, the recently confirmed Henry Waldo. The attorney general was William Breeden, former supreme court clerk and lead organizer of the territorial Republican Party. The U.S. attorney was Thomas Catron, and the clerk of the territorial supreme court, who also served as clerk for the First District, was Rufus J. Palen, son of the recently deceased former chief justice.

Waldo, Catron, and Stephen Elkins, territorial delegate and past Maxwell Land Grant and Railway Company president, all hailed from west-central Missouri, where they had known each other as boys and university students. As a student, Breeden had also lived in the area and may have met one or more of the others there. Elkins, Catron, and Breeden formed the nucleus of the political alliance known as the Santa Fe Ring. Because of his association with the other men from Missouri, and as Breeden's law partner, Waldo was commonly identified as a Ring member, but he was a Democrat in party affiliation, and was rarely involved with the others politically or in business. He was respected by many for his independence and integrity.[7]

From 1869 to 1887, the First Judicial District was comprised of seven northern counties, including Colfax, Mora, Rio Arriba, San Miguel, Santa Fe, Taos, and a county later abolished in a reorganization of counties in the northwestern part of the territory, Santa Ana.[8] This was by far the largest of the three districts in population and number of counties served, making it the most active of the three districts. The chief justice sat as district judge for the First District, making him a very busy man. Judges of the Second and Third Districts had many hot, dusty miles to cover, but they did not have to hold court in seven counties twice a year and manage the docket and other business of the supreme court.

For all of the judges, each year began with the supreme court session. The appellate load was normally light, most years lasting little more than a week, if that. After this was finished, the judges returned to the work of their districts and the chief justice began his spring circuit through the counties of the First District. Most court sessions, but not all, began on Monday, and Saturday was sometimes a court day. Traveling to all of the county seats for court in the First District were the chief justice, the attorney general, and the clerk. Often the U.S. attorney had business before the court. Sometimes the U.S. marshal attended. Lawyers came from around the district and beyond as they had clients and interests to represent before the court. The predominant mode of travel in pre-railroad days was the stagecoach. Semiannual sessions usually included a grand jury review of persons accused but not yet indicted and trials, as scheduled, for pending criminal and civil cases.

At the first merged court session to consider matters arising in Colfax and Taos Counties, some notable cases and defendants were scheduled to come before the grand jury. Among these were charges against Clay Allison for murder and other offenses. Robert Longwill and Florencio Donoghue were charged with involvement in procuring the murder of the Reverend Franklin J. Tolby, and O. P. McMains was charged in the murder of the Cimarron constable and murder suspect Cruz Vega. Given the high levels of excitement surrounding these cases, it was deemed prudent to provide a military presence for the purpose of maintaining peace and order during the session at Taos. The governor forwarded a request for support to the district headquarters in Santa Fe, and on March 30, 1876, a detachment of fifteen soldiers was ordered to Taos in advance of the court session.[9]

The April term of court for matters arising in Colfax and Taos Counties opened at Taos on Monday, April 3. The process was not without controversy. It was charged that jurors were being vetted by Pedro Sanchez of Taos, presumed local agent of the Santa Fe Ring.[10] According to the *Colorado Chieftain*'s report, "The jury consisted of seventeen Mexicans, not one of whom could understand a word of English, and only one of whom could write his name," that being the foreman, Sanchez's father-in-law.[11] Frank Springer later complained that the entire jury pool was chosen from Taos County, so that accused persons from Colfax County could not be said to have been judged by a jury of their peers.[12] Springer and other detractors took exception to the judge's instruction that Attorney General Breeden was to attend all grand jury deliberations, and that the jurors should be guided by Breeden's advice.[13]

Whatever the merits of these criticisms, the grand jury was seated and forged ahead with its work. But before they were set to the task of hearing and sifting the allegations and evidence, Chief Justice Waldo had somewhat to say. He had been present for the informative hearings and citizens' meeting at Cimarron on November 10, 1875, and he had followed reports of seemingly rampant violence in the region with alarm. He was deeply affected by the unfeeling and careless disregard of laws, civil behavior, and legal processes, and he was troubled about the epidemic of gun violence. He chose to convey his thoughts to jurors chosen to act on behalf of the territory in upholding law and justice. Waldo spoke in English, and his words were translated into Spanish.

Judge Waldo Unloads

Henry Ludlow Waldo learned about frontier violence at an early age.[14] He was just three when his father, Lawrence Ludlow Waldo, met death in an uprising of Pueblo Indians, who with some of the Spanish-Mexican people of northern New Mexico, rose against the American regime in 1847. The episode has been known as the "Taos Revolt" or "Taos Massacre," for the principal flashpoint, the site of greatest violence and destruction; but the revolt also spread to other places in the northern mountain region. Unaware of the trouble, Lawrence Waldo's party of traders rode into the Mora Valley, where they had been welcomed on previous journeys. Heading back toward their homes in western Missouri, the six men of the party were captured by rebel forces under the command of Manuel Cortez and were summarily executed on Cortez's order.[15]

Despite this unhappy episode of family history, Henry Waldo trekked across the plains to New Mexico in 1862. The next year, he struck out for California, where he read law and began a legal career. He married in 1870. By the time Waldo removed to New Mexico in 1872, he was a family man and an experienced attorney. He joined Tom Catron and Stephen Elkins in Santa Fe and took on part of the workload in their firm, freeing Elkins for his work as New Mexico's

Henry Ludlow Waldo. Waldo grew up in west-central Missouri. After several years as an attorney in California, he moved to Santa Fe. Waldo served as territorial chief justice and attorney general before leaving public office to serve as solicitor for the Atchison, Topeka and Santa Fe Railway Company. Denver Public Library, Western History Collection.

delegate to Congress.[16] After the death of Joseph Palen, the controlling faction in Santa Fe put Waldo's name forward for the vacant office of chief justice. Waldo served two years as chief justice and the following year as attorney general, during some of the most turbulent times of the territory's history, including trouble in Colfax, Lincoln, and Grant Counties. Waldo wanted to do something about the shocking wave of violence if he could. This was the theme of his message to the Taos grand jurors.

Waldo started his speech to the jury with a pro forma reading of statutes concerning the nature and limits of responsibilities delegated to juries by law, offering precautionary advice and emphasizing the vital importance of the grand jury in upholding the law, maintaining an orderly society, and ensuring fidelity to processes of self-governance. He exhorted the men of the jury to approach their work with great care to ensure a "fair, calm, dispassionate but thorough, vigorous, and fearless" discharge of their duties.[17]

Having disposed of formalities, Waldo came to the heart of the matter. He was distressed at the frequent and calamitous nature of gun violence occurring in the district, and he wanted the jury to consider its decisions in light of the damaging effect of the violence in their communities. Judge Waldo saw danger in the ready access to deadly weapons, especially when worn openly in violation of laws prohibiting the carrying of weapons in settlements or plazas. In his thinking, the act of bearing firearms was "directly conducive to violence and bloodshed." The judge observed, "It is presumed that there is a purpose, and a meaning in every man's acts. He who carries a deadly weapon carries it to use it. He thus habituates his mind to fierce and violent expedients. In case of a quarrel, his first impulse is a resort to his pistol or knife."[18]

The result of this situation, Waldo believed, was a culture of violence. "It may be easily demonstrated," he remarked, "that when any considerable number adopt the practice of carrying deadly weapons we are sure to find among them the dominion of the revolver and the bowie knife with a contemptuous disregard of order and a reckless defiance of law, and accordingly among such we may expect that scenes of violence, bloodshed, and murder, must occur with frequent, constant and almost invariable regularity."[19] In support of his contentions, the judge pointed to a record of murders, assassinations, brawls, and shoot-outs occurring in Cimarron and vicinity in recent months—amounting to some sixteen or eighteen in the area, with six violent deaths in a single drinking house. He expressed contempt for the practice and apparent public toleration of lynch law. He cited the cases of Cruz Vega and Manuel Cardenas, both suspected assassins of Reverend Tolby, pronouncing their unknown killers guilty of the crime of murder.

Having said his piece, the judge moved ahead with the business at hand, but his personal campaign against public violence was not over. Because Colfax County was not the only section of the territory in which heinous acts occurred, and because Santa Fe had experienced recent outrages resulting in the deaths of innocents, he delivered a similar charge to the grand jury at Santa Fe when it convened in July 1876.[20]

In Re: Allison

The prosecution of Clay Allison was a particular design of the governor of New Mexico, Samuel Axtell. The depth of the governor's obsession with Allison was made clear in the course of a conversation that Frank Springer had with Axtell in his office in Santa Fe in February 1876. Springer was there to talk about the removal of the district court from Cimarron, and to see if he might persuade Axtell to change his mind on the attachment of Colfax County to Taos County "for judicial purposes." Springer was not successful, but he learned more about the governor's intent and rationale than he had known before.

Recalled Springer, "Said Axtell was, during this conversation, very bitter in his allusions to Colfax County, and especially in his allusions to one R. C. Allison, whom he denounced as a murderer, and who, he said, was guilty of several murders both in Colfax County and other parts of the territory, and declared that he, Axtell, was going to have him indicted and punished for all of them, or else compel him to leave the country." Axtell's obsession with the effort to have Allison arrested, convicted, and punished or persuaded to leave the territory was evident in the odd plan that he concocted for Allison's arrest at a meeting at the stagecoach station in Cimarron the previous month.[21] Axtell doubtless was pleased to hear of Allison's travel to Taos in custody of the Colfax County sheriff, there to make his appearance in the district court and to face a grand jury that he presumably had not already charmed or frightened into submission.

At the session in Taos, Allison was called on to answer charges that had been referred for consideration by the grand jury, including murder charges. Surviving records of the proceeding are incomplete and news reports scant. According to one source, since repeated by others writing about Allison, he was charged with the murders of Francisco "Pancho" Griego, "Chunk" Colbert, and Charles Cooper, the sole witness to the shooting death of Colbert at the stage stop of Clifton in northwestern Colfax County.[22] This account, as narrated by Dale Schoenberger, was informed by writings of William G. Ritch, the longtime territorial secretary and an avocational historian. However, the arrest warrant cited by Ritch and the reward proclamation signed by Axtell named only Cooper as the victim of a homicide with which Clay Allison was charged.[23] James S. Peters, a careful student of Allison's career, could confirm only two murder indictments returned by the Taos grand jury, one charging Allison in the death of Cooper, and another for his involvement in the lynching of Cruz Vega. Neither resulted in a murder conviction.[24] Allison had been cleared in the killing of Pancho Griego by the Colfax County justice of the peace, based on Allison's claim of self-defense, but Breeden, acting as territorial prosecutor, may or may not have reinstated this charge for consideration of the Taos grand jury.

Anecdotal tales about Allison abound in the accounts of old-timers, from recollections, or from hearsay. One such tale, told by George Crocker, illustrates Allison's sense of responsibility, as revealed in the Taos grand jury session of April 1876. According to Crocker, Allison, under a bond signed by friends, appeared as required and immediately asked the judge whether his bondholders were released, now that he had presented himself in court. When Judge Waldo replied in the affirmative, Allison calmly walked out of the courtroom and rode away. He was indicted by the grand jury, Crocker recalled, but Sheriff Rinehart "made no effort to arrest him, knowing that it was useless."[25]

Allison, however, was worried about indictments still pending against him. When Axtell traveled through Colfax County on June 3, following the April grand jury session, Allison hailed the governor's coach as it rumbled over the open prairie northwest of Cimarron. Taking passage to Trinidad, Allison boarded the coach and engaged Axtell in conversation. If, as Axtell recalled, the meeting was not prearranged, Allison possibly had learned of the governor's travel plans and had made a point of seeing him.

According to Secretary Ritch, Allison wanted to see what sort of man "had so interfered with his personal liberty" to the extreme of offering a five-hundred-dollar reward for his arrest and having the troops from Fort Union help with the arrest.[26] According to Ritch, Axtell wanted to know why a brave man like Allison did not "surrender himself and stand trial like a man"; Allison replied that he was entirely willing to face charges against him if guaranteed a fair trial which, in his opinion, would be impossible in Taos.

Allison did return to Taos in April 1877 as required by the court. He was found guilty of assault and paid a fine of one hundred dollars. The territory apparently decided against prosecuting the murder charges, and Allison again walked away from serious charges—a free man, cleared by virtue of claims of self-defense, or dismissed by the territory for want of sufficient evidence of his guilt.

Allison found more trouble during the year between the indictments and final dispositions of the charges against him in New Mexico, returning fire and killing a local officer who had shot Allison's brother, John. The brothers had traveled to Las Animas, Colorado, to engage in a cattle transaction, and had refused to comply with a local ordinance requiring that patrons check their firearms upon entering the local dance hall.[27] The Colorado grand jury declined to indict Allison, citing its finding of self-defense in the shooting death of constable Charles Faber.[28]

Conspiracy on Trial

Manuel Cardenas's accusation that Franklin Tolby had been the victim of a homicide paid for by four men was clouded by Cardenas's retraction in a jailhouse visit from friends of the men accused, occurring prior to the November 10 hearing, and was further complicated by the murder of Cardenas after the hearing.[29] Of those accused by Cardenas—Florencio Donoghue, Francisco Griego, Robert Longwill, and Melvin Mills—Griego had already been sentenced and executed by Clay Allison, and Mills had been released at the conclusion of the November 10 hearing due to insufficiency of evidence against him. Enough evidence had been found to justify grand jury consideration of Donoghue's case. Charges against Longwill were still pending following his flight from Cimarron upon being identified as a suspect in Tolby's killing.

To many in Colfax County, there was still reason to suspect Longwill and Donoghue and perhaps other leaders of Santa Fe's ruling political faction. There was sufficient evidence against both men to give a thoughtful grand jury pause. But despite circumstances that Tolby's avengers believed were damning to the accused, the effort to have Donoghue and Longwill indicted by the grand jury could not rise above contrary allegiances of the prosecutor, Attorney General William Breeden; presumed bias of the jury chosen in consultation with local politico Pedro Sanchez; and the fact that much of the evidence against the accused men was circumstantial or hearsay.

The *Santa Fe New Mexican* took pleasure in announcing the grand jury's exoneration of Longwill and Donoghue. Melvin Mills had already been cleared in the hearing at Cimarron, but the inquiry and conclusion in the Taos proceeding reiterated his innocence. The *New Mexican* remarked that "about fifty witnesses residing in Colfax County" had been questioned, with no evidence presented to incriminate those accused. According to the paper, the charges had been based on rumors and suspicions.[30]

Donoghue, though given a lower billing in the *New Mexican*'s account, was particularly fortunate to be cleared, in that he alone among the accused men still living had been accused in both circulating theories of Tolby's killing—the one contending that a group of four men aligned with the Santa Fe Ring had paid for Tolby's death; and the less well-publicized theory, according to which Francisco Griego and Florencio Donoghue had arranged the murder to keep Tolby from telling the grand jury about the assault Tolby had witnessed, in which Griego and Donoghue had allegedly shot at some "Americans."[31]

Springer and Morley and their Colfax County associates did not agree with the grand jury finding regarding Longwill and Donoghue, but there was little they could do other than complain about grand jury bias and Ring domination of the courts. Freed of the threat of a pending murder charge, Longwill and Donoghue left Colfax County behind and made their permanent homes in Santa Fe.

Melvin Mills, cleared of complicity in the Tolby murder, had a long life and career in Colfax County. In Springer, he built a twenty-two-room mansion in the "Second French Empire" style and made a home there with his parents, his wife, Ella, and their children.[32] He lived nearly sixty years in the county, spoke to civic groups, sat for interviews, and became a fount of information on the history he had seen from Maxwell's time to the 1920s. His memory was not perfect at distances of fifty years or more, but he gave authentic impressions of events and people he had known. Despite his constructive citizenship, the experience of being accused in the Tolby murder left a mark. Recalling those bad times before his passing, Mills noted that the stigma had sometimes blocked his way in life, saying, "I have found it difficult to raise [sic] above it."[33]

The Case of O. P. McMains

In addition to its focus on criminal allegations related to the death of Reverend Tolby, the Taos grand jury devoted considerable attention to the deaths of Cruz Vega and Manuel Cardenas by mob violence—with emphasis on the lynching of Vega. According to the court records, some fifteen men of Colfax County were indicted in the murder of Vega. Most cases were dismissed in a few weeks or months by means of a nolle prosequi—notice of the territory's intent to forego prosecution. Three men had been arrested after indictments. One was Jimmy Thorp, who was not in the area at the time of Vega's death and whose charges were dismissed. This left William Terhune and O. P. McMains to face prosecution.[34]

How McMains became a distinct scapegoat in the eyes of territorial officials who worked the apparatus of prosecution and judicial decision making was a mystery to friends of McMains. Perhaps it was because his determination to "ferret out and bring to justice" those responsible for Tolby's death pointed a finger toward officials and allies of the Santa Fe power coalition, but the evidence against him in the killing of Vega was slight. McMains seemed surprised to be indicted, much less made the target of the prosecution. Six months earlier, he had taken part in the hearing of November 10, 1875, questioning witnesses as an advocate of those seeking justice for Tolby.[35] Now he was accused of first-degree murder, awaiting trial. McMains had shown himself to be an impulsive, passionate, sometimes bombastic advocate for the causes he undertook. In the attempt to extract information from Cruz Vega, he had exercised appalling judgment in exposing Vega to interrogation by an angry mob, at a time and place in which it could be assumed that the men had been drinking. McMains's contention that he had left the scene after imploring those questioning Vega not to harm him physically was substantiated by others present. No witness had accused McMains of ordering the torture or murder of Vega, or of condoning or taking part in these acts.

McMains had attended part of the Taos grand jury session, but left before it was finished, unconcerned about his own status. He learned of his indictment after the court had adjourned and the parties had dispersed, and upon his return to Cimarron, he submitted to arrest and was locked up in the stone jail. He agreed to be represented by Frank Springer. Springer soon arranged for a hearing with Chief Justice Waldo in Santa Fe; he requested release for McMains and Terhune on writs of habeas corpus. Waldo declined the writs, but agreed to release the prisoners on bonds of twenty thousand dollars each.[36] As conditions and amounts of the bonds were prohibitive, the men were returned to their cells in Cimarron to await trial. Said the *Colorado Chieftain* in support of McMains, "As Judge Waldo is the person who presided at the notorious Taos Court, and is a prominent member of the 'ring' nothing else could be expected."[37] When the cases came up for trial, the territory did not, after all, prosecute Terhune.

The pending prosecution of McMains dragged along for more than a year, but it was clear from their persistence that McMains's enemies were determined to see him damaged. According to the *Chieftain*'s report in May 1877, the case was twice dismissed, and he was reindicted each time for the sole purpose of keeping him incarcerated until the trial, despite the fact that he posed no danger to anyone.[38] McMains's case was dismissed at least twice to foil legal attempts to have him released, first by means of an appeal of the denied habeas corpus writ, later by an attempt of the U.S. attorney general to take the case from territorial officials and handle it in his office.

When the Taos district court convened in September 1876, still hearing matters from both Colfax County and Taos County, the trial of McMains, along with most other criminal cases, was continued to the following spring term. At that session, in March and April 1877, Springer asked for another continuance and a change of venue to Mora County, where the likelihood of seating a fair jury might be improved. The changes were granted, and the case finally proceeded to trial on August 22, 1877. At some time after the Taos court session, McMains had been freed on bond.

Aside from its importance to McMains, the trial at Mora was valuable for the information it provided concerning the capture, interrogation, and lynching of Cruz Vega and the parts played by William Low and McMains in the affair. The scene described was ugly and tragic, not only in the manner of Vega's death and the sham justice meted out to him, but in the complete failure of due process, presumption of innocence, and other legal protections put in place in order to secure justice for those accused of crimes. The *News and Press* published the witness testimony in full, and the *Las Vegas Gazette* and the *Santa Fe New Mexican* printed substantial portions as well.[39]

The jury's decision, announced on August 24, was perplexing, finding McMains "guilty in the fifth degree," and specifying a fine of three hundred dollars. The *Colorado Chieftain* was incredulous, finding murder in the fifth degree "a dilution a little beyond anything we have heard of before."[40] The practical-minded Springer, however, was drawn to the jury's failure to name a specific crime for which the defendant was guilty. Springer brought this lapse to the attention of Judge Waldo and observed that McMains had not been found guilty of any crime. Waldo agreed that the verdict was legally defective and decreed that McMains be given a new trial.[41]

By the time McMains was to be tried again in spring of 1878, Cimarron had regained its district court, and Henry Waldo had resigned as chief justice and trial judge for the First Judicial District. The designated replacement was not yet in the territory, so for the April court session at Cimarron, Judge Samuel Parks of the Second District was on the bench. Judge Parks had recently arrived from Illinois and may have concluded that the long and tortured prosecution was due to be put to rest. He dismissed the case "for want of jurisdiction." McMains's ordeal as a criminal defendant was designated by the *Colorado Chieftain* as "a long persecution of the most rascally and outrageous character." In the paper's view, McMains deserved his freedom.[42]

Considering, in retrospect, the high-profile prosecutions emanating from Colfax County in the violent season of fall 1875, the courtroom power struggle between the Santa Fe Ring and the Cimarron locals may be said to have ended in a draw. The Taos grand jury declined to indict alleged Ring allies Robert Longwill and Florencio Donoghue, while Allison and McMains sustained only slight damage as a result of having been prosecuted for their actions against the interests of the presumed Ring partisans. There were, however, losers, considering the failure of the territory to hold anyone accountable in the killings of Franklin Tolby, Cruz Vega, and Manuel Cardenas, or in the saloon shoot-out that ended in the death of Pancho Griego. In the lofty business of reaching just outcomes through fair and consistent application of its statutes, clearly the Territory of New Mexico still had work to do.

The Santa Fe power elite, dominated by Steve Elkins, Tom Catron, and William Breeden, could also be considered losers, in the sense that, although not convicted, two of their friends in Colfax County, Longwill and Donoghue, had essentially been run out of the country, and Catron and Axtell would be dealt with later. Elkins may have believed it prudent to retire from the quest for land and money from the Maxwell grant and press his advantage in new fields of opportunity in Washington and West Virginia. The Santa Fe men may have been ready to call off the dispute that had been ignited in northeastern New Mexico, but the angry men of Colfax County were not.

CHAPTER 12

A Most Audacious Ring

The transition of the Maxwell Land Grant claim from a benevolent autocracy to corporate ownership and management, and the chaotic period that followed the new company's assumption of authority, coincided with the rise of another power known broadly and somewhat derisively as the Santa Fe Ring. This was an era of "rings"—combinations of political figures and businessmen who allegedly used connections and powers of office in shameless pursuit of political dominance and personal financial gain. In New Mexico, such a political alliance had emerged in the early 1870s, when its leaders managed to capture virtually all significant territorial offices, by appointment or election, or by enticing uninitiated appointees to join the club and share in the spoils. This clique, in common with similar groups, had no official character or structure, and its supposed members were identified by its political rivals.

With insiders Stephen Elkins, Thomas Catron, and William Breeden holding the offices of territorial delegate to Congress, U.S. attorney, and attorney general by 1873, and with affable appointees on hand as governor and surveyor general and in the judiciary, their hand was strong. By virtue of Elkins's involvement with Lucien Maxwell and the English company, his group had an early foothold in the scramble for profits to be realized from the property claimed by them. Over the decade following the sale of the Maxwell grant, at least twenty men associated with the Ring, by reputation, had a hand in its affairs.[1] The alleged Ring became known nationally through exposures in the *New York Sun*, one article styling the elite group, "a most audacious ring."[2]

By the time O. P. McMains went to trial, outbreaks of partisan violence in Colfax County had subsided, but William Morley and Frank Springer, leaders of the Cimarron opposition, were still fuming and were disinclined to forgive and forget. The target of their anger was the Santa Fe Ring, and its bullseye was the governor. They were feeling humiliated as a result of the unilateral decision of a Ring-friendly legislative assembly and Governor Samuel Axtell to attach Colfax County to Taos County for judicial purposes, and of the governor's requesting soldiers to maintain order in Cimarron. They were angry about an apparent stunt—Axtell's sending Benjamin Stevens with an escort of troops to arrest Clay Allison. The governor's orders included a contingency plan for dealing with local men who tried to interfere; they were to be killed. Morley, Springer, and Henry Porter were named as possible objectors who might have to be killed. This, at least, was Axtell's intent, according to Springer's later perusal of the governor's instructions to Stevens. Despite the *Las Vegas Gazette*'s article advising the men of Colfax County to "abandon the past," give their grievances a rest, and look to a brighter future, they were nowhere near ready to let it go.[3]

The partisan divide and smoldering rancor about Colfax County matters might have been abated, perhaps entirely defused, had Axtell been the sort of even-handed leader who could go to Colfax County and sit, listen, and talk with citizens to whom his recent actions and policies were obnoxious. He had been urged to do so several times, but his refusal even to meet the people and hear their views turned a disagreement into a mutual grudge. Axtell's inflexibility concerning the situation in Colfax confirmed his identity as a tool of the Elkins-Catron ring and invited a hostile reaction. Before coming to New Mexico, Axtell had been appointed governor of the Territory of Utah in December 1874. He had held the office less than half a year before being removed, to the great relief of many citizens in Utah. Despite the support of powerful friends, he was soon on shaky ground in New Mexico.

An Angry and Determined Woman

To use a common expression, William Morley "married up," meaning he married above his circumstances. Orphaned and raised by his uncle in Iowa, Morley's heart's desire was golden-haired Ada McPherson, whose father, Marcus McPherson, had served for eight years in the Iowa state senate and was district attorney for the Third Judicial District at the time of his death. The family's means had

Mary Tibbles McPherson. McPherson, mother of Ada Morley and mother-in-law of William R. Morley, took an active role in the fight to rid New Mexico of an allegedly crooked territorial administration. With a partner, she filed charges and evidentiary documents, attempting to bring about a federal investigation that would reveal corruption and topple corrupt officials. New Mexico State University Library, Archives and Special Collections, Cleaveland Collection.

provided a comfortable lifestyle, musical training, and a university education for Ada. Morley and Ada met as students at the State University of Iowa, later known simply as the University of Iowa. Following a three-year courtship, during much of which Morley was busy building western railroads for General William J. Palmer, they married in January 1873, and took rail and stagecoach transportation for Cimarron. As executive officer for the Maxwell Land Grant and Railway Company, Morley could offer as comfortable a home as could be found in Cimarron, but the amenities were far less elegant than those Ada had left behind.

Through his marriage, Morley brought two strong women into the orbit of Colfax County and the struggle of resistance to domination by the territorial ring. Ada's mother, Mary Elizabeth Tibbles McPherson, was to be the most significant female character of the conflict. Widowed by Marcus McPherson's death a year before Ada's marriage, Mary McPherson was ready and more than capable of asserting herself in public causes that interested her, and there were several. She came from a family of preachers, political and social activists, and writers, and for over a quarter century after her husband's death, she moved with ease and confidence in political and reformist circles. Her family was deeply rooted in the Methodist Church. Her father and two brothers were ministers and her dedication to the work of the church was lifelong.[4] One brother, Thomas Henry Tibbles, achieved national recognition as an abolitionist, an advocate for Indian rights, a lawyer, a newspaper editor, and an author. McPherson's late husband had also shown a strong reformist streak, seen in his activism as a state legislator and advocate. As her great-grandson, Norman Cleaveland, wrote a century later, it is not hard to see how "a Tibbles, fired up by a McPherson about injustice and corruption, could become a fierce crusader."[5]

McPherson's first chance to survey the situation in Colfax County came in spring 1875, when she traveled to Cimarron to see her firstborn grandchild, Agnes.[6] She had likely heard, via letters from her daughter, about the territorial ring and the tension between its leaders and agents, and the local managers of the Maxwell Land Grant and Railway Company, including her son-in-law, Morley. Mrs. McPherson, with a natural affinity for Methodist preachers, met and admired Rev. F. J. Tolby. She must have liked him all the more, upon learning of his reputation for vocal criticism of political corruption—naming names and exposing allegations, or so it was rumored, in articles published in eastern papers. The Santa Fe Ring had been noticed and named in widely separated counties in the territory in the early 1870s. By the time McPherson arrived, grievances concerning its malign influence were common.

The Purloined Letter

McPherson apparently made the first of several attempts to complain about the territorial administration in spring of 1875, not long after her arrival, when a letter mailed from the Morley household became the subject of controversy, resulting in an indictment of Ada Morley for theft of the U.S. mail. This came about when she took it upon herself to retrieve an envelope mailed at the Cimarron post office, a small and casually run operation.[7] Upon learning of its content, Ada walked quickly to the post office, went to the box in which the outgoing mail was collected, and found the piece she wanted, then turned to exit the building and return to her home. The identity of the writer and the object of the letter may have been known locally via an efficient rumor mill. Recalling the affair in an 1878 deposition, Frank Springer said only that the item had been posted by "a family member," but according to Morley family history, the writer was Ada's mother, and her purpose was to report rampant corruption in the territorial government of New Mexico.[8] Ada seemingly wanted to head off more trouble.

The postmaster, John B. McCullough, confronted Mrs. Morley about the unauthorized extraction of a letter already posted by the sender. Unsatisfied with her response and angry from a heated exchange on the matter with William Morley, McCullough referred the matter to U.S. Attorney Thomas B. Catron for criminal prosecution under federal statute.[9] The episode did no lasting damage to Ada Morley or her family, but Catron's response to the complaint, as depicted in sworn testimony, likely contributed to his resignation as U.S. attorney for New Mexico.[10]

In accordance with McCullough's complaint, Catron submitted the matter to the federal grand jury. That panel returned an indictment in July 1875, and there the issue rested for almost two years, with no arrest made. Whether the delay in arresting Mrs. Morley suggested a desire to keep the threat of arrest and punishment hanging over the Morleys' heads, Catron's disinterest in prosecuting the matter, or a humane hesitation to harass a mother of infant children is unclear; but the plot thickened in March 1876, when Asa Middaugh made a sworn affidavit that reflected poorly on Catron. The purpose of giving the affidavit at that time is also unclear, unless it was to support charges to be made against Catron, but the affidavit was cited in a letter from William R. Morley to U.S. Attorney General Alphonso Taft in March 1877 and was an attachment to Frank Springer's deposition of August 1878, given in response to a federal inquiry into possible official misconduct by public officeholders in New Mexico.

The substance of Middaugh's testimony was that Catron had brought charges against Ada Morley because she had taken a buggy and team when Catron wished to use them during a recent session of the district court in Cimarron.[11] Retaliation against William Morley for his criticism of territorial officials in the *Cimarron News and Press* and in the *New York Sun* was also thought to be one of Catron's motives in prosecuting Ada Morley. When confronted with accusations about possible use of his office to pursue a personal grudge, Catron denied that he had used his position for a personal or political purpose. In the judgment of Catron biographer Victor Westphall, those eager to excoriate the Ring may have read too much into Catron's involvement; Westphall notes that, as U.S. attorney, Catron was obligated to pursue the complaint until it was resolved in court or dropped by the accuser, McCullough.¹²

A Cause in Search of a Champion Meets a Champion in Search of a Cause

Over the next few years, Mary McPherson divided time between Cimarron and her home at Council Bluffs, Iowa, with periodic travel to Washington as her involvement in New Mexico matters deepened. Her membership in and loyalty to the Methodist Church engendered sympathy for O. P. McMains, relative to the lengthy prosecution of McMains for his role in the lynching of Cruz Vega. She took up the cause and began to seek support for McMains outside New Mexico. McPherson sought out influential church leaders, asking that they intervene to halt the injustice to McMains. She hoped to see Bishop Thomas Bowman of Saint Louis, Bishop Matthew Simpson of Philadelphia, and a future bishop, Dr. John P. Newman of Washington, D.C., when traveling in the eastern states in fall of 1876. All were important figures in the church. McPherson sought and obtained letters of introduction, and at least met with Bishop Bowman at Saint Louis.¹³

As McPherson was trying to help McMains and topple the regime in Santa Fe, Morley's friend, Frank Springer, was on a parallel track, seeing political allies and appealing to authorities in Washington. In fall 1876, McPherson intended to visit influential attorney William Fishback, McMains's brother-in-law, in Indianapolis, but Fishback was traveling and she failed to connect with him. A few weeks later, however, Springer had a productive meeting with him that resulted in a decisive, if ultimately fruitless, attempt to assist McMains.¹⁴ Through an acquaintance in the federal administration, Fishback secured a meeting with newly inaugurated President Rutherford B. Hayes. Hayes referred the matter to Attorney General Charles Devens, who wired instructions to the territorial attorney general for New Mexico, William Breeden, ordering him to suspend the prosecution of McMains. Breeden refused on grounds that the issue was under territorial law and jurisdiction and was not a concern of the federal administration. Devens appealed to Governor Axtell to intercede, but Axtell also refused, leaving McMains to stand trial.¹⁵

Prior to the change in administration, McPherson had traveled to Washington, where her attention increasingly turned to pressing corruption charges against federally appointed officials in New Mexico. By letter of February 7, 1877, she fired an initial volley, writing to Attorney General Taft, complaining about a variety of abuses, but focusing on Catron's apparent use of his office to torment the Morleys. Taft was soon to go out with the rest of the Grant administration, leaving the matter to Charles Devens, attorney general in the new Hayes administration. Catron was also accused of using his powers to oppress the innocent while protecting guilty allies, and of threatening frivolous prosecutions to gain votes for Stephen Elkins in the last election. McPherson accused courts and judges of colluding with political allies and concluded, speaking of the corruption in New Mexico, "I do not know myself but it is prevalent among the people that all U.S. officers out there are in league together, and the people are the sufferers."[16]

On receipt of McPherson's accusations, Taft immediately referred the letter to Catron for his response. Catron denied pressing the prosecution against Ada Morley in retaliation for use of a buggy and team that he wanted to use, denied prosecuting political enemies while letting guilty allies go free, denied using threats of prosecution to extort fees for himself or votes for his party, and defended the attachment of Colfax to Taos County for judicial purposes as a measure needed to curb violence in a county out of control. Other charges were denied. Countering McPherson's accusations, Catron accused William Morley of inciting murder and assassination as editor of the *Cimarron News and Press*.[17] For the time being, McPherson and Catron had argued to a draw; no official sanction was levied against Catron.

McPherson had written to apprise Ada and William Morley of her actions, including the letter sent to Attorney General Taft and her acquisition of an associate in the effort to redress the venality in Santa Fe. Apparently, this was William B. Matchett, a former Methodist minister who had experience working with Congress and federal agencies. He joined McPherson in her efforts to draw attention to the irregular actions of federal officials in New Mexico.

The response to this completely surprising news in the Morley household was a mixture of alarm and concerned approbation. To seek the help of church officials in McMains's defense was one thing; taking on the Ring through the federal hierarchy in Washington was another. On March 6, 1877, William Morley wrote his mother-in-law, "I was astonished beyond measure, at your proceedings, and have fears as to the result: at the same time, I will not throw a straw in your way, but will do what I can to help matters."[18] Morley was thoroughly discouraged with the state of affairs, including the incoming new Republican officials at all levels, who were expected to extend the self-serving policies of past administrations, including the use of public appointments in the territories to reward political support rather than to ensure good government. But warming to his mother-in-law's better intentions, Morley exhorted, "If you can remove any of these men, do so by all means." He thought having a secret agent sent from Washington might be the best way to engender the trust of local citizens who knew plenty, but might be afraid to tell what they knew, lest it be used against them. Ada followed up the next day, voicing her fears for a failed effort to oust the corrupt officials, but reinforcing William Morley's suggestion of a secret agent to probe corruption in New Mexico on behalf of the federal government.[19]

The next initiative for McPherson and her new partner, W. B. Matchett, was an appeal to Secretary of the Interior Carl Schurz, the official most directly responsible for oversight of civil governance in the territories. In their letter of March 1877, Morley and Matchett concentrated on the misdeeds and failings of the governor, stating two general charges against his administration: one concerning his participation in a "corrupt combination," and the other alleging manipulation of Spanish and Mexican grants for personal gain, with a view to facilitating the establishment of Mormon enclaves on the lands acquired.[20]

In April, Matchett and McPherson took the matter a step further, appealing directly to the new president, Rutherford B. Hayes. Named in their complaint were Catron; Associate Justice Warren Bristol, district judge in the Third Judicial District; Henry Waldo; Governor Samuel Axtell; and "others of the said Territory" who had tried to "corrupt and defraud justice and defeat the ends thereof." The McMains prosecution was also cited as an issue. The request was that those found complicit in corrupt activities be removed from office. The petitioners requested a thorough and rigorous investigation.[21]

The letter was referred to Interior Secretary Schurz, who in turn sent the complaint to Axtell for response. The governor replied by letter on June 14, denying all charges except that of writing letters to a Utah newspaper when serving as governor of Utah, and signing himself "El Obispo," the bishop, which he explained was in the nature of a pleasant rapport with the Mormon people of the region. Axtell admitted that he had not gone to Colfax County to meet with citizens there, stating that he was well informed concerning the circumstances there, and was not required by duties of his office to travel around the territory or provided with the means to do so.[22]

Samuel Beach Axtell, 1874. Following a brief, stormy tenure as governor of the Territory of Utah, Axtell was appointed territorial governor of New Mexico. He had previously represented the state of California in Congress. Photo by C. R. Savage. The photo is presumed to be in the public domain. Image courtesy of the Church History Library, Church of Jesus Christ of Latter-Day Saints.

The news concerning charges filed against Axtell was received with special interest in his home state of Ohio; in California and Utah, where he had held public office; and in New Mexico. Newspapers often took sides, some condemning and some defending Axtell and his associates in Santa Fe. Of Axtell's alleged complicity in a plan to create Mormon settlements in New Mexico, the *San Francisco Chronicle* declared that the allegations should be thoroughly investigated, and if true, he ought to "be removed from the Governorship of New Mexico."[23] The *Colorado Weekly Chieftain* published the charges as submitted to the secretary of the interior in March 1877, and made clear its belief in, and censure of, a corrupt political combination in New Mexico.[24] The *New Mexican* denounced the charges as "false and unfounded," denying that Axtell had collaborated in efforts to plant new Mormon settlements, or had conspired to use land grants for that or any purpose.[25]

In May, Matchett and McPherson sent Schurz a copy of charges as submitted to President Hayes, along with supporting materials to be entered in any proceedings concerning Governor Axtell and his status.[26] In August, they distributed a printed pamphlet, *In the Matter of the Charges Vs. Governor Samuel B. Axtell and Other New Mexican Officials*, consisting of case history, meeting minutes, correspondence, congressional testimony, and other evidentiary documents in which the charges were substantiated.[27] The document was prepared for submittal to the Departments of the Interior and Justice. Presumably copies also went to other officials who might influence decisions on the charges, and perhaps to recipients positioned to sway public opinion.

Reviewing the McPherson-Matchett efforts of the past months, the *Deseret News* of Salt Lake City observed in July 1877 that the effort to unseat Axtell in New Mexico was proceeding, "though apparently without making much headway with the administration." The paper reported that Axtell had denied the charges and that Stephen Elkins and other associates had sent letters to the capital defending him and casting doubt on the intentions of his accusers.[28] Morley, again in the business of building railroads, wrote to Attorney General Devens in September to protest the delay in Catron's long-threatened prosecution of Ada Morley, but the case was soon to be settled, by virtue of postmaster McCullough's withdrawal of the charges.[29]

Two other communications sent to Washington on behalf of Colfax County residents in the summer or fall of 1877 raised other issues of possible corruption by New Mexico officials as they touched the interests of Colfax County residents. Whatever the effect of the messages, they opened a new line of criticism of the Santa Fe–based officials, relating to commerce in Spanish and Mexican land grants. Documents sent in support of these complaints became part of the Interior Department's file on Axtell, and of the body of evidence to be considered in later inquiries.

Lewis Kingman who, like Morley, was a displaced railroad locating engineer waiting out effects of the financial panic of 1873 in Colfax County, was alarmed at what appeared to him to be efforts to legitimize and sell the forged Uña de Gato grant in the northern part of the county. He conveyed his concerns in a letter to Henry Arms, a neighbor and sheep rancher in the region, and Arms sent the letter on to William M. Evarts, later U.S. secretary of state, but then serving as assistant commissioner of the General Land Office. The information implicated

U.S. Attorney Thomas Catron in knowing involvement in a fraudulent scheme. Arms's letter, and Kingman's, prompted a full inquiry into the validity of the Uña de Gato grant by Surveyor General Henry M. Atkinson, and helped to forestall legal validation of the grant.[30]

At about the same time, probably in September 1877, a Trinidad, Colorado, attorney and businessman, Horace Merriam, sent off a list of charges purporting to justify Axtell's removal, accompanied by supporting affidavits from Ezra Beardsley, Lewis Kingman, William D. Lee, J. B. Norton, Frank Springer, and Harry Whigham. Merriam's accusations reprised some of those conveyed by McPherson and Matchett and addressed the issue of fraud in relation to the Uña de Gato claim, faulting Governor Axtell for trying to interest U.S. senator Stephen W. Dorsey in the tract.[31] The documents were included as evidence in the investigation of the Uña de Gato grant.

A Temporary Reprieve

Federal officials, including the secretary of state, secretary of the interior, and president, had given some notice to the allegations presented by Mary McPherson, W. B. Matchett, Arms, and others, referring the charges to Axtell and Thomas Catron for response, and opening files on the complaints received. It was not, however, clear that an official proceeding had been opened, until at the end of September 1877, a finding was announced. On September 29, the *Washington Evening Star* and other papers across the nation published a brief notice to the effect that charges against Governor Axtell had been found to be "vague and unsupported by proof."[32] In response to the decision, and in an expression of her annoyance, Mary McPherson wrote to Secretary Schurz on September 30, to inquire as to when she might be heard through her attorney, presumably W. B. Matchett, since she had been assured that there would be a hearing, in which she could expect to introduce more evidence. Stating that she had been advised of the recent decision through notices she read in the *Star* and the *Nation*, McPherson wrote, "I shall not accept newspaper reports as a decision in a case of the Interior."[33]

McPherson may have had little choice but to accept the decision of Secretary Schurz and the president. She and Matchett had made the case concerning corruption in New Mexico as best they could. After the decision, they moved on. McPherson made Washington her home and was unstinting in service of multiple causes, including women's suffrage, the temperance movement, the Women's Press Association, and mission activities of the Methodist Church. William Morley remained intensely interested in the defeat of the Ring as a center of political power, but he had business to attend to. The resumption of railroad building, along with obligations to his young family, curtailed his direct participation in the effort to free Colfax County of Ring rule.

The efforts of Mary McPherson and William B. Matchett on behalf of dissatisfied Colfax County citizens should not be considered a failure. On the contrary, the complaints that they had articulated and the evidence they developed remained on file in the official records of the U.S. Departments of Interior and Justice and would be used in further inquiries that would come about soon enough. McPherson and Matchett had begun, in earnest, a chase that others would finish.

Frank Springer, still practicing law in Cimarron and representing interests of the Maxwell Company, was left to press the allegations against Axtell and other officials. He remained deeply committed to the effort, and soon had help from events transpiring in other parts of the territory, especially in Lincoln County—developments that would make it hard for Hayes's administration to ignore or downplay the serious charges at issue. Springer continued pursuing the grievances of disaffected Colfax County citizens, and he worked to achieve satisfactory redress in an effort that would extend well into the following year, 1878.

CHAPTER 13

A Reckoning

Had the accusations brought by Mary McPherson and William Matchett been the extent of charges raised in Washington regarding the integrity of governance in New Mexico, the powerful men of Santa Fe might have weathered the controversy and returned to business as usual, but this possibility was nullified by an outbreak of violence bloodier, and if possible, more vengeful than anything seen in Colfax County. As in Colfax, money and political control were at the root of the conflict. It was not surprising to find the usual seekers of power and privilege associated with the reputed Santa Fe Ring deeply involved and looking out for their own interests.

In Lincoln County, many of the same forces were at work as in Colfax: a competition for control in business and politics; a deep factional division, one side with the territorial ring behind it, the other fending for itself; and a country still ruled as much by strength and daring as by law. Conflicts spawned by economic competition sometimes turned personal, and elements conducive to violent behavior were present in abundance—a preponderance of men, a fight over money and power, and an engrained impulse for resorting to violence to redress a slight or settle a grudge. Surely no citizen would have welcomed the bloodshed and animus that had been loosed in the foothills around Lincoln and Fort Stanton. Still, residents of Colfax County may have felt some relief from the stigma of being seen as belonging to a uniquely dysfunctional society.

Trouble in Lincoln County

The Lincoln County War had its roots in a struggle for economic dominance in a growing region of cattle ranching in the Sierra Blanca Mountains and along the watercourses falling away from them—the Rio Ruidoso, Rio Hondo, Rio Bonito, Rio Feliz, and at some distance, the broad valley of the Pecos River. The army post of Fort Stanton and the Mescalero Indian Reservation and Agency offered lucrative opportunities for contracting, and a steady influx of settlers provided an expanding retail market. Former army officer Lawrence Gustave Murphy was the first person to consolidate economic power in the area, securing contracts to supply beef and other goods for the army and the Mescalero Reservation. Expelled as post trader at Fort Stanton in 1872, Murphy had relocated to the village of Lincoln, establishing a mercantile store in partnership with James J. Dolan and Emil Fritz in a firm known locally as "the House," later taken over by Dolan and John H. Riley. Murphy sold cattle purchased at favorable prices from small ranchers, some of whom reportedly acquired beeves free of charge by rustling them from larger producers like John Chisum who, by the early 1870s, had driven herds into the Pecos Valley and made a reputation as the reigning cattle baron, and as a major target for cattle thieves. Said Emerson Hough, author of the first generally accepted account of the Lincoln County War, "Murphy was king of the Bonito country. Chisum was king of the Pecos."[1]

Beginning toward the end of 1876, the competition for business in the area became more of a three-cornered affair with the arrival of Englishman John Henry Tunstall from London by way of Canada, San Francisco, and Santa Fe. Tunstall, just twenty-three years of age when he arrived in Santa Fe, was highly motivated to invest in the western territories of the United States. Fate and Alexander McSween propelled him to Lincoln County, in the Territory of New Mexico. Tunstall met cattle king John Chisum and learned that his own interests and Chisum's were, more often than not, aligned in opposition to the House of Murphy and Dolan, with its ties to the profit-minded territorial officials in Santa Fe. McSween, Scottish by ancestry, Canadian by birth, had opened a law practice in Lincoln, working for L. G. Murphy and Company until a falling out sent him to the other side of the gathering conflict. In March 1877, L. G. Murphy withdrew from the business. He died in Santa Fe in October 1878.

In the spring of 1877, John Tunstall bought land for a ranch on the Rio Feliz and began stocking it with cattle. In a more direct challenge to the House, he opened a general merchandise store in Lincoln, with McSween holding a limited financial interest. The rivalry intensified, both sides hiring rough men who could handle guns, and who were willing to protect their employers' interests. A dispute over a life insurance policy, a debt allegedly owed to the old Murphy-Dolan company, and McSween's role in handling the matter for the heirs, created a convenient point of conflict that Dolan could press. At Dolan's urging, a relative of Emil Fritz, the deceased man, sued McSween over alleged embezzlement of proceeds from the insurance policy and obtained a court order for attachment of McSween's property to satisfy a judgment against him. The joint interest owned by Tunstall and McSween pertained to the store in Lincoln, while the ranch and cattle were generally known to be "Tunstall's independent and private venture," but this fact was unknown to, or disregarded by, the party dispatched to bring in livestock belonging to Tunstall.[2] Threatened with the removal of animals from his ranch, Tunstall attempted to drive his horses to safety, but in the chaotic encounter with the party sent to enforce the writ, he was shot dead. To Tunstall's friends, including Robert Widenmann and William Bonney—alias Billy the "Kid"—the killing amounted to murder, and it unleashed a torrent of violence that, aside from clashes between the army and Native warriors, was as bloody as any seen in the post–Civil War West.[3]

Details of the Lincoln County War have been catalogued well and often. In relation to the trouble in Colfax County, the Lincoln County story is significant in that aggrieved parties in that struggle succeeded, where citizens of Colfax had so far failed in attempts to bring about a serious investigation of alleged corruption. A similarity in the two conflicts arises from the extraordinary extent to which men commonly associated with the Santa Fe Ring were already involved in local financial and political matters. Murphy and Dolan had long done business with the First National Bank of Santa Fe and its officers and directors, including Stephen Elkins and Thomas Catron. Governor Samuel Axtell had received a loan from L. G. Murphy and Company in April 1876, a debt that investigator Frank Warner Angel later concluded "was probably repaid in November 1877."[4] Murphy, Dolan, and Riley, along with district judge Warren Bristol and district attorney William Rynerson, were political allies of the Santa Fe men in the southern counties.

Catron, in particular, was heavily vested in Lincoln County, and in the firm of J. J. Dolan. In January 1878, Catron loaned money to the failing company, taking a mortgage on the building and land, inventory and accounts, grain, hay, cattle, and horses comprising the firm's assets. Suddenly he had more reason to hope for the company's success.[5] He owned other cattle in the region and was naturally concerned about their security when the shooting started; Catron did not hesitate to ask the governor's help in providing for protection of his Lincoln County property.

The wrongful death of Tunstall and the failure of federal officials in New Mexico to take much interest in the case prompted calls from British officials for a thorough investigation and report. Urging the British officers and members of Tunstall's family to demand action were two outspoken men. Neither became long-term residents of the territory, but the men were intensely interested in the case and eager to see Tunstall's death avenged. These were Robert Widenmann, from the German region of Württemberg, Tunstall's close friend and confidante, and briefly a deputy U.S. marshal; and Montague R. Leverson, a British subject who wrote frequent, rambling letters to Washington officials, seeking justice for Tunstall.

Advised of Tunstall's violent death, Edward Thornton, British ambassador to the United States, wrote Secretary of State William Evarts on March 9 to raise the subject and express the concern of his government, telling Evarts, "Under these circumstances I cannot doubt that the Government of the United States will promptly cause enquiries to be made into the matter and will take such measures as it may deem expedient for investigating the Sheriff of Lincoln County and for ensuring the arrest of the accused, and their being brought to trial."[6] In quick succession, Leverson dispatched letters to President Rutherford Hayes, Ambassador Thornton, U.S. Marshal John Sherman, and Secretary of the Interior Carl Schurz, with the intent of more fully informing them about the circumstances of Tunstall's death as he had learned them, and of the corruption in Lincoln County and in the territorial government at Santa Fe. He urged a full investigation of the matter by federal authorities or, failing in that, by the appropriate committees in Congress.[7]

Unrelated to the violent outbreaks in Colfax and Lincoln Counties was the line of inquiry opened by Henry W. Arms, a New Englander who briefly tried ranching in Colfax County before returning to his native state of Vermont. In a letter to Secretary Evarts in March 1878, Arms renewed a concern expressed earlier, when he had raised the issue of land grant fraud, relative to the questionable Uña de Gato grant. Arms's letter was referred to Secretary Schurz in the Interior Department. If the authorities in Washington were fully apprised of the situation, he wrote, "I am morally certain an investigation would be had and some important changes would be ordered."[8] The letter reinforced calls for an investigation of alleged misconduct among New Mexico public officials, including Catron, who was said by Arms to be mixed up in the Uña de Gato matter.[9]

Frank Springer kept his and his Colfax County allies' grievances against Axtell and other members of the Santa Fe combination simmering. Regarding the Lincoln County chaos, he wrote to tell Iowa congressman Rush Clark that the territorial government, backed by military forces in New Mexico, was fervently working to "protect and assist a small combination of corrupt men—speculators in military and Indian contracts—against the best men in the county."[10] Clark had the letter forwarded to U.S. Attorney General Devens.[11] At the same time, Springer renewed charges against his favorite nemesis, Axtell, touting new evidence of Axtell's having threatened the lives of several prominent men of Colfax County in March 1876, in connection with the planned arrest of Clay Allison.

Hayes, Devens, and Secretary Schurz continued to hear from writers complaining about corruption in New Mexico through the spring of 1878. A compelling letter from Montague Leverson written on April 2, 1878, reached President Hayes and his cabinet department heads "at the precise moment when the administration was being made painfully aware that it could no longer avoid conducting an investigation of affairs in Lincoln County."[12] An inquiry was ordered for the purpose of investigating controversies arising in Lincoln County, including allegations of corruption in government, improper use of federal military forces, and corrupt practices of Indian agents—as well as alleged land grant fraud and the lingering grievances of Colfax County citizens in the northeastern part of the territory.

The Angel Investigation

Within days, Frank Warner Angel, a thirty-three-year-old New York attorney, had been appointed special investigator for the Department of Justice, commissioned to find the facts and render reports and recommendations concerning the circumstances of the death of John Tunstall and, more broadly, the trouble that had led to so much bloodshed and turmoil in Lincoln County. Having learned of Angel's appointment, Secretary Schurz of the Interior Department contacted Angel on April 16, 1878, to request that he also investigate the long-smoldering charges against Governor Samuel Axtell, whose office came under Schurz's official purview. Schurz stipulated that Angel was to have access to support and documents that might be needed to conduct a thorough investigation, adding that officials in New Mexico would be instructed to provide access to such records as might be useful there. "Upon the conclusion of your investigation," Schurz stated, "I desire to have a full report made to me hereon, with your opinion as to any and all charges made against any officer under the supervision of this department."[13]

Examination of the Uña de Gato claim was added to a growing list of assignments. Angel was also asked to complete an unfinished investigation of charges against Indian agent Frederick Godfroy at the Mescalero Reservation, where irregular, possibly fraudulent transactions were said to have occurred.[14] He was further assigned to examine charges against Benjamin Thomas, agent for the Pueblo Indians.

Tasked with these varied issues upon which he was to find facts and compile reports and recommendations, Angel conferred with numerous officials in Washington and departed for New Mexico. He traveled as a gentleman bound for Santa Fe usually did in the last months before the railroad reached New Mexico, taking a train to the Denver and Rio Grande terminus at El Moro, Colorado, near Trinidad. From El Moro, he caught a buckboard down Raton Pass and across the prairie that skirted the Sangre de Cristo Mountains. He presumably was able to travel by coach in the last phase of his journey, stopping at Fort Union and Las Vegas, arriving in Santa Fe by May 4, when he was listed in the *New Mexican* as a guest at the Exchange Hotel.[15]

The order in which Angel arranged his work in New Mexico reflected the priorities of the Justice Department, by which he had first been engaged to conduct investigations. The trouble in Lincoln County was raging, with much bloodshed and confusion concerning the authority vested in local officials. Angel stayed several days in the capital and made himself known to significant contacts in Santa Fe, then headed out to learn what he could at first hand.

On May 10, Angel left Santa Fe for Fort Stanton in Lincoln County, where the larger part of the work was concentrated, arriving on May 14.[16] He collected witness statements and talked less formally with persons on both sides of the conflict, finding opinions deeply divided between the McSween faction and forces led by James Dolan and John Riley. Angel hoped to understand the pattern of alliances and influences at work in Lincoln County, and to form early impressions of right and wrong; he could not avoid observing that there was ample wrong on both sides.[17] An early priority was the completion of the Godfroy investigation. On July 2, Angel witnessed and certified a count of the men, women, and children drawing rations on the Mescalero Reservation, finding a large discrepancy between the number of persons accounted for, relative to numbers submitted for federal reimbursement of ration costs.[18]

The rest of Angel's time in Lincoln County was spent in developing evidence concerning the violent conflict between the "House" of Dolan and Riley and the "Regulators" who supported Alexander McSween. With the documents provided concerning Colfax County's troubles, Angel could reflect on common and divergent aspects of the two disorders. Notable among the common themes in Axtell's responses to the two conflicts were a failure to listen to all sides before taking drastic action, and his bald partisanship favoring the factions embraced by his Santa Fe allies and joining them in denigrating their rivals. These items would appear in Angel's most consequential reports, on the turmoil in Lincoln County and concerning the charges made against Axtell.

Angel was also working on a separate but closely related investigation ordered by Devens at the behest of the British government and Tunstall's family, on the cause and circumstances of John Tunstall's death. As to the circumstances of the killing, Angel related credible stories of the chase and the shooting and concluded that it was impossible to say who had fired the fatal shots; Tunstall's body was found with mortal wounds from two different guns, and two of the men who had pursued Tunstall had shortly been killed. Significantly, Angel did not find that any officer of the government had been involved in causing Tunstall's death.[19]

In the course of his three-and-a-half-month tour of New Mexico, Angel collected seventy or more statements, including ones taken by other officers commissioned to swear witnesses and notarize their statements. Angel took over twenty statements and was present for others in which he propounded questions to the witnesses but relied on local officials for help in writing out the needed affidavits and depositions. While in southern New Mexico, Angel twice ventured to Doña Ana County, where he took more testimony. He was back in Santa Fe by July 16, and reportedly was awaiting funds for travel to the northern counties.[20]

After the time in Lincoln and Doña Ana Counties, the pace of Angel's inquiry slowed. In conducting investigations and preparing reports on the two Indian agents, Godfroy at the Mescalero Reservation and Benjamin M. Thomas with the Pueblos, Angel was finishing the work of Edwin C. Watkins, inspector for the commissioner of Indian Affairs. Watkins had taken substantial testimony in the cases, and William Griffin, Santa Fe banker and U.S. commissioner, took at least three affidavits from witnesses. Angel's report essentially exonerated Thomas. He was sympathetic concerning Godfroy's case but found irregularities in practice that he judged substantial enough to require a change in supervision at the Mescalero Agency.

Angel may have stopped in Las Vegas and San Miguel County during a tour of northern counties, but if so, he collected no affidavits or other documents that made it into official reports. At Cimarron, he focused on Frank Springer, who was prepared to dish on the governor regarding his alleged misdeeds with respect to Colfax County. Angel left Cimarron for Santa Fe on August 10, carrying Springer's deposition of some thirty-two handwritten, legal-size pages, plus attached exhibits "A" through "F," purporting to show, among other things, that local Ring figures Melvin Mills and Robert Longwill had colluded with powerful associates in Santa Fe and that Axtell had conspired to have Colfax County rivals, including Springer, murdered with the help of soldiers.[21]

Springer's testimony included stunning allegations, but Angel evidently found it credible. The time with Springer in Cimarron has been cited as a turning point in his investigation, causing Angel to reconsider earlier conclusions regarding Lincoln County and the influence of territorial and federal officials there.[22] On Sunday, August 11, a day after arriving back in Santa Fe, Angel surprised the governor with a list of thirty-one interrogatories, requesting that he respond within twenty-four hours. Thinking he had been cleared after Angel's extended visit to Lincoln County, Axtell was stunned, and requested an extension of time to answer the questions. Angel's thought was that, if confronted with similar serious charges, he would not take even twenty-four hours to respond. Still, he reasonably granted the governor thirty days. Angel evidently was motivated by a strong desire to wind up his time in New Mexico and head home. He left Santa Fe on or about August 14, spent the night of August 16 in Denver, and may have stopped in Washington before arriving in New York on August 24, to begin writing up his findings and recommendations.[23]

Judgment Days

Secretary Schurz received Angel's preliminary recommendation concerning the governor soon after his return from New Mexico, in advance of his written report. Satisfied that Axtell was not fit to serve in the office of governor, Schurz saw no reason to delay; Axtell's suspension was approved by President Hayes as early as

August 31, 1878. Word of the governor's removal was appearing in eastern papers by September 3. Axtell would be relieved by Lew Wallace, a Union general who since the Civil War had been an attorney, a writer, and an aspirant for public office.

In Colfax County, response to the news was spontaneous and euphoric. George Crocker, then a boy of twelve, recalled, "The night we got word that Axtell was removed from office, the citizens of Cimarron shot off anvils all night long. Shooting anvils meant that they took these huge anvils from the blacksmith shop and put two of them together, one on top of the other. They filled the center with powder and set it off with a hot iron. They made a terrific noise."[24] Blasts at Cimarron reportedly were answered with anvil shots and rifle salutes from outlying ranches.

On September 6, the *News and Press* celebrated with an "extra," topped by the image of a crowing rooster and the heading "The Bishop Boosted!! Axtell's Head Falls at Last." The paper reported on local responses to the news, which included a fifty-gun salute to celebrate the retiring governor's departure. The editors unleashed a deluge of derision in response to Axtell's downfall and expressed enthusiasm for the appointment of Wallace to succeed him.[25]

Elsewhere, reactions varied. The *Mesilla Valley Independent*, a consistent critic of Axtell, shed no tears. The *Santa Fe New Mexican* reflexively defended the governor and others generally named as Ring figures and attacked their critics. The paper had done so since Axtell's arrival in the territory and was consistent in its opposition to his removal. The *Las Vegas Gazette*, perhaps the most thoughtful among the territorial papers, covered Angel's investigation in greater depth and evolved from an open-minded posture to one more skeptical of Angel's conclusions. Beyond the territory, at least one writer viewed Axtell's removal as the result of "attacks by unprincipled men, by whom he has been misrepresented and vilified," but the judgment met with indifference elsewhere.[26] Greater attention was given the nominee to succeed Axtell, Lew Wallace of Indiana, and much of it was not favorable. Some saw the appointment as repayment for Wallace's help in getting Hayes elected president.[27] Others interpreted the move as a means of getting Wallace out of Indiana, where he was opposing the election of Godlove Orth, a man of questionable integrity, who was running for Congress.[28] Nonetheless, Wallace was soon confirmed by the U.S. Senate. It remained to be seen whether the office would be a fitting prize for the new appointee.

With Axtell gone, attention turned to Catron's future as U.S. attorney for New Mexico. Angel's interest in questioning Catron strongly indicated that he

News and Press.

Extra.

CIMARRON, SEPTEMBER 6, 1878.

THE BISHOP BOOSTED!!

AXTELL'S HEAD FALLS AT LAST.

The Mills Of The Gods Grind Slow, But They Grind Exceeding Fine.

REJOICING IN CIMARRON.

Fifty Guns Fired in Honor of the Event.

General Lew. Wallace Appointed Governor.

It has been known in Cimarron, through private sources for about a week past, that Gov. Axtell's official head was about to be lopped off, and that his successor had been named, and last evening the Washington dispatches announced it as an accomplished fact.

The reception of this news created more enthusiasm in Cimarron than anything since the restoration of our courts. The exultation of victory, well earned after a long fight, took possession of our people, and general joy and congratulation prevailed. This feeling soon took shape in active demonstrations. Powder was offered on every hand, and a pair of heavy anvils, managed by experienced hands, served as an implement for saluting purposes, fully equal to a 12-lb cannon. A parting salute of fifty guns was given in honor of the decapitation of El Obispo. The loud explosion resounded over the plains, and thundered in soft repeated echoes among the hills, and as the ringing reports reverberated from peak to peak, and leaped from cliff to crag among our rugged mountains, each answering echo seemed to say, "farewell Bishop Axtell!"

The firing was heard by the ranch men, some of whom rigged up an anvil and answered gun for gun.

It was the voice of Colfax county, wishing him a speedy departure, and in this we feel sure that all New Mexico will join, unless perhaps some isolated spots, where his pardoning some murderer has raised up for him that "fellow feeling" which "makes us wondrous kind." There will be no mourning for him, save by the few who could use him as a tool, for whose personal advantage he prostituted the high powers of his position, brought the name of Governor into disrepute, and sunk the high and honorable office which he was sent here to fill, into the depths of degradation. There may be some, who, in charity, may "pity the sorrows" of a dyspeptic old man, whose occupation is gone, but there will be few indeed, except those who used him, to regret his fall.

He has talked much about the dignity of his office, but dignity went out when he came in. If he ever had any dignity of his own he left it in Utah with his Mormon Masters, or if perchance be brought with him to New Mexico any small remnant of it, he laid that aside when he wrote to "Dear Ben" to carry out a sanguinary scheme of slaughter in Colfax county, to get rid of those who stood in the way of his partisans. He has no dignity left to take with him, nor any reputation but that of infamy and disgrace. When he was appointed to New Mexico, the Utah anti Mormon papers said, "What has New Mexico done that she should be cursed with Axtell?" We sincerely hope we shall not have to ask this question with regard to any other unfortunate territory. We wish to see the poorest of them, even Alaska, spared the infliction of his presence in an official capacity.

We do not believe the republican party will want to carry him any longer. It has, in the governorship of two territories, rewarded him for his desertion of the democrats in congress, when a vote was needed. The democrats of course will have no use for a repentant traitor. Both parties have had enough of him, and he will probably become a sort of political owl or bat, outcast by both, and allowed to get forth only in the obscurity of twilight, or the darkness of night, out of those whom he has either disgraced or betrayed.

The people of Colfax county have now the satisfaction of being even with El Obispo. When called upon to do justice, he said he had no compromise to make with them. They never asked it, nor offered him any. He talks about the "Cimarron Ring." We don't know what that is unless it be the NEWS AND PRESS. Whatever it is, it's got away with him, and for this happy result the NEWS AND PRESS is entitled to a large share of credit. We began the fight. We made our charges against him, and persistently urged them, until they have been heard at Washington and fully sustained. We have made no charge against him that we have not been fully able to explain or deny.

We hope he is satisfied with the result, and that our brethren of the territorial press, who have been disposed to think lightly of our complaints, will now appreciate that with the smoke there was an extremely hot fire.

We are satisfied and so is our rooster.

Now he may pack his grip-sack for the Live House.

It will be now in order for the *New Mexican* and *Las Vegas Gazette* to wear the usual badge of mourning for 30 days.

WHAT BOOSTED HIM.

"Our man signed the invitation for me to visit Colfax with others who were at the meeting, Porter, Morley, Springer, et al. Now if they expect me Saturday, they will be on hand. Have your men placed to arrest him and to kill all the men who resist you, or who stand with those who do resist."—*Axtell to Ben.*

Don't you wish you hadn't written it!

THE NEW GOVERNOR.

As Axtell's successor the President has appointed General Lew Wallace, of Indiana, the son of the late Governor David Wallace of that state. General Wallace was a soldier in the war with Mexico, and he mustered the first company and regiment in the service from Indiana on the call of President Lincoln in the war of the rebellion. He served with distinction during the war and was promoted to the rank of Major General. After the war he returned to his profession, the practice of the law, at Crawfordsville, Ind., where he now resides. He has gained quite a reputation in the literary world as the author of The Fair God, a legend of the conquest of Mexico by Cortes, and other works of repute.

General, now Governor Wallace is a man of energy and great will power. He would put down a Lincoln county war in ten days. He enjoys the confidence of his fellow citizens as a man of ability and integrity. During his sojourn in Mexico he became familiar with the language, customs and institutions of her people, and will come here with a better understanding of our native population than our public men generally have.

We give him a hearty welcome.

"I see clearly that we have no friends in Colfax."—*Axtell.*

Right, old boy, for once.

He will send no more insulting messages to the Legislature.

OUR ROOSTER.

The energetic and high spirited bird which embellishes the head of these columns is a Colfax county production. Not having on hand a rooster of proper style and attitude to do justice to the occasion, we called in our special artist to get up one last night. He has done his work well. This chicken is of vigorous constitution and striking appearance, and we will back him against anything of his kind in the Territory.

Where was Stephen B.? Is it possible that he has lost his grip?

"A good man, a worthy officer, and a Republican."—*S. B. Elkins.*

But it didn't save him, Stephen B.

"It is not probable that the courts will ever be restored to Cimarron. At least I shall not recommend it."—*Axtell.*

Say it again, and say it slow.

Whigham & Henderson,

JOB PRINTERS,

CIMARRON, N. M.

Cimarron News and Press, September 6, 1878. This "Extra" edition of the *News and Press* was published in celebration of the suspension of Samuel Axtell as governor of the Territory of New Mexico in September 1878. Courtesy private collection of the CS Cattle Company.

was under suspicion concerning his conduct as U.S. attorney. Complaints against him included allegations that he used his office to satisfy personal motives and punish his enemies, as well as to pursue his political interests and those of his party. Catron was also accused of unseemly and possibly illegal involvement in land grant matters.[29]

When it became generally known that federal officials, and Angel in particular, were hot on Catron's trail, friends of Catron responded with letters of support on his behalf. An important ally in the attempt to save Catron's job was his lifelong friend, Stephen Elkins, who contacted the attorney general three times, hand delivering Catron's petition for time to answer the charges against him in early September 1878. Elkins again plied Devens in Catron's favor on September 13, and again on September 24, reiterating a request that Catron be allowed more time to answer Angel's questions and respond to charges made against him in various affidavits.[30] Catron finally submitted substantial responses to the questions and charges, but on October 10, possibly having concluded that his cause was lost, he sent Devens a letter of resignation, effective November 10, 1878.[31] By mutual agreement, Catron's tenure was extended to ensure that the duties of the U.S. attorney were duly executed, pending qualification of a successor.[32]

The Angel Reports

In New York, Angel still had work to do. Evidence continued to trickle in, in the form of affidavits and letters. His sponsors in Washington expected to be briefed informally, and reports remained to be written. Angel did not have the New Mexico job off his hands before November 27, when he submitted his report on the death of John Tunstall, along with all evidence on which the Tunstall report and his report on the disorders in Lincoln County were based.

Historians sometimes refer informally to the "Angel Report." In fact, Angel prepared and submitted no fewer than six reports on the subjects he had been asked to investigate. These were, by title, agency to which the report was directed, and date of completion or submittal:

1. *In the Matter of the Uña de Gato Grant.* Department of Justice; August 1878.
2. *In the Matter of the Examination of the Charges against C. F. Godfroy, U.S. Indian Agent, Mescalero Apaches, N.M.* Department of the Interior; October 2, 1878.

3. *In the Matter of the Investigation of the Charges against S. B. Axtell, Governor of New Mexico.* Department of the Interior; October 3, 1878.
4. *In the Matter of the Lincoln County Troubles.* Department of Justice; October 7, 1878.
5. *In the Matter of the Examination of Charges against Dr. B. M. Thomas, U.S. Indian Agent, Pueblo Indians of New Mexico.* Department of the Interior; October 7, 1878.
6. *In the Matter of the Cause and Circumstances of the Death of John H. Tunstall, A British Subject.* Department of Justice; November 27, 1878.

The investigation of charges against Axtell appears to have required the least effort and attention on Angel's part, while producing the most significant consequences. Angel had attempted to obtain testimony from the governor, but a direct and timely response was not forthcoming; Angel could only include in his report the published response that Axtell sent to the *Santa Fe Sentinel*.[33] Angel's report was strongly influenced by testimony and documents provided by Frank Springer and was further informed by documents on file from the failed effort to have Axtell removed in 1877.

A lingering mystery concerns the absence of a report addressing issues related to Thomas B. Catron and his conduct as U.S. attorney. Catron's biographer and sometime defender, Victor Westphall, was convinced that Angel had planned to produce such a report for the Department of Justice. Adding to the intrigue is an exchange of letters between Catron and Stephen Elkins, then serving as secretary of war in the Hayes administration, when Catron was running for the office of territorial delegate to Congress in the fall of 1892. Catron wrote to Elkins, asking that matters be so arranged with the attorney general that no such report would be issued to anyone.[34] Elkins sent Catron's letter on to the attorney general, who returned it marked, "O.K."[35] Elkins's private secretary so advised Catron. Nothing related to the investigation came up during the election, but Catron continued to worry. Early in the following year, he raised the issue again, telling Elkins to "get that report and destroy it," so that it could never surface to hurt Catron at some future date.[36]

It remains unclear whether a report was or was not submitted, relative to charges against Catron. He does, however, appear in an unfavorable light in Angel's report on the fraudulent Uña de Gato claim, in which Angel speculates that Catron altered grant documents and, though aware of the fraudulent nature of the grant, worked to persuade former U.S. senator Stephen Dorsey to purchase it. In Westphall's opinion, the circumstances of the contemplated transaction were more complex than Angel knew, and it was far from proven that Catron was at fault.[37] Morris Taylor, a student of the Uña de Gato saga, also concluded that evidence did not support Angel's belief that Catron had deceitfully tried to get Dorsey to buy the grant, in that Dorsey had already known that the claim was suspect, but "backed out only when the forgery had become public knowledge."[38]

It is probably impossible to know whether Catron's resignation in October 1878 was the result of a free-will decision or, as seems likely, a decision made under duress. There may simply have been too many allegations against him, and too much distrust, for Catron to remain as U.S. attorney with the support of his superiors in Washington. In any event, he resigned, and charges concerning his conduct as U.S. attorney were not pursued further by the Justice Department.

Angel's performance as special agent in New Mexico in 1878 has drawn mixed reviews from historians. Some believed that he was too easily influenced by strong, vociferous witnesses like McSween and Springer—attorneys who perhaps spoke Angel's language and engendered a natural affinity.[39] In the view of Robert M. Utley, the governor was unfairly portrayed in Angel's reports. Finding Angel's conclusions more hyperbole than fact, Utley wrote, "Compared with his predecessors, Axtell had been a good governor."[40] Joel Jacobsen, an assistant attorney general in New Mexico when he was studying Lincoln County matters, judged Angel a "first rate attorney," with a facility for getting witnesses to offer details that reinforced their credibility. In Jacobsen's estimation, Angel was unbiased in pursuing the truth, and based his conclusions on a reasonable evaluation of the evidence.[41] Regardless the judgment on Angel's performance, his reports left a priceless trove of information on a significant sequence of events in New Mexico's territorial history.

The filing of Angel's reports, Catron's resignation as U.S. attorney, and the dismissal of Samuel Axtell as governor marked an end to the Colfax County War, viewed as a brutal clash of interests dating from the departure of Lucien Maxwell and climaxed by the assassination of Rev. F. J. Tolby and the recriminations that followed. Consequences of Angel's investigation included a temporary suppression of the Santa Fe Ring as an instrument of political and economic control. There was, however, no immediate end to the violence in Lincoln County, where there remained much for Lew Wallace to do in restoring peace and order. Nor was there any closure in Colfax County, where a clash among multiple interests distilled into a longer struggle between the Maxwell Land Grant Company and settlers who continued to believe that the company's bloated claim encroached on land rightly belonging to the public domain and available to home seekers.

CHAPTER 14

Settling the Maxwell Grant Conflict

With a blast of celebratory anvil shots, a hastily organized fifty-gun salute, and a special edition of the *Cimarron News and Press*, the people of Colfax County reveled in the downfall of an odious governor and all that his removal meant. In September 1878, it had been three years since the assassination of Franklin Tolby had sparked such rage—the beginning of an agonizing time of chaos and consternation. Axtell's dismissal and the appointment of Lew Wallace to take his place as governor, and Catron's resignation under duress, were cause for relief, but Angel's inquiry did not resolve all outstanding issues. Colfax County residents had an acrimonious land grant dispute to be settled, and a territorial government that was susceptible to manipulation for the benefit of a privileged few. The concerned citizens of Colfax could enjoy the moment and the general decline in tension that followed, but thorny difficulties and lingering enmities stalked the country for some years more, sometimes breaking out in renewed hostilities. By 1900, the long-running Maxwell Land Grant conflict was settled legally, and calm had largely been established, which is not to say that all controversy was or ever would be fully resolved.

An Exodus of Factions

A notable condition leading to the trouble in Colfax County in the mid-1870s was the presence of multiple interests, most of them embodied in people who were passionate about their urgent desires and their varying, often disparate, views of justice with respect to landownership and use, social order, and legal process. The region drained by the Red River and its tributaries had never enjoyed peace for long, from the earliest clash of rival tribes, through the succession of intruders who came across the plains seeking satisfaction, mostly in the way of material gain. With the assortment of economic and cultural forces that had gathered in the Cimarron country by the early 1870s, and with the associated collision of wills and prevalence of guns and liquor, Colfax County was likely to be a rough and rowdy neighborhood for most of the decade. Then, after the suspension of Governor Axtell and the joyous firing of anvils and rifle salutes, and the arrival of Lew Wallace as the new governor, a curious thing happened. Some of the parties most contentious in pursuing their aspirations quit the country, leaving a simpler, if still bitter, dispute between the Maxwell Company and settlers who believed themselves to be legally situated on lands in the public domain. Disputes over ownership and control of usable land were still hotly contested, but the departure of diverse, competing factions provided some relief from constant turmoil.

THE SANTA FE RING

The first to go among competitors for power and resources in Colfax County were the men of the alleged Santa Fe Ring. The suspension of Samuel Axtell as governor and Thomas Catron's departure as U.S. attorney in 1878 did not kill the Ring. Catron came back strong, eventually winning one of New Mexico's first U.S. Senate seats in 1912. Axtell also resurfaced, winning appointment and confirmation as the territory's chief justice in 1882—only to lose the post when the Democratic administration headed by President Grover Cleveland took office in 1885. The Ring, though altered through changes in composition as older members died or moved away and new alliances were formed, continued as a force in the last years before statehood. With the events of 1878, however, the Ring was roundly boosted from Colfax County, and the combination never again had a strong hand in the affairs of the Maxwell Company, or in local political affairs of the county.

THE MOUACHE UTES AND JICARILLA APACHES

Next to go, after centuries of occupation in and around the Cimarron country, were the Mouache Ute and Jicarilla Apache Indians. Their eviction had been assured when Lucien Maxwell sold the land grant to investors whose only interest was in realizing a profit from the land. Financial returns would come chiefly through the efforts of those who settled and worked the property's resources—miners and prospectors, farmers, cattle raisers, and entrepreneurs offering varied

Jicarilla camp on the Mescalero Reservation, ca. 1886. Some of the Jicarillas lived at the Mescalero Reservation in southern New Mexico between 1883 and October 1886. This photo appears to have been made in 1886, when the photographer was traveling from his base at Topeka, Kansas, and taking photos at New Mexico locales, including Mescalero. Photo by J. R. Riddle. New Mexico State University Library, Archives and Special Collections.

products and services. After false starts halted by the protests of miners and other parties who coveted the areas proposed for reservations, Utes living at Cimarron and Abiquiu were situated on lands in southern Colorado, later comprising the Southern Ute Reservation.[1] This occurred in July and August of 1878.

The quest for a satisfactory home for the Jicarillas was more complicated. Their fortunes suffered from opposition by settlers already living in the area of the proposed reservation, others coveting the land for their own use, and political meddling in the Indian Bureau's efforts to solve longstanding dilemmas concerning relocation of the bands. There was also substantial dissension among the Jicarillas. The tribe, or part of it, was moved to the Mescalero Reservation in southern New Mexico in 1878, while some members stayed near Abiquiu. Some Jicarillas returned to the Cimarron area, living there during the summer of 1879, before moving to land in the vicinity of Tierra Amarilla, New Mexico, that had been proposed for a reservation.[2] The odyssey of the Jicarillas was not over, however, as local opposition to the reservation and vacillation by federal officials combined to keep the Natives homeless. Over the next several years, bands were scattered among the Mescalero Reservation, the Abiquiu Agency, and several Rio Grande pueblos.[3] In 1887, the Jicarillas were at last situated on a permanent reservation in northwestern New Mexico with Dulce as its administrative center.[4]

THE TEXANS

Another development that altered the social landscape of Colfax County was the departure of many of the men informally known as "Texans." The early-day merchant Henry Porter explained in his memoir, "The same cause that brought the Texans into the Maxwell Grant sent them away. The ranges were covered with good grass. Later they became badly overstocked and the grass so poor and short they had to seek other ranges and went over the mountains west near Durango, where the country was new, with their herds."[5] By 1878, the conditions for "open range" livestock herding were declining, at least in Colfax County. It must have been clear to the men running herds on the Maxwell grant that the company's contested title would eventually be settled, and that they had best be going, unless they could buy all the land and water they needed.

By 1879, a general exodus was under way. Big operations under Hiram Washington Cox and Irvin Lacy migrated to the San Juan country of northwestern New Mexico. Others went east to the Texas Panhandle.[6] Clay Allison left the area in 1878, traveled the West, married, and had a daughter.[7] He ranched in several locations, settling down near Pecos, Texas. Marriage and family life apparently had a calming effect, but Allison came to an early demise when the wagon he was driving one day in 1887 capsized and landed on him, ending a remarkable life and career.

The Texans who stayed in Colfax County were mainly those who built homes and raised families there. Some had purchased land from Lucien Maxwell or from the company or would yet acquire land of their own. Most were citizens and community members who worked hard and prospered. These included the Dawsons, the Curtises, the Chases, the Littrells, and the family of Mathias Stockton.

THE MINERS

"Miners," for present purposes, include prospectors and gold rush followers, mine and mill owners and laborers, solo placer operators, barkeeps, cooks, store owners, and all others attracted to work in nineteenth-century western mining camps.

Though already reduced in population from the palmy days of 1868 to 1870, when hopes for a bonanza in the Baldy-Moreno goldfield were high, the miners of Elizabethtown remained a force not to be trifled with in 1875. The census recorded eight hundred residents in 1870, and Elias Brevoort's estimate in 1874 was six hundred.[8] The 1880 census reported just 175 people at Elizabethtown.[9]

In 1881, a visitor found the town a pitiful shell of itself, giving the impression of "a sort of grave yard stillness, deserted buildings, and a general tumble down appearance."[10] By now the few who remained presumably had steady work, while fortune seekers and dissidents had moved on. The ranks of the miners had been reduced by the illiberal policies of the Maxwell Company, depletion of easily accessible ore deposits, a shortage of water for hydraulic mining, and want of affordable freight transportation. The mining district survived through "two decades of low-level activity," before seeing a renewal of interest and population in the 1890s.[11]

THE BLUECOATS

By the end of 1879, a posse comitatus act curtailing military intervention in local affairs had been enacted by Congress and signed into law. Thereafter, deployments from Fort Union to Colfax County were few.

Between 1851 and 1891, when the post was abandoned, Fort Union accounted for a small but notable population of Black people in Colfax County, these being soldiers in army companies comprised mainly of African American enlisted men. The presence of Black soldiers in the Ninth Cavalry (1876–81) in Colfax County coincided with the peak years of Texas cattle ranching in the region, making for potentially volatile contact. By 1881, the rowdier Texans had gone, as had the buffalo soldiers.[12]

Grand Plans and Monumental Failures

The corporate life of the former Beaubien and Miranda grant, beginning with its sale by Lucien and Luz Maxwell in 1870, got off to a rocky start. The dysfunction persisted over twenty years, from 1870 until 1892. John Collinson assumed the presidency of the Maxwell Land Grant and Railway Company with visions of riches from gold mining, a busy and prosperous colony of farmers from the British Isles, and a neat little town platted on the site of Maxwell's ranch on the Cimarron. Because he did not know the people or the country, and because he was not a capable manager, what he got were three years of failed efforts, an uprising from miners and settlers, and shrinking mortgage bond values. Collinson had succeeded in spending a good deal of money and building "American style" houses in Cimarron. By 1873, management of the company had been turned over to new officers—Elkins and Morley—but their hopes lay in other directions, and in a few years, they had moved on. By 1878, the Maxwell Company was in deep financial trouble.

Following a forced sale of the claim, the Maxwell Company entered into a reorganization that placed supervision of the company in the hands of Frank Remington Sherwin, a New Yorker who had bought a large quantity of the company's securities and entered into an agreement with the Dutch bondholders, under which he was to manage the property and operations. The transfer was finalized in April 1880. Along with new management, the organization also received a new title. The "Maxwell Land Grant and Railway Company" name was left behind when the concern was incorporated by Royal Decree of the United Netherlands, to be known as the "Maxwell Land Grant Company."[13]

As president, Sherwin took a hands-on approach, but his enthusiasm and confidence exceeded his competence as a manager, and he took only about four years in landing the company in a new slough of financial distress. Sherwin invested heavily in cattle, incorporating the Maxwell Cattle Company under a separate board of directors and placing valuable assets in its hands without the prior knowledge or approval of the Dutch bondholders. He pursued a plausible exploitation of the grant's massive coal deposits but locked the company into a long-term contract under which the largest customer paid so little that coal was being sold at a loss.[14]

By 1882, the company was again in financial straits and a majority of the Dutch investors were alarmed. Concerns persisted, and the following year, a committee representing the bondholders traveled to Cimarron and negotiated an agreement under which Sherwin relinquished the presidency and sold his interest to the company. This relieved a main source of irritation to other investors, but at the cost of a crushing financial debt.[15] More financial machinations ensued, and it was not until 1892, when company attorney Frank Springer was elected president, that cycles of failure ended with the adoption of sensible plans for profitable use of the grant's assets.

Few settlers were dissuaded in their resistance to Maxwell Company demands when the federal government issued a patent affirming the company's title in 1879. The reluctance to settle or move was reinforced in 1882, when the Justice

Department filed suit challenging the validity of the title and boundaries of the Maxwell grant. Given new hope by the government's lawsuit, many settlers refused to give up their homes or settle with the company.

As the struggle continued, two notable blowups occurred, one in Colfax County, and the other in southern Colorado. These evoked old grievances and brought on futile suffering. Deaths in these incidents were officially caused by fatal gunshot wounds, but contributing factors were blind passion, chronic mistrust, and human failure. The aftershocks occurred in 1885 and 1888.

The Springer Court House Fight

In the eighties and beyond, critical struggles over ownership and direction of the Maxwell Company were pursued through financial negotiation and legal action. In the field, the encounter most apt to spark violence was one involving a Maxwell agent demanding that a settler purchase, lease, or vacate land occupied without title, opposed by an angry settler who refused all options. Sometimes tempers flared and parties came to blows. Occasionally an agent or settler was killed. Maxwell men thought they were giving reasonable terms, offering to buy settlers' improvements and livestock at fair prices. Dispirited at their prospects, some squatters were willing accept the company's offer and leave, but others resolved to stay and fight.

In 1884, the political order in New Mexico was shaken with the election of a Democrat as president of the United States, and the certainty that there would be changes in territorial officials subject to presidential appointment. These included the governor, the surveyor general, the U.S. attorney, and judges for the district courts and territorial supreme court. A violent disturbance in Colfax County resulted from Maxwell officials' anticipation of a coming change in party control of the federal administration. A few company leaders contrived to gain leverage against squatters before new federal appointees could take office. Their idea involved authorization of a territorial militia that could help serve legal documents and enforce writs of ejectment under color of law. Conceived by interim managers of the Maxwell Company, the scheme was acted on favorably by a notably average governor, Lionel Sheldon. The resulting debacle was later referred to by some as the "Springer court house fight."[16] The deadly skirmish was rooted in the Maxwell Land Grant conflict, but by the time blood was shed, it had morphed into a collision animated almost entirely by personal antagonisms.[17]

The trouble started in Raton, a growing town at the foot of the all-important pass through which the Atchison, Topeka and Santa Fe Railway had laid track in 1878 and 1879. It reached its climax at Springer, a relatively new town established by the railroad, named for Frank Springer in recognition of his help, as the Maxwell Company's attorney, in facilitating construction across grant land between Raton Pass and Las Vegas in 1879.[18]

In those days the general election was held in November, but the president was not sworn in until March 4. In case of a change in the party winning the White House, a lag of a few weeks might follow the inauguration of the president before new federally appointed territorial officials were named and confirmed. After Grover Cleveland's election, Republicans had a few months in which to request political favors of the outgoing governor. According to George Curry, a Colfax County resident at the time, Maxwell Company officials saw a chance to strengthen their hand in the effort to evict settlers who refused to lease or buy the land they occupied, and who would not accept the company's terms. It was important to proceed while officials under the spell of the old Santa Fe political ring were still in power.[19]

At this time, following the ruinous Frank Sherwin administration, the Maxwell Company did not have a capable executive in place. The titular head of the company in America was Hans Mattson, a Swede who had assisted other Dutch investors in extricating themselves from prickly business entanglements. Mattson never moved his home from Minneapolis and spent little time in New Mexico. He served mainly as a financial agent.[20] The request for help from the New Mexico governor was probably presented by Harry Whigham, who had been associated with the Maxwell Company since the mid-1870s, functioning variously as company secretary and as the company's court-appointed receiver in a bankruptcy proceeding and, for a time, as editor for the *Cimarron News and Press*. The request was that the governor approve the creation of a militia company for Colfax County for defense purposes. In reality, the intent was to use the force for Maxwell Company purposes. The unit was created with James Masterson, brother of the noted "Bat" Masterson, as its commanding officer. As the company's lawyer, Springer reportedly had advised against the idea, which was pursued over his objection.[21] Masterson proceeded to recruit.

With few exceptions, the troop was said to be staffed with gunmen and gamblers who did not live in the territory. Perceptive anti-grant settlers and other citizens were incensed and lodged protests with the governor, who backtracked and disbanded the unit. The force ceased operations as ordered, but Masterson took out his anger on those who had criticized him. Locals organized a countervailing citizens' posse and took action, disarming Masterson's militiamen and escorting some of them to the Colorado line with a warning to stay out of New Mexico. Concerned citizens formed a vigilante group, appointing Dick Rogers, a popular cowboy and gunslinger, as captain. Rogers and his companions from the cattle country showed that there remained at least a remnant of raucous Texans herding livestock in the Red River and Vermejo areas, and that they could still "run the town." The town in this case meant Raton, rather than Cimarron. These men repeatedly clashed with members of the defunct militia. A feud between the factions intensified, leading up to the tragedy that unfolded over five days in March 1885.[22]

The problem began when John Dodds, a member of the cowboy vigilante group, was sent to Springer with another cowboy, Sam Littrell, to buy a wagonload of corn. The corn was likely purchased on Saturday, March 14. After this Dodds evidently spent the day drinking. On Sunday, March 15, Dodds was again in liquor, and he began to make trouble. He had a verbal altercation with acting sheriff Jesse Lee, a militiaman, and a more physical disturbance with James Carter, the constable.[23] Dodds was arrested for disturbing the peace, paid a fine, and was released. Riding home with Sam Littrell, he was chagrined to be hailed down by Lee and Carter, who proposed to arrest him for the assault on Carter. Dodds refused to be arrested, so Lee and Carter gave up and turned their horses around. Instead of going on to the ranch, Dodds went back to town and wired Dick Rogers. Rogers headed for Springer with friends and ended up drinking liquor and nursing resentments toward Lee, Carter, and Charles Martin, editor of the *Springer Stockman*. Feeling his liquor, Rogers declared that those men would have to leave the territory. Dodds had another go at Carter, beating the constable for trying to arrest him earlier. Hearing the rumors of a growing mob and fearing an attack in which they might be overrun, Lee and two deputies, "Duce" Hixenbaugh and William Kimberly, took refuge in the Colfax County Court House and jail.

When word got out that Dick Rogers was headed to Springer with a force of men, it was widely assumed that he was coming to help Dodds and would make war on the men in the courthouse. Rogers routinely displayed his weapons, often wearing two at a time, and he had been in recent shooting affrays in which he had killed one man and gravely wounded another.[24] There was substantial sympathy for the local officers, but early on March 16, Rogers went to see the justice of the peace to discuss Dodds's case, then walked to the courthouse to speak with Jesse Lee. Lee had wired acting governor Samuel Losch, to say that his men were penned up in the courthouse with Rogers's gang prowling outside, apparently bent on mischief.[25]

Serious confusion set in when Rogers and his party reached the jail, agitated and heavily armed. Rogers had arranged to have a local man, Jack Williams, who was said to be a deputy U.S. marshal, walk with him up to the jail to talk with Lee, but this did not improve his standing in the eyes of Lee and Kimberly. When Rogers stepped toward the courthouse door, they reacted. According to George Curry, the officers told Williams to move aside, then fired on Rogers. As Rogers fell, John Curry and Tom Whealington, cowboy friends of Rogers, advanced and were cut down before the shooting stopped. George Curry insisted that Rogers's intent was peaceful, but the need for his visit to the jail was not clear, and his judgment in wearing his weapons was questionable. Some observers, including friends of Rogers, understood Lee's unease that he and his men were about to be attacked. Regardless, three men lay dead when the smoke cleared.

Before more damage could be done, cooler heads intervened, including one belonging to Marion Littrell, who later earned public respect as a capable and honest sheriff of Colfax County. Littrell and others calmed matters at the courthouse, and Melvin Mills drove a team of horses to Wagon Mound to telegraph the governor an appeal for military intervention. Twenty soldiers and two officers were sent from Fort Union, arriving in Springer the same evening.

On Tuesday morning, March 17, a party including acting governor Losch arrived from Santa Fe. Their presence evidently had a calming influence on the shaken community.[26] It was decided that the men who had shot down Rogers, Whealington, and John Curry—Lee and Kimberly being prime suspects—should be transported to Las Vegas to be examined before Chief Justice Samuel Axtell, pending possible prosecution. The lawmen were escorted by guards from the courthouse to the railway station, where the party boarded a railway car for the short run to Las Vegas. John Dodds was arrested later, presumably on charges stemming from alleged assaults on Lee and Jim Carter. Most of the cowboys returned to their home ranches and their work, leaving questions of criminal liability and guilt to be sorted out in the courts. Lee and Kimberly ultimately went free.

Funeral services for the fallen cowboys were held at Raton on March 18, 1885, two days after the shooting. Some twelve hundred mourners reportedly attended the services conducted by three local ministers. At the cemetery, Rev. Eli Burch, a Baptist preacher, brought a message that he described as a call to learn from the recent trouble. The remarks, he said, would be "of and to cowboys." An easterner by birth, Burch had taken an interest in cowboys and their ways. Work on the range, Burch had observed, "must be done with all their might and must be done quickly," nurturing a tendency to impulsive behavior. He also noted that as good cowboys became used to danger, they ceased to know fear. Burch had also found that cowboys who relied on one another formed close bonds of mutual loyalty. These attributes, virtues under normal circumstances, had, in Burch's view, contributed to a tragic result. His plea to citizens was to watch over cowboys in their midst, mindful that "these boys were somebody's boys."[27]

A Question with Two Sides

In a season of extraordinary discontent, when the storms of controversy over the Maxwell grant were raging across Colfax County and adjacent areas in southern Colorado, a writer for the *Las Vegas Daily Optic* took stock and observed, "Probably no more vexed question ever arose than that between the Maxwell Land Grant Company and the settlers on the tract. It is certainly a question with two sides."[28] There may have been knowing deception in the manner by which the entities that followed Lucien Maxwell in ownership of the old Beaubien and Miranda grant laid claim to such a sprawling parcel of real estate. Regardless, there were by the 1880s both settlers in New Mexico and Colorado and investors in Europe with competing claims to the lands of the Maxwell grant, both meritorious. On each side, claimants had invested money, sweat, or both, in the belief that the land was theirs to claim, in law and in fact. It was this unavoidable conundrum that made the struggle for control and ownership such a wrenching ordeal, especially for settlers who thought they were seizing the opportunity of a lifetime.

In 1882, the U.S. Department of Justice, egged on by O. P. McMains and other interested parties, acceded to the wishes of those who believed that the Beaubien and Miranda or Maxwell Land Grant claim had been illegally enlarged through fraud and manipulation, and that the patent guaranteeing ownership should be canceled. It was the intention of the government lawyers to invalidate the patent and reduce the area of the grant to approximately ninety-seven thousand acres, as provided in Mexican law when the grant was made. In negotiating the Treaty of Guadalupe Hidalgo at the end of the War with Mexico, the U.S. government had pledged to honor Spanish and Mexican land grants in accordance with legal provisions governing the original award of land.[29]

In response to questionable moves of the administration of Frank Sherwin as president of the Maxwell Land Grant Company, the committee representing the company's majority investors in the Netherlands sent an experienced manager of colonial properties, Martinus Petrus Pels, to take a hand in its operations in New Mexico. He arrived in New York on February 24, 1885, and proceeded west, traveling to the property as needed, but making his headquarters in Denver. Pels served as an advisor to Harry Whigham, who managed the company's affairs and functioned as its court-appointed receiver from August 1885 until it emerged from receivership in 1888. In the new Maxwell Land Grant Company, Pels became the general manager and Whigham stayed on as local administrator.

Pels's arrival came at a time when the lengthy conflict between settlers and the company seemed to be moving toward a climactic decision that would satisfy the desires of one side while dealing a devastating defeat to the other. The issue had divided Colfax County for almost fifteen years, but with the patent suit pending in federal court, a decision was in sight. Both parties could not be accommodated, and neither was willing to lose. With or without an official position in the Maxwell Company, Pels represented a majority of Dutch investors, and his views were regarded accordingly. He entered the intensifying dispute with a determination to pursue investor interests and he adopted, as his first priority, the subjugation of an ornery league of settlers not recognized by the company as landowners. He intended to remove, by forcible eviction, any who would not buy the land they occupied, lease it from the company, or leave peacefully.

Prior to Pels's arrival, perhaps with greater intensity under Pels's influence, the Maxwell Company methodically moved to confront squatters and force or incentivize their compliance, offering lease arrangements or buying settler-made improvements. During these years—between 1885 and 1890—there were numerous face-offs as the company tried to survey the property, put untitled settlers off the claims they occupied, and otherwise press the company's right to possess and use the entire 1,714,764-acre tract, minus the validated claims of prior purchasers.

During the same period, the title suit filed by the U.S. Department of Justice was making its way through the federal court system. The decision of the Denver circuit court in 1885 upheld the company's position and discouraged many settlers, but it did not dissuade O. P. McMains and other claimants who were certain that their cause was just. A U.S. Supreme Court ruling of April 1887, affirming the circuit court's decision, was widely viewed as the final word on the validity of the entire claim, a death knell to the dreams and demands of settlers without lease or title. Technically, the ruling applied only to land in Colorado, but it could be, and was, applied to the New Mexico part of the grant in a later suit. Other challenges were raised, but ultimately they were of little consequence.[30] The decisions buoyed the Maxwell Company position, but victory in court did not immediately translate to compliance on the ground, and resistance on the part of settlers unwilling to deal with the company persisted for some years more.

Success in court emboldened the Maxwell Company in its determination to evict settlers who were living on its property in violation of the company's ownership rights. It also produced resignation in some settlers and anger in others. Rumors and actual threats of an armed rebellion cropped up around the grant. In October 1887, President Grover Cleveland furnished officials in New Mexico with a letter intended for publication, stating that the decision of the Supreme Court was "authoritative and conclusive," and warning that an act of insurrection, such as the "rumpus" referred to in a screed from McMains, would certainly "be visited with the penalty appropriate to the crime."[31] With McMains stirring up passions among the settlers and Pels impatiently pushing for a coerced removal of people he looked upon as trespassers and embezzlers of grant resources, the feud spiraled toward a seemingly inevitable, violent climax.

In a study of land grant conflict in northern New Mexico focusing on the Tierra Amarilla grant, David Correia observes that the concepts of property and law are inseparably related and, further, that "violence is inherent to law and property." The idea is somewhat counterintuitive, in that "legal interpretation appears disinterested but requires violent enforcement by legal agents," whose work normally involves use of force and sometimes bodily harm.[32] The "Stonewall War," coming after a Supreme Court ruling that was considered conclusive with respect to the Maxwell Company's claim of ownership, reinforces this idea, in that the company managers were seeking assistance from law enforcement officers and military forces when amicable negotiation with the settlers failed. Violence could be initiated by an "agent of the state," or by the resistance of those facing legal ejectment.

In the summer of 1888, tensions began to roil across the grant. Maxwell officials believed they needed to be more aggressive in their posture toward squatters, but moves like the attempted removal of the George Blosser family from their Willow Springs ranch near Raton served only to enrage settlers against the company. The family was away attending a settlers' meeting when the company's agents came. The incident drew a strong response from a mass of armed settlers, who quickly restored the Blossers to their home, then paraded through the streets of Raton trailing a makeshift "Dutch flag" in the dust.[33]

Both sides appeared willing to be guided by a bona fide ruling of the federal government, clearly stated. The Maxwell Company considered the Supreme Court's decision of April 1887 to constitute such a ruling, but settlers wanted something more definitive from the executive branch and Congress. President Cleveland had offered a letter for publication, urging settler compliance with the Supreme Court decision, but had stopped short of declaring that the 1869 determination of the secretary of the interior, that most of the land claimed by the company was public domain and open to settlement, had been reversed. Early in 1887, the House Committee on Private Land Claims had been delegated to look into the Maxwell claim; but a subcommittee given the task of determining whether the 1869 ruling had been officially reversed still had not reported.[34] As the months rolled by without any clarification, the settlers' frustration mounted.

The Stonewall area in southern Colorado, where the company had been applying pressure in an attempt to dislodge intransigent settlers, became the locus of the conflict. Some residents of the valley held documentary proof of conveyance from the U.S. government and did not meekly submit to the notion that a court decision for the company required them to leave homes in which they had invested years of effort and expense. The settlers' papers were patents issued by the U.S. government, suspended when the lands were found to lie within the Maxwell Grant survey as declared valid by the nation's highest court.[35] Violent resistance was increasingly seen as an option, and preparations were made accordingly. Both sides—the Maxwell Company and the settlers led by McMains—were blameworthy in a series of provocations that ultimately led to the tragic confrontation at the settler stronghold of Stonewall, Colorado.

In the weeks leading up to the flashpoint, both sides engaged in acts of aggression. Pels, then general manager of the Maxwell Company, considered asking for military help in enforcing ejectment orders against settlers, and sought assistance from local authorities. The company also tried to secure leases and offered to buy the settlers' livestock and other assets as an inducement to their voluntary departure. The more pugnacious settlers countered by threatening or harassing other settlers who acknowledged the company's rights and accepted its terms. In a notable case, a leading Stonewall resident, Richard Russell, reached a satisfactory bargain with the company. However, clumsy handling of the matter by Pels and a determined effort by McMains to change Russell's thinking evidently sabotaged the agreement, setting back the effort to achieve amicable resolution with the settlers.[36]

Two incidents accelerated a seemingly inevitable trajectory toward violent conflict. Both were initiated by actions of local settlers who had adopted a policy of noncooperation with the Maxwell Company. In the first instance, J. W. Lewelling was digging an irrigation ditch on land bought from the company for use as a summer resort, when he allegedly was warned of danger to his life if he continued. He resolved to arm himself and his laborers and continue working but changed his mind and left after being visited by a mass of armed settlers, most wearing masks.[37] Separately, E. J. Randolph and his wife, who had leased a ranch in the area, were threatened with hanging over their acknowledgment of the company's authority. They fled for Trinidad, "having escaped with nothing but the clothes they wore." The *Pueblo Daily Chieftain* advised readers, "Ejectment suits are being prepared against 77 settlers. The settlers go armed, and say they will resist. A collision and bloodshed seem imminent."[38]

Bent on keeping the peace, the Las Animas County sheriff in Trinidad sent a detail of six deputies to Stonewall and telegraphed the governor, Alva Adams, to report on the crisis and ask for military assistance. Adams deferred sending the militia, but sent the regimental commander, Colonel Benjamin Klee, to assess the situation and report back to him.[39] Whether the sheriff's posse was intended to maintain peace, to serve papers, or to enforce writs of ejectment is unclear. In the Stonewall country, the sending of the posse was understood as an act of aggression and treated accordingly.

The deputies left Trinidad on Thursday, August 23, and by Friday afternoon they were at Stonewall village, where their arrival generated a sense of impending hostility. By telegraph and rider, word of their presence was spread to allied settlers, including McMains, who was on the Red River in New Mexico. McMains soon headed to Stonewall, accumulating a cavalcade of anti-grant men as he traveled. Allies reportedly came from several New Mexico grants, including the Maxwell, Taos, Tierra Amarilla, and Costilla tracts.[40]

On Saturday morning, August 25, McMains rode in at the head of a column of men who would stand with the Stonewall settlers. The contingent stopped near the Pooler Hotel, where the six deputies from Trinidad were lodging, and where a large gathering of local men were waiting, making a total of about two hundred settlers and allies on hand, many armed. McMains and one or two local men made contact with the sheriff's men, demanding that they hitch up the wagon they had brought and leave.[41] Following a consultation with his companions, the posse's leader, William Hunn, said that the men would not leave. McMains reportedly directed others to surround the building, and someone in the crowd outside fired a shot, touching off an exchange of gunfire in which at least one of the Stonewall men, Rafael Valerio, was killed, and Richard Russell was mortally wounded. At about noon, the deputies called for a cease-fire and hotel employees were allowed to leave the building. Apparently, terms for withdrawal of the deputies were discussed, but a demand that they surrender their weapons seemingly killed the negotiation and the standoff continued, with sporadic gunfire. By grace or luck, the deputies managed to escape undetected that night under cover of a barn fire that distracted the crowd and left a dark, shaded way into the country behind the hotel. The deputies bushwhacked through the broken country and back to Trinidad. At some point, the hotel burned.

Marion Sloan Russell was not present for the confrontation at the hotel. Her husband of twenty-three years, with whom she had worked to build a home place and make a family in the Stonewall Valley, was brought to her with severe gunshot wounds. Through five agonizing days, with no doctor to attend Russell and no way to summon one, his life ebbed away. He was buried on a mesa above the wide valley. Presumably based on stories brought to her, Marion Russell referred to her husband's having been "assassinated" when approaching the hotel, "carrying a flag of truce."[42] It was not clear to others how or by whom the fatal shot was fired, or whether Russell was engaged in the exchange of gunfire between the settlers and the sheriff's men.

After discovering that the deputies had escaped, the settlers remained on alert for several days before dispersing. Recriminations followed and criminal charges were filed. McMains was acquitted on a charge of manslaughter in the deaths of Richard Russell and Rafael Valerio, who were said by prosecutors to have died as a result of McMains's incitement of violence. McMains was later arrested on a federal criminal charge of "inciting and aiding resistance to the service of official

Oscar Patrick McMains at Stonewall, Colorado, 1890s (*standing in front, hand on a wagon wheel*). After the debacle at the Pooler Hotel in Stonewall, McMains and his wife moved from Colfax County to Stonewall and lived there for the remainder of his life. His battle against the Maxwell Company was slipping away, but in the pristine isolation of the Stonewall country, he was among friends. Courtesy History Colorado, accession no. 84.193.1613.

papers."[43] Convicted, he served about six months in the common jail at Pueblo. Upon his release, McMains returned to his work as the "Agent for the Settlers," lobbying Congress and the executive branch in Washington while railing against the government and the Maxwell Company in handbills that had little effect on the status of the grant or the settlers. In mid-June 1889, Oscar and Mary McMains moved to Stonewall. There the near-indefatigable agitator lived out his final years.[44]

An End of Strife

The Maxwell Company continued the work of trying to dislodge settlers who did not own or lease presumed company properties on which they were living, sending agents to serve papers and otherwise move the lengthy processes of settlement and ejectment along. Perhaps inspired by the popular movement of Las Gorras Blancas, the "White Caps," in nearby San Miguel County, Spanish-speaking settlers along the Ponil and Vermejo drainages commenced more aggressive tactics of resistance in the early 1890s, destroying fencing and other property owned by persons associated with the Maxwell Company, or purchased from squatters to secure their departure.[45] Holdouts among the Euro-American settlers also expressed their outrage, publishing statements of protest and warning, and continuing to resist the Maxwell Company's entreaties. Encounters between law officers or Maxwell agents and resisting settlers in the early months of 1891 led to the violent deaths of Zeb Russell, a deputy U.S. marshal, and Manuel Gonzales, a leader of the Vermejo settlers.[46] Urged on by McMains, a declining number of settlers in New Mexico and southern Colorado continued to resist. As the campaign to remove or settle with the remaining squatters continued, violent confrontations decreased.

With Frank Springer's election as president of the Maxwell Company in 1892, and other changes in board membership, persistent tensions among the trustees were alleviated. Relations with the company's investors in the Netherlands also improved, owing to their longstanding trust in Springer's competence and judgment. Pels's departure as general manager in 1895 expedited a shift in the company's approach to the conflict with settlers from one of confrontation to one that emphasized negotiation and accommodation. An agreement was reached in a meeting at Trinidad in October 1899, whereby settlers agreed to recognize the Maxwell Company's title and accepted leases that allowed them to retain their homes.[47]

O. P. McMains had passed on April 15, 1899, having spent almost all of his adult life working in the interest of settlers in conflict with the Maxwell Company. In spring of 1901, the Maxwell Company sold its remaining holdings north of the Colorado–New Mexico boundary to the Colorado Fuel and Iron Company.[48]

Under a small headline, "Maxwell Grant Troubles Ended," the *Santa Fe New Mexican* reported in October 1899 that eviction notices served on squatters who had not already agreed to terms with the company had been resolved amicably, with "liberal" leases offered to all who had made improvements to the lands they occupied.[49] Whether the comment was strictly accurate or on the optimistic side, it was true that a long and painful struggle over the Maxwell claim was nearing its end. For good or for ill, disputes over land tenure and ownership had been settled for the foreseeable future. It was left to the managers and investors of the Maxwell Land Grant Company, and to future landowners, to see what could be done with the varied resources of the once wild Cimarron country.

CHAPTER 15

Time and Change

On August 15, 1846, General Stephen Watts Kearny, commander of an occupying force of U.S. troops, mounted an adobe building on the north side of the old Las Vegas plaza and told assembled townspeople, "We come amongst you as friends, not enemies; as protectors, not conquerors. We come among you for your benefit, not for your injury."[1] This was his version of a darkly humorous phrase heard in later years: "We're from the government, and we're here to help you." The words were meant to convey goodwill and invite acceptance but were more apt to evoke skepticism. Some Mexican citizens probably did welcome Kearny's troops; Governor Manuel Armijo's administration in the remote and largely ignored northern province of Mexico had been notably corrupt and autocratic. Still, having one's country overrun by a force imposing a new system of government, different values, and an alien language and culture, all wrapped in attitudes of moral and cultural superiority, does not always wear well with the conquered.

Central to the economic conquest of New Mexico, and of the Cimarron country, was "the evolution of land from matter to property," or in language preferred by María Montoya in a study of economic and race-class issues contested in the Maxwell Land Grant conflict, "translation" of property in the transition from one governing regime to another.[2] *Translation* demolished Plains Indian tradition that recognized zones of occupation and defense around a homeland, but that did not involve surveys or deeds of ownership. For Spanish-Mexican people whose occupation in the region preceded that of non-Hispanic Euro-Americans, conversion to a scheme that reduced land to fee-simple ownership by private parties or public land managed by the government, meant that structures like community grants with common lands and division of drainages into cross-stream strips ensuring access for all to essential resources such as water, arable land, pasture, and timber, might not be honored under a U.S. administration.

Translation of property in the Cimarron country can be said to begin with the conferral of the Beaubien and Miranda Land Grant in 1841. The process of translation was complete by about 1900, by which time nearly all settlers living on land claimed by the Maxwell Company, without benefit of lease or title, had given in to the company's claims of ownership. The legal conclusion of the Maxwell Land Grant conflict and the abatement of hostilities in the mountains, valleys, and plains of the grant area—a defeat for squatters, and perhaps more relief than triumph for the Maxwell Company—yields a few ponderable questions concerning the experience of a thirty-year struggle in federal and territorial courts and in the hills and valleys of the Cimarron country, and along the high valleys of the Purgatoire in southern Colorado.

Violence in Colfax County: How Wild Was It?

The question regularly arises as to whether the late nineteenth-century Old West was more violent in comparison with other times and other places, or whether that notion is a fabrication of the make-believe industry. While uniform crime statistics were not compiled in the lively days of Tombstone and Deadwood, some scholars have used retroactive data collection and analysis to calculate measures that could facilitate comparisons of the severity of violence across locales and eras. In order to reduce the effect of year-to-year fluctuations in areas with relatively few people, numbers are often aggregated over a period of several years. The techniques are less than perfect but may support credible and comparable estimates. So how wild was the Cimarron country in its rough and rowdy days?

Using data gleaned from period newspapers, published histories, government reports, and court records, a list of apparent homicides was compiled for the period between 1870 and 1880, inclusive (see table 1). A total of ninety-two cases of homicide or manslaughter were considered.[3] Fifty-two cases were viewed as valid instances of local homicide not mitigated by claim of self-defense or other extenuating circumstance. Taking the population figures for Colfax County from the 1870 and 1880 U.S. Census reports and adding in data on the Ute and Jicarilla people from the Indian Commissioners' annual reports, average and aggregate population figures were derived. Using common practices in calculation of

TABLE 1
AGGREGATE HOMICIDE AND LYNCHING RATES IN COLFAX COUNTY, NEW MEXICO, 1870 TO 1880

	Avg. Census Population	Native American	Total Colfax County Pop.	Homicides	Lynchings
1870	2,695	1,361	4,056	2	1
1871	2,695	1,509	4,204	8	1
1872	2,695	1,500	4,195	9	0
1873	2,695	1,170	3,865	2	1
1874	2,695	750	3,445	4	1
1875	2,695	900	3,595	7	2
1876	2,695	650	3,345	7	1
1877	2,695	749	3,444	5	0
1878	2,695	400	3,095	3	0
1879	2,695	277	2,972	3	0
1880	2,695	30	2,725	2	1
Totals	29,645	9,296	38,941	52	8
Calculated Homicide Rate for 1870–1880, 0.95 CI [101.9, 175.1]				**133.5**	
Calculated Lynching Rate for 1870–1880, 0.95 CI [10.4, 40.5]				**20.5**	

Notes: Colfax County U.S. Census totals were 1,992 for 1870 and 3,398 for 1880. An estimate for the eleven-year period was determined by averaging these numbers and multiplying by eleven.

Native Americans were not counted in the U.S. Census until 1890. Figures for Native Americans in Colfax County were derived from the census conducted by W. F. M. Arny in 1870, and reports of the commissioner of Indian Affairs for all other years. The sum of figures from 1870 to 1880 yielded an estimate for the eleven-year period.

Population figures indicated include all persons, all ages.

Ninety-two credibly reported homicides were examined. An 1874 Plains Indian raid responsible for an estimated twenty-six deaths was viewed as an "outlier," not an instance of local violence; these were excluded from calculations. Fourteen "justifiable homicides" were also excluded, leaving a total of fifty-two homicides. Calculated rates may be understated due to unreported and undetected homicides. Confidence intervals (CI) were computed by the Wilson method, using the Ausvet online calculator.

the homicide rate, expressed as a ratio of homicides per 100,000 population, and making conservative judgments in interpreting data used, a rate of 133.5 homicides per 100,000 residents was calculated for the period of 1870 to 1880, inclusive.

By way of comparison, annual homicide rates for 2009 to 2019 for the United States, as published through the federal Uniform Crime Reporting Program, ranged from 4.4 to 5.4. New Mexico reported rates ranging from 4.8 to 9.9 for the same years.[4] For an earlier span, using data compiled by Kevin J. Mullen, Eric H. Monkkonen, and Claire V. McKanna, Jr., Randolph Roth, a historian associated with Ohio State University's Criminal Justice Research Center, calculated homicide rates for nine California counties, 1850–1865, and reported an aggregate rate of 65.45 over a sixteen-year period for an adult population.[5] Roth notes that factors affecting comparison of homicide rates in the nineteenth century with rates observed in later times include the advent of emergency services and advances in nonemergency medical care. These developments almost certainly have prevented some deaths from injuries that were commonly fatal in olden times.[6]

As a corollary to the calculation of homicide rates, Robert R. Dykstra used data sets from California, New Mexico, and Colorado to figure aggregate "lynching rates," stratified by decade, from 1861 to 1900.[7] The rates varied from 0.7 to 7.5. Dykstra was not surprised to find that rates declined after 1880, such that lynching had practically disappeared in the trans-Mississippi West by 1900. The high rate among the four decades was 7.5 lynchings per 100,000 people, from 1871 to 1880. For a comparable period in Colfax County, 1870 to 1880, eight lynchings were reported, for a calculated lynching rate of 20.5 per 100,000 residents. Small numbers in data used to make calculations and draw inferences invite skepticism, but it is difficult to escape the conclusion that Colfax County in the 1870s was extremely violent, relative to other places and other times.

Whose Land?

The story of contention and violence in Colfax County and on the Maxwell Land Grant is largely a saga of conflict over land, and of the varied persons and groups who coveted something from the land. The tale, as usually told, is of spirited competition between a corporate entity that claimed ownership of a vast section of northern New Mexico and southern Colorado and all the settlers, miners, and ranchers who believed they had legal rights to lodge competing claims. But who really owned the land? Struggling to answer the same question about a peak rising out of the southern New Mexico desert, a character created by novelist and environmental writer Edward Abbey traced the title back from the current claimant, the U.S. government; through the ranchers from whom the government had forcibly purchased it; to the Natives who had preceded the stock raisers; to the original owners—eagles, mountain lions, and coyotes.[8]

Considering the same question for the greater American West—or the whole continent—Margaret Jacobs, author of *After One Hundred Winters*, a study of "takings" of land and efforts to resolve injustices, put the matter about as starkly as anyone could: "Unless you are an American Indian or Alaskan Native, you are living on stolen land."[9] She meant all of it—the great ranches, farms, national parks and forests, and sprawling cities, down to the tiniest lot on which a "garden home" is planted. This is not to say that all non-Indian property owners are jumping land without paying for it. Victor Westphall, historian of New Mexico land grants and public lands, pointed to Thomas Catron's acquisition of the Tierra Amarilla grant. Catron had treated the grant as though wholly owned by its principal settler when, in reality, there were other legitimate claimants. "He probably paid $200,000 for that land," Westphall wrote, "but the question is did he pay it to the right people?"[10] Most U.S. landholders surely own property that was paid for with real money or otherwise acquired legally, but chances are, some party in the chain of ownership leading to the current owner either seized the land in disregard of prior occupation and use vesting presumptive rights of ownership in indigenous people, or paid for the land but did not pay the right people.

Indian claims to western lands were hardly on the radar to a non-Indian population and its supportive federal government, eager to occupy the West and exploit its resources. When contact turned hostile, Native people had inferior weaponry with which to hold off the onslaught. More to the point, they lacked effective political power and legal representation, and their efforts to resist, sometimes including the killing of innocents or taking of scalps, furnished fuel for intruding non-Indians to rally citizens back east and in the halls of Congress to their cause. With Native peoples effectively dismissed as claimants or owners of western land, the focus, as on the Maxwell grant, shifted to competition among factions of westering seekers of homes and treasure.

The governments of Spain and Mexico recognized indigenous ownership of land in the Rio Grande region that they colonized and occupied before 1846.[11] The U.S. administration, in contrast, could not see beyond its tenets of fee-simple ownership, documented in written deeds and patents. With the Treaty of Guadalupe Hidalgo in hand, officials proceeded to review and confirm or deny land grant claims and referee property disputes among parties, with little or no regard for historic occupation and use by Native people, especially those of the "wild" class. In the case of the Maxwell grant, the conflict became a struggle between two factions: settlers who believed the lands they occupied were or ought to be public land; and investors who believed the Maxwell grant to be a valid claim, blessed by federal officials and confirmed in court decisions.

Under the U.S. system of government, courts exist to settle disputes, examining the facts and the law to reach rational and informed decisions. In the dispute over the Maxwell grant, the U.S. Supreme Court did its job in reviewing evidence, hearing arguments, and rendering a finding. The Maxwell Company won its case, and by application of a prior ruling that Congress had the power to exceed its obligation under the Treaty of Guadalupe Hidalgo and create a "new grant," the Maxwell grant was affirmed as claimed by the company, at 1,714,764 acres, a decree pleasing to the company's managers and investors, but an outrage to many others.[12] Whether the justices "got it right" is a matter of opinion.

Before 1946, provisions for Native American entities to seek redress for illegal taking of lands were difficult or, for long periods, nonexistent. Before adoption of the Indian Citizenship Act in 1924, Native Americans living in the United States were not even recognized as citizens; early efforts to provide paths for their pursuit of land claims were largely ineffectual and perhaps half-hearted. With the 1946 creation of the Indian Claims Commission, tribes had legal recourse that recognized "use and occupancy from time immemorial" as a basis for aboriginal title.[13]

By authority of the Indian Claims Commission, qualifying entities could be compensated for lands within a defined "award area," with awards reduced by "offsets" and other deductions. Awards would be based on the land's value at the date of its taking, such that the awards presumably would be considerably under current value. Depending on the size of the award area, payments could still be substantial, and were welcomed by the tribes, some investing proceeds in revenue-producing activities that could advance self-sufficiency. An early claim was filed by the Confederated Ute Bands. Southern Utes, including the Mouache and Capote Bands at Ignacio and the Ute Mountain Utes, shared approximately $6,000,000 following a favorable ruling.[14] The Jicarilla Tribe initiated its claim in 1958; the lengthy process resulted in an award of $9,150,000 in 1970.[15]

The Jicarillas and their attorneys disagreed with the commission's finding that excluded confirmed land grants within the award area in calculating the acreage for which the tribe would be compensated. In the commission's view, the tribe's title to those lands had been extinguished by the Spanish and Mexican governments when the grants were made, thus the United States was not to blame for that taking of Jicarilla lands.[16] Perhaps as significant as the funds received by the Jicarillas was the commission's finding that nearly all land in the award area, including the land grants, had belonged to the Jicarilla people and had been wrongfully taken from them.

Also likely getting short shrift were some among the area's earliest settlers, Spanish-Mexican people who had moved north from more established parts by the mid-1840s, in the earliest years after the Beaubien and Miranda grant was awarded, or during Maxwell's time. "Obtaining and keeping grants required settlement," wrote a Maxwell biographer, and inducement of settlers by the promise of landownership was a near universal expectation, in custom if not in law.[17] But Maxwell's aversion to written agreements, and the nature of the transaction in which he disposed of the property, left settlers who might have been entitled to land occupied under his authority to remain as sharecroppers under the dispensation of a corporate entity having no interest in such an arrangement.[18] "Settler rights" not specified in American law, or in the purchase agreement, were of little or no concern to a foreign company bent on consolidating control and maximizing profit.

More than a century and a half into U.S. administration of land laws in the southwestern borderlands, surely every piece of land, large or small, is backed by legal documents establishing some form of private, corporate, or public ownership. But questions as to how the pattern of landownership reached its present state, and the extent to which the processes were fair and outcomes consistent with a faithful reading of applicable laws and treaties, remain tangled and vexed.

What about the Women?

The recorded history of the Colfax County War and the Maxwell Land Grant conflict and the violence associated with those clashes is overwhelmingly a story of men, as told primarily by non-Hispanic white men through contemporary newspaper reports and later historical narratives. In the analysis of violent deaths in Colfax County between 1870 and 1880, all fifty-two victims of local homicides were men, killed by other men. All public officials and eligible voters were also men. Women were hardly visible in most accounts of these times in the Cimarron country, but many women were present to experience the pain and passion of bad times in Colfax County and on the Maxwell grant.

The difficulty confronting Ute and Jicarilla people in the struggle to survive through the 1870s and 1880s was aggravated by two circumstances. First, the buffalo herds were decimated through the seventies, due to overhunting and wanton slaughter, perhaps abetted by some in the government who adopted extermination of the buffalo as an overt strategy to "starve out" Native people and force them onto reservations.[19] Second, because the Cimarron Agency or issue site was located on a private grant, the Native people could not engage in farming or grazing without arousing the wrath of settlers, nor could they escape pressure to move to a reservation.[20]

Faced with the double blow to the Jicarilla economy, some women acted to develop new means of support. In 1875, the agent at Cimarron found it notable that an unnamed "old woman," the matriarch of her clan, leaned on members of her family to make a serious attempt at farming or gardening. The family reportedly made a good corn crop, dividing the yield with others of the band.[21] Jicarilla women also increased production of their micaceous pottery, already a desirable object of trade.[22] In December 1886, it was reported in newspapers that "For purposes of helping along, the women of the tribe have gone into the pottery business."[23] The pottery of the Jicarillas was valued for the clay from which it was made and for its unusual glaze.[24] The vessels evidently withstood high temperatures and resisted breakage better than did other clay pots. The pots were welcome in the villages of northern New Mexico, and the Jicarilla women who made them hoped their value would help sustain the people in a changing economy in which trade was vital.[25]

The experiences of Hispanic women in Maxwell's time, when his ranch was organized on the order of a traditional New Mexican hacienda, varied according to one's social class. María de la Luz Beaubien Maxwell, with her brother and four sisters, grew up in a family of wealth, power, and property. As heirs to the Beaubien and Miranda Land Grant, Luz's siblings readily sold their shares in the grant, enabling the Maxwells to secure full ownership of the estate. The most active of Luz's siblings in settling on the land and developing its economy and resources was her sister, Petra, who, with her husband, Jesús Abreu, sold her share to the Maxwells, but bought a ranch in the Rayado area, on which they raised their family and did well in agriculture and business. The sisters who sold shares in the Beaubien and Miranda grant may have been attracted to the notion of trading their land for cash, believed by some to be a safer asset for married women.[26] In María Montoya's estimation, Luz Maxwell was an able businesswoman, "not a quiet and passive doña of the Maxwell hacienda, but an active and integral part of New Mexico's cattle industry."[27]

The Abreu family at Rayado, ca. 1912. Petra Beaubien Abreu (*seated*), daughter of Carlos and Paula Lobato Beaubien and sister of Luz Maxwell, is surrounded at the family home by her adult children (*from left*): Victoriana Abreu, Sofia Abreu, Adelina Abreu Valdez, Josefa Abreu Clothier; and the Abreu men: Santiago, Jesús Librado, Carlos, Narciso, and Ramon. Petra died in 1914. The last of the Abreus remaining at Rayado had left by 1930. Courtesy private collection of James Abreu.

Little is known of the lives of working-class Hispanic women on the Maxwell grant in the late nineteenth century, except that many of their families lost the lands on which they had been living and working, when company agents and attorneys enforced writs of ejectment or prodded them into lease agreements between 1870 and 1900. Some of the families may have been able to purchase land from the company and remain in their homes, but most could not.[28]

The Hispanic women directly impacted by the chaotic events of 1875 in Colfax County, family members of the men who had been lynched or shot down, had roots in Santa Fe and Taos Counties. Joaquina Griego de Vega, the widow of Cruz Vega, lived with her husband in Colfax County during the three years prior to his death in 1875. They had been married in the old Parroquia, or parish church, at Santa Fe in 1869. Following Vega's death, she returned to Santa Fe and lived in poverty until her death in 1902. In 1895, she applied for and received a widow's pension of eight dollars per month, payable on account of Vega's Civil

War military service.[29] In applying for the pension, Griego de Vega stated, through a recorder, that she lived in a one-room adobe owned by a neighbor. She explained, "I do some chores now and then for my neighbors (who are also poor people) who, in return give me [a] little coffee, bread, flour, etc."[30] She had no children, and had no husband before or after her marriage to Vega, whose death she attributed to "desperados."

Among Euro-American women whose paths crossed the Maxwell property in these dark times, the stories of three women and their responses to hardship are noteworthy. Two came west as wives; another married an infantry lieutenant after traveling to New Mexico over the Santa Fe Trail. Each suffered the sudden death of a husband. They were mothers of children, but all stayed in the region or left and later returned. The women wrote of their experiences in the West, and on other topics that interested them. Despite the grievous losses of their spouses, the women seemed somehow liberated to pursue varied issues and causes, including animal welfare, services for the blind, and women's suffrage. The women who found exhilaration after the pain were Olive Ennis Hite, Ada McPherson Morley, and Marion Sloan Russell.

Olive Ennis appears in this work as the author of a revealing portrayal of Lucien Maxwell and his home ranch at Cimarron in the late 1860s, from observations she made as an army spouse visiting from Fort Union. Lieutenant Joseph Ennis, her sweetheart from their hometown in Ohio, died of his injuries after falling from a horse near Cimarron in 1869. As Olive rode with his body back to Fort Union, the ambulance in which she was riding toppled over, and she was seriously injured.[31] Such trauma might have quashed the adventure for many travelers, but not for Olive Ennis. After some fifteen years working for newspapers in Cincinnati and Saint Louis while raising her son, Ennis returned to New Mexico to visit in 1884, and to live for some years beginning in about 1887. She remarried, lived on a ranch in the Manzano Mountains, and published a newspaper in Albuquerque with her husband, Wallace Hite.[32] The Hites later moved to Washington, D.C. They retired to California for reasons of health, but Olive spent time in New Mexico during several summers and was known to associates as a journalist whose work nimbly merged sharp criticism, ethical judgment, and good humor.

Ada Morley fought the Santa Fe Ring in the 1870s with her mother and husband. William Morley was mortally wounded by an accidental gunshot in January 1883, while locating a route for the Mexican Central Railroad, and his body was transported to Las Vegas for burial. Ada's world and those of their children were shattered. She remarried briefly, and perhaps unwisely, not long after the accident. Deserted by her husband, she settled with her family on a remote ranch in southwestern New Mexico. In the Datil Mountains, she raised her children and became involved in the women's suffrage movement, an interest likely inherited from her mother. Ada occasionally wrote for publication, and reared a successful writer in her daughter, Agnes Morley Cleaveland.

After Richard Russell's shooting death in the standoff at Stonewall, Marion Sloan Russell bargained with the Maxwell Company to buy most of the ground they had settled and continued raising their children. Aided by her daughter-in-law, she wrote an engaging memoir of life on the Santa Fe Trail in the 1850s and 1860s.[33] She stayed in Las Animas County, and passed at the age of ninety-two in 1936, after being hit by an automobile in Trinidad. The loss of her beloved Richard was a constant sorrow, but she never wearied of the apple-green valley in which she had lived, or the mountains that soared above it.

Mary Tolby Smith and family at Battle Ground, Indiana, ca. 1892. Mary Tolby's life after tragedy included marriage to Erastus Smith (*far right*) and a blended family including (*from left*) Charlotte Smith, Grace Tolby, Alta Smith, and the sons born to this couple, Wilson Smith and Horace Smith. The elder Tolby daughter, Rachel, married in 1889 and lived with her husband in California. Courtesy private collection of Lisa Reichard and James Klaiber.

These were women for whom strength and destiny did not depend on a spouse. Their stories also demonstrate that men held no monopoly on the impulse to go West, acquire land, and settle. High, open skies, the beauty of mountain and desert landscapes, freedom from security and boredom, and perhaps the diversity of people and places in the western territories, seemed to make these women want to be there, with or without the men with whom they had shared dreams of homes and families, and long, happy lives.

Mary Tolby could hardly be blamed for taking a different path following the vile murder of her husband, Rev. Franklin Tolby. With their two young daughters, she returned to her family in Indiana. She remarried in 1884 and had two sons with her second husband, Erastus H. Smith, owner of a livery business. She passed in 1923 at age seventy-three and was buried at the Battle Ground Cemetery in Tippecanoe County, Indiana.

Racial Identity and Prejudice: A Permanent Scourge?

While some determinants of the turmoil of the 1870s were related to specifics of time and place, and to broader issues respecting landownership and alleged attempts to impose "ring rule" in Colfax County, other conditions that fueled the emotion and violence in the Cimarron country long ago have been enduring and widely shared, and they appear to be thriving in the twenty-first century. These include the national obsession with racial identity, and the prejudice and disorders that sometimes result; high rates of extralegal gun violence in society; and an apparent incapacity of government to effectively address large and long-term issues like those concerning indigenous people and management of western lands in the nineteenth century, or threats concerning climate change and the environment in later times.

The most egregious stain on the national character of the United States may well be the persistent race-related prejudice and turmoil that have beset the society from pre-colonial times to the present. New Mexico's northern precincts did not escape this blight, and given the economic and social influences at work in the 1870s, it would have been a miracle if they had. In Maxwell's time, the Cimarron country was certainly multicultural, and not exactly free of prejudice, but with a strong hand in dealing with his servants and employees, Maxwell managed to make custom conform to his preferences most of the time. After his departure in 1870, prejudice and race-related hostility were elements of a milieu that produced a great many violent incidents over the next decade. In 1875 and 1876, years of intense chaos, a familiar spectacle was on exhibit with the assassination of two Hispanic murder suspects and the shooting deaths of three African American cavalrymen at Cimarron. In neither case was there any apparent effort to identify or punish those responsible for the deaths, beyond the prosecution of O. P. McMains for organizing the interrogation that led to the hanging of Cruz Vega. Local Indians were victims and perhaps perpetrators of race-related acts, and raiding Plains tribes inflicted wanton violence on non-Indian settlers in Colfax County.

In some instances, immigrants and travelers exported their prejudices to other parts of the country in their letters, diaries, and memoirs, and in the judgments of newspaper correspondents concerning Hispanic and indigenous residents. Fray Angelico Chavez wrote of these denigrating portrayals, "In practically all such publications, the average New Mexican fares badly, as he did when many of those things actually happened." Continuing, and referring to the brotherhood that famously engaged in self-flagellation and enactment of the crucifixion as part of its Easter ritual, Chavez remarked, "Once in a while, there has to be a lurid and most often imaginative reference to the Penitentes, as if these represented all of the New Mexican people and their faith."[34] Those sensational and unsavory depictions could not have been helpful to the majority of Hispanic New Mexicans, nor for the hopes of people coveting the prize of statehood for New Mexico.

Into a New Epoch

The Atchison, Topeka and Santa Fe Railroad topped Raton Pass in the final days of 1878 and built across Colfax County in the early months of 1879, bringing good news and some not so good. Nearly all "Americans," meaning non-Hispanic white immigrants, were thrilled, or at least relieved, to have rapid, reliable transportation for people, goods, livestock and materials between New Mexico and the commercial and population centers of the more industrialized eastern states. The aspiration that Cimarron would thrive as a place of importance in the territory, however, was frustrated when the railroad bypassed Cimarron in laying track from Raton Pass to the prevailing mercantile hub of Las Vegas. In 1882, Cimarron yielded the seat of Colfax County to the town of Springer, named in honor of attorney and Maxwell Company advocate Frank Springer. Springer, the man, accepted the inevitable decline of Cimarron, moving his family and law practice to Las Vegas in 1883, while remaining firmly tethered to Colfax County through his ongoing work with the Maxwell Company, and the ranch that he owned in partnership with his brother, Charles. By late 1881, the *Cimarron News and Press* had a new home in Raton and was publishing under the banner of the *New Mexico News and Press*, and later, the *Raton Range*.

As the Maxwell Land Grant Company's business operations normalized under Springer's leadership as president starting in 1892, significant investments were made to develop the grant's wealth in coal and timber. Though gold mining remained an unstable and often marginal industry on the grant, new and friendlier policies encouraged more prospecting, mining, and processing of gold ore, and helped optimize income. Cattle grazing remained the major use of rangeland on the Maxwell grant, though increasingly decentralized as large parcels were sold for ranches. Farming on the grant never reached levels envisioned by some of the early managers of the property, but a project designed to increase water for irrigation—construction of the Eagle Nest Dam—gave rise to a greatly expanded industry in recreation and tourism. The development of Vermejo Park as a site for resort homes and sporting activity in the early twentieth century also reinforced the area's potential for such activities. The advent of polo clubs, a summer camp for girls, and the Philmont Scout Ranch, brought more visitors to the area in the first half of the twentieth century.

The Maxwell Land Grant Company's success in winning a federal patent on its immense claim and prevailing in lawsuits aimed at canceling the grant's confirmation, had the significant consequence of keeping much of the land intact under administration of the Maxwell Company. This led to the preservation of the historic grant as an area of large holdings. In a 2015 study of land status, some 85 percent of Colfax County was classified as private property, with more than half of that total held by ten owners of large operations holding properties that were situated entirely or largely within the bounds of the Maxwell grant. These were mainly ranching concerns, including the half-million-acre Vermejo Park Ranch, the CS Cattle Company, the Express UU Bar Ranch, Philmont Scout Ranch, and the Silver Spur Land and Cattle Company. Owners of other large properties included Taos Pueblo and Sandia Pueblo, and the Vermejo Coal Company. It is a paradox of sorts that a 33,000-acre tract in northern Colfax County, in a country once occupied by herders known as "Texans," and known for legendary gunslingers, was bought by the National Rifle Association for use as a recreational shooting sports center.[35] The region's popularity as a vacation destination is evident in year-round use of public and private recreational properties, including state wildlife areas, the Valle Vidal Unit of the Carson National Forest, Philmont Scout Ranch, and the Angel Fire Resort.

The removal of Ute and Jicarilla Apache Indians to distant reservations and the voluntary out-migration of the "Texan" cattlemen from the Canadian River country and of miners from the Baldy region left modern Colfax County with a population dominated by Hispanic people (49 percent) and non-Hispanic whites (47 percent), with Native Americans accounting for approximately 3 percent of the county population, according to 2021 estimates.[36] While Hispanic residents, on average, lag non-Hispanic whites in household income, political power appears to be equitably shared, judging by the composition of local governing bodies and the identities of other elected officials.

The story in the southern Colorado portion of the former Maxwell Land Grant property is similar to that of Colfax County. Average income levels of residents are low to moderate, but the region has shown potential for significant tourism, based in part on its history associated with the Santa Fe Trail and a formerly robust mining industry. Ranching remains a modest but sustainable activity in parts of the old grant, including the broad valleys of the Stonewall country. Coal once provided good incomes for miners and families in the Purgatoire Valley, but production fell after World War I, with revivals occurring intermittently since.

Time and Tide

For all its notoriety as a place of conquest, violent conflict, lawlessness, and political and economic chicanery during territorial times, the area embracing Colfax County and the Beaubien and Miranda or Maxwell Land Grant has been better known in recent decades as a place of great beauty and a prime destination for outdoor education and recreation. Prosperity remains elusive. A once-valuable mining industry withered and seems unlikely to return. The Angel Fire ski resort and community, high in the southern part of the Moreno Valley, was a welcome attraction for the area in the 1960s, but the loss of Raton's La Mesa Park Racetrack and the failure to secure a new track was discouraging. Colfax County's only hospital, Miners' Colfax Medical Center in Raton, contends with struggles that afflict many small facilities providing services to rural communities. A onetime hotbed of frontier journalism, Colfax County has been without a print newspaper for much of the twenty-first century. Ranching is one of the few relatively stable economic activities in the region, despite the uncertainties of weather and climate, public policy, and changes in the national and global economy.

The people who met in the wild country of northern New Mexico and southern Colorado in the 1870s and 1880s were of diverse racial and cultural origins. They also represented groups with varied economic interests, and they were animated by divergent motives. They met in New Mexico, in an American territory, previously a Mexican province superimposed on the homeland of the Mouache Utes and Jicarilla Apaches, to struggle with competing factions having different attitudes and aspirations, and with the hazards of a wild land. Their striving resulted as did many such encounters in the West, with cultures merging in part but remaining distinct, as the machine of progress forged ahead, claiming resources formerly in the domain of nature and of people with less complicated needs, advancing the ideal of a continental nation established in accordance with the legal traditions and governing institutions of the American states.

Notes

ABBREVIATIONS

AC/NMHU	Arrott Fort Union Collection, New Mexico Highlands University
FS/CS	Frank Springer Papers, CS Cattle Company
MLG	Maxwell Land Grant Collection, Center for Southwest Research
NARA	National Archives and Records Administration
NMSRCA	New Mexico State Records Center and Archives
RG	Record Group
TANM	Territorial Archives of New Mexico
TBC	Thomas Benton Catron Papers, Center for Southwest Research

PREFACE

1. Sonnichsen, *I'll Die Before I'll Run*, 7.
2. *Merriam-Webster's Collegiate Dictionary*, 1330. Zimmer, "Colfax County War."

INTRODUCTION

1. *Chicago Daily Inter-Ocean*, Feb. 4, 1876.
2. F. J. Tolby to "My Dear Sister," Jan. 29, 1874, Collection of the Old Mill Museum, Cimarron, NM.
3. La Farge, "New Mexico," 46.
4. Unidentified source quoted in the *New York Sun*, Dec. 3, 1894.
5. Correspondence of April 26, 1871, in the *Cincinnati (OH) Commercial*, May 8, 1871.
6. *Arizona Citizen* (Tucson), May 6, 1871.
7. Limerick, "Trail to Santa Fe," 76.

CHAPTER 1. THE PLAINS PEOPLE AND THE CEDAR BARK PEOPLE

1. Tiller, *Jicarilla Apache Tribe*, 4.
2. Concerning names used to designate these Native Americans by Spanish- and English-speaking people who explored or invaded their homeland, see Eiselt, *Becoming White Clay*, 146–47. See also Simmons, *Ute Indians of Utah, Colorado, and New Mexico*, 22.

209

3. See Delaney, *Southern Ute People*, 1–53; and Russell, *Land of Enchantment*, 131–36.
4. Gunnerson, *Jicarilla Apaches*, 160.
5. Gunnerson, 165.
6. Tiller, *Jicarilla Apache Tribe*, 9.
7. Eiselt, *Becoming White Clay*, 12.
8. Kiser, *Borderlands of Slavery*, 2.
9. Ebright, Hendricks, and Hughes, *Four Square Leagues*, 6–7.
10. Ebright, Hendricks, and Hughes, 18–20. See also Westphall, *Mercedes Reales*, 108–9.
11. Murphy, *Indian Agent in New Mexico*, 38–39.
12. See West, *Contested Plains*, 237–63; and Jacobs, *After One Hundred Winters*, 23. Sources cited in this paragraph came to attention through Jacobs's summary of the impact of settlement on Natives of the central Colorado mountains and plains.
13. W. W. Bent, Agent for the Indians on the Arkansas, to A. M. Robinson, Superintendent, Central Superintendency, Office of Indian Affairs, *Report of the Commissioner of Indian Affairs*, 1859, 138–39.
14. See Quintana, *Pobladores*, 69–70.
15. Quintana, 180. See also Eiselt, *Becoming White Clay*, 123.
16. Delaney, *Southern Ute People*, 25.
17. Tiller, partial manuscript review at the request of the author, October 2021.
18. Simmons, *Ute Indians of Utah, Colorado, and New Mexico*, 61. See also Westphall, *Mercedes Reales*, 43–65.
19. Westphall, *Mercedes Reales*, 52, 295n20.
20. Concerning origins of the Beaubien and Miranda or Maxwell Land Grant, see Murphy, *Lucien Bonaparte Maxwell*, 34–54.
21. The Mouache Utes moved to a reservation on the Rio de los Piños in Colorado in July 1878. Delaney, *Southern Ute People*, 57. The Jicarillas were not finally settled on the reservation at Dulce, New Mexico, until spring of 1887. Tiller, *Jicarilla Apache Tribe*, 96–97.
22. Manypenny, *Our Indian Wards*, 177.
23. Acting Gov. William Messervy to George Manypenny, Commissioner of Indian Affairs, March 31, 1854. Quoted in Michno, *Depredation and Deceit*, 191.
24. This account and assessment are based on a study of military records and an archeological investigation of the battle site following its discovery in 2002. Johnson et al., "Taos, the Jicarilla Apache, and the Battle of Cienguilla," 137–51.
25. Michno, *Depredation and Deceit*, 237–40.
26. Young, *Ute Indians of Colorado in the Twentieth Century*, 25.
27. Tiller, *Jicarilla Apache Tribe*, 56.
28. Guild and Carter, *Kit Carson*, 198.
29. See Murphy, *Frontier Crusader—William F. M. Arny*, 247–53.
30. *Report of the Commissioner of Indian Affairs*, 1861, 128.
31. *Report of the Commissioner of Indian Affairs*, 1862, 242–46. Murphy, *Lucien Bonaparte Maxwell*, 123–24.
32. Tiller, *Jicarilla Apache Tribe*, 60.

33. Brevet Major Gen. George W. Getty to Brevet Brig. Gen. C. McKeever, Aug. 28, 1867, RG 98, NARA, AC/NMHU.

34. Rupert N. Richardson put the number of warriors encountered at one thousand in *The Comanche Barrier to South Plains Settlement*, 286. Higher estimates came from sources cited by Thelma S. Guild and Harvey L. Carter in *Kit Carson*, 330n3, including Carson's official reports of Dec. 4 and Dec. 16, 1864.

35. Guild and Carter, *Kit Carson*, 250–55.

36. Richardson, *Comanche Barrier to South Plains Settlement*, 286–87.

37. *Report of the Commissioner of Indian Affairs*, 1872, 10.

38. *Report of the Commissioner of Indian Affairs*, 1866, 144–45.

39. Brevet Major Gen. George W. Getty to Brevet Brig. Gen. C. McKeever, Oct. 23, 1867, RG 98, NARA, AC/NMHU.

40. *Report of the Commissioner of Indian Affairs*, 1867, 191.

CHAPTER 2. LUCIEN MAXWELL

1. Murphy, *Lucien Bonaparte Maxwell*, 79–84.

2. Murphy, "Rayado Pioneer Settlement in Northeastern New Mexico," 49.

3. Murphy, *Lucien Bonaparte Maxwell*, 106.

4. See Pearson, *Maxwell Land Grant*, 8–14.

5. Murphy, *Lucien Bonaparte Maxwell*, 154.

6. Pearson, *Maxwell Land Grant*, 11; U.S. Census, Territory of New Mexico, 1880.

7. Goldrick, "From Denver to Santa Fe, No. VII," in *Daily Rocky Mountain News* (Denver), Feb. 6, 1864.

8. Hawthorne (pseud. of Olive Colvin Ennis), "Looking Back: How Issue Day Was Observed in Cimarron in Long Years Gone By," *Las Vegas (NM) Daily Optic*, June 7, 1888. The writer was the wife of Lieutenant Joseph Ennis, who served at Fort Union and suffered a fatal fall from a horse on August 12, 1869. His widow's recollection was from the years 1866 to 1869, an active period at Maxwell's ranch on the Cimarron.

9. Inman, *Old Santa Fe Trail*, 373–88.

10. A shorter version of the portrayal of Maxwell in *The Old Santa Fe Trail* was published in numerous newspapers, mostly in small midwestern towns, in 1891. See, for example, Inman, "The Maxwell Ranche," in *Ness County News* (Ness City, KS), Nov. 21, 1891.

11. Goldrick in *Daily Rocky Mountain News*, Feb. 6, 1864.

12. Cleaveland, *Satan's Paradise*, 13–14.

13. Cleaveland, 7–8.

14. Inman told of Maxwell's allowing chiefs of local bands to sleep on the floor of his great room when they were in the area. Melvin Mills, an eyewitness in Maxwell's last year or so in residence at Cimarron, also spoke of Maxwell's familiar relationship with the Indians and their regular presence around the home ranch. Mills, "Mr. Mills' Address Before Kiwanis Club," *Raton (NM) Reporter*, July 18, 1922.

15. Goldrick in *Daily Rocky Mountain News*, Feb. 6, 1864.

16. Ryus, *Second William Penn*, 108–10.

17. Howbert, *Memories of a Lifetime in the Pike's Peak Region*, 170.
18. Hawthorne, "Looking Back: How Issue Day was Observed in Cimarron."
19. Cleaveland, *Satan's Paradise*, 12–13.
20. Jones, testimony in Transcript of Record: Charles Bent et al. v. Guadalupe Miranda et al., 158–59.
21. Goldrick in *Daily Rocky Mountain News*, Feb. 6, 1864.
22. Mills quoted in the *Raton Reporter*, July 18, 1922.
23. "Interesting Letters from Captain Marcy," *Daily Ohio Statesman* (Columbus), July 6, 1858.
24. "Maxwell's Ranch," *Daily Rocky Mountain News*, Feb. 15, 1866. The piece was signed by "Russell," possibly John T. Russell, editor of the *Santa Fe Gazette* at about this time.
25. Inman, *Old Santa Fe Trail*, 374. Cleaveland, *Satan's Paradise*, 13.
26. Goldrick, *Daily Rocky Mountain News*, Feb. 6, 1864.
27. For a study of regime change and property law on the Maxwell Land Grant, see Montoya, *Translating Property*.
28. Edward Bergman, interviewee, "Duke of Cimarron," *Omaha (NE) Morning World Herald*, Aug. 11, 1895. "Bergman" and "Bergmann" are common spellings of this name.
29. Hawthorne, "Looking Back: How Issue Day was Observed in Cimarron."
30. See Murphy, *Lucien Bonaparte Maxwell*, 198–99. Murphy notes that details of Maxwell's investment are vague, but it is clear that Maxwell lost heavily in the venture.
31. Bergman, "Duke of Cimarron." Inman, *Old Santa Fe Trail*, 375.
32. Mills, *Raton Reporter*, July 18, 1922.
33. Bell, *New Tracks in North America*, 109.
34. George W. Getty, Bvt. Maj. Gen., to Bvt. Brig. Gen. N. H. Davis, Aug. 12, 1869, RG 98, NARA, AC/NMHU.
35. Conard, *"Uncle Dick" Wootton*, 458–59.
36. Bell, *New Tracks in North America*, 110.
37. "Letters from Denver, C. T.," *Boston Herald*, Feb. 8, 1868.
38. Mills, *Raton Reporter*, July 18, 1922.
39. "The Cimarron Mines: A Protest Against Taxes," *Daily Rocky Mountain News*, March 4, 1868.
40. Bergman, "Duke of Cimarron."
41. Lambert, *Stephen Benton Elkins*, 31.
42. Mauzy, *Century in Santa Fe*.
43. In its edition of Oct. 31, 1874, the *Las Vegas (NM) Gazette* reported the theft of some 180 horses and 20 mules from Maxwell's ranch in the Bosque Redondo, but by Dec. 5, the paper could report that a force led by Maxwell had recovered a large number of stolen animals, at least reducing his loss.
44. Longwill, testimony in Transcript of Record: Charles Bent et al. v. Guadalupe Miranda et al., 432–36.
45. Bergman, "Duke of Cimarron."
46. Mills, *Raton Reporter*, July 18, 1922.

CHAPTER 3. GOLD ON THE MAXWELL GRANT

1. Christiansen, *Story of Mining in New Mexico*, 20.
2. Paul, *Mining Frontiers of the Far West*, 156.
3. Paul, 155.
4. See Miller, *California Column in New Mexico*, especially 43–62. Data for members settling in New Mexico are derived from Appendix 1: California Veterans Residing in New Mexico after Discharge, in tandem with U.S. Census records.
5. Miller, 43–60.
6. An effort was made to develop mining properties in an area designated as the "Cimarroncito Mining District," but the promise of viable ore bodies never materialized, and mines first developed in the early 1880s were abandoned in the 1920s, having supported little productive activity in approximately forty years of their existence. Murphy, *Philmont*, 160–64.
7. Raymond, *Statistics of Mines and Mining*, 388–89.
8. Jones, *New Mexico Mines and Minerals*, 141–42. According to Jim Berry Pearson, William H. Moore, William Kroenig's partner in efforts to develop the new strike, received the copper-bearing rock from a Ute man who was grateful for Moore's having helped him when he was severely wounded. This information was from a 1953 interview with William Moore's son, George Moore. Pearson, *Maxwell Land Grant*, 16n24.
9. Murphy, *Boom and Bust on Baldy Mountain*, 10n16.
10. Anderson, *History of New Mexico*, 2:954.
11. Twitchell, *Leading Facts of New Mexican History*, 3:64–68nn21–22.
12. These historians include Twitchell, Jim Berry Pearson, Lawrence R. Murphy, and Darlis A. Miller, in works cited above.
13. Jones, *New Mexico Mines and Minerals*, 142.
14. Clever, *New Mexico*, 33.
15. Watts in "Maxwell's Quartz Mine," *Santa Fe Weekly Gazette*, Nov. 28, 1868.
16. Jones, *New Mexico Mines and Minerals*, 149. Raymond, *Statistics of Mines and Mining*, 385.
17. Morris Bloomfield to John T. Russell, editor, June 9, 1868, *Santa Fe Weekly Gazette*, June 20, 1868.
18. Anderson, *History of New Mexico*, 2:955.
19. *Hartford (CT) Courant*, Dec. 28, 1867.
20. Report of Mills's address to the Kiwanis Club of Raton, New Mexico in *Raton (NM) Range*, Feb. 28, 1925.
21. Sherman, *Ghost Towns and Mining Camps of New Mexico*, 73.
22. *Santa Fe Weekly Gazette*, April 18, 1868.
23. Sherman, *Ghost Towns and Mining Camps of New Mexico*, 73.
24. *Daily Rocky Mountain News*, April 4, 1870.
25. U.S. Census, 1870, Territory of New Mexico, Colfax County, Precinct 1.
26. *Daily Rocky Mountain News*, June 22, 1868.
27. Longwill, testimony in Transcript of Record: Charles Bent et al. v. Guadalupe Miranda et al., 438–43.
28. Martin, testimony in Transcript of Record: Charles Bent et al. v. Guadalupe Miranda et al., 146–47.

CHAPTER 4. IN PAIN AND TROUBLE

1. Fergusson, *Grant of Kingdom*, 158.
2. Concerning details of the sale, see Murphy, *Lucien Bonaparte Maxwell*, 168–86.
3. *Santa Fe Daily New Mexican*, Aug. 2, 1870.
4. Murphy, *Lucien Bonaparte Maxwell*, 189–91. *Daily Rocky Mountain News* (Denver), Nov. 5, 1870.
5. Murphy, 196–205. Concerning Maxwell's use of assistance from Ute and Jicarilla warriors in fighting Plains Indian raiders, see *Galveston (TX) Daily News*, Feb. 25, 1875; and Goddard, *Jicarilla Apache Texts*, 250–51.
6. Collinson and Bell, *Maxwell Land Grant*.
7. The estimate of 3,000 people living in Colfax County in 1870 is based on the 1870 census total for the county, of 1,992, plus a separate tally or estimate of Native Americans serviced by the Cimarron agency, 1,361 as given in the report of a special census by William F. M. Arny in August 1870. See Murphy, *Indian Agent in New Mexico*, 44–45. Most people in Colfax County were situated on lands claimed as part of the Maxwell grant.
8. For a discussion of the "myth of the unsettled West" and the misunderstandings and conflicts fueled by the notion, see Montoya, *Translating Property*, 80–87.
9. *Daily New Mexican*, Sept. 15, 1870.
10. Longwill, testimony in Transcript of Record: Charles Bent et al. v. Guadalupe Miranda et al., 432.
11. Cleaveland, *Satan's Paradise*, 64.
12. *Las Vegas Gazette*, May 24, 1873. "Magnificent Swindle: History of the Maxwell Grant," *Cimarron (NM) News and Press*, Feb. 9, 1879. Copy in files of the author.
13. *Colorado Transcript* (Golden), Oct. 5, 1870.
14. *Colorado Transcript*, Oct. 5, 1870. The *Transcript* published an excerpt from an article in the *Press and Telegraph* of Elizabethtown.
15. *Colorado Miner* (Georgetown), Nov. 3, 1870. The *Miner* presumably was quoting another paper since, by the date of publication of this issue, the New Mexico election had already occurred.
16. *Topeka (KS) Daily Commonwealth*, Oct. 30, 1870.
17. 1st Lt. Edmund Luff to Lt. J. H. Mahnken, Oct. 28, 1870, RG 98, NARA, AC/NMHU.
18. *News and Press*, June 27, 1878. This account, preserved in a clipping in the papers of Frank Springer at the CS Cattle Company, may be the only surviving narrative describing the incident. The writer of this account, published several years after the fact, conveys a somewhat explicit bias against the Maxwell Company concerning its early efforts to evict settlers and, in some cases, to abrogate the claims of miners.
19. *News and Press*, June 27, 1878. According to the *News and Press* account, "All this took place in December 1870."
20. "Petition of 257 Citizens of Colfax County, New Mexico," Records of the U.S. House of Representatives, 41st Cong., Committee on Public Lands, Petitions and Memorials, Folder 15 (HR 41A-H11.1), RG 233, NARA.
21. Cong. Globe, 41st Cong., 3d Sess. 289 (1870); Cong. Globe, 41st Cong., 3d Sess. 1458 (1871).

22. Tameling v. United States Freehold and Emigration Company 93 U.S. 644 (1877). By the Treaty of Guadalupe Hidalgo and its protocols, it was understood that grants made by the Mexican government were to be recognized by the U.S. government subject to Mexican laws in effect when grants were made. This principle, which would have limited the Maxwell grant to approximately 97,000 acres, was upended by the *Tameling* decision, in which the U.S. Supreme Court found that Congress could make a "new grant" larger than that allowed under Mexican law, and that such a grant could be legally confirmed by Congress.

23. The Maxwell Land Grant conflict is generally recognized to have been resolved legally in the U.S. Supreme Court decision in United States v. Maxwell Land-Grant Co. et al. 121 U.S. 325 (1887), which found that Congress had the power to confirm the grant as claimed by the company, and that the claim and survey were free of fraud.

24. *Daily New Mexican*, Jan. 7, 1871.

25. *Cincinnati (OH) Commercial*, Feb. 21, 1871.

26. *County Observer and Monmouthshire Central Advertiser*, March 4, 1871.

27. *Western Home Journal*, April 13, 1871.

28. Collinson, *Report of the President to Holders of Stocks and Bonds*. English text quoted in a retrospective piece in the *Cimarron News and Press*, Feb. 9, 1879.

29. Collinson and Bell, *Maxwell Land Grant*, 15.

30. *Report to Holders of Stocks and Securities of the Maxwell Land Grant and Railway Company 1871*.

31. *Report to Holders of Stocks and Securities of the Maxwell Land Grant and Railway Company 1870*.

32. *Leavenworth (KS) Times*, April 14, 1871. A Santa Fe correspondent is cited as the source of this information.

33. *Idaho World* (Idaho City), March 23, 1871.

34. *Colorado Transcript*, April 5, 1871. The item was reprinted from the *Denver Tribune*.

35. *Colorado Weekly Chieftain* (Pueblo), April 27, 1871. The *Chieftain* stated that twenty-seven English miners were disarmed by twelve "American" miners. Another source reported that twenty-two Cornish miners "armed with Colt's revolvers," had been disarmed by eleven Americans. *Daily Rocky Mountain News*, May 5, 1871.

36. *Daily New Mexican*, April 21, 1871.

37. *Daily Rocky Mountain News*, May 5, 1871.

38. *Las Vegas Daily Gazette*, Oct. 31, 1874.

39. *Elizabethtown Argus*, quoted in *Albuquerque Republican Review*, April 29, 1871.

40. *News and Press*, July 11, 1878.

41. See Lamar, *Far Southwest*, 146–47.

42. *News and Press*, July 11, 1878.

CHAPTER 5. A BREW MADE FOR MAYHEM

1. Morris Bloomfield to Dr. D. W. C. Peters, NARA, Department of the Interior, U.S. Geological Survey, Ferdinand V. Hayden Papers, Hayden correspondence book, Jan. 29, 1870 to Dec. 31, 1872. Reproduced as appendix B in Brayer, *William Blackmore*, 347.

2. From the author's compilation of murders, including lynchings, in Colfax County, New Mexico (and the portion of Mora County that became part of Colfax County in 1869) between 1868 and 1880. Files of the author.

3. For an informative discussion of "the Texans" as a force in Colfax County and other parts of New Mexico and Colorado after the Civil War, see Maddox, *Porter and Ike Stockton*, 3–22.

4. Mills, quoted in Fulton, *New Mexico's Own Chronicle*, 226.

5. *Prescott (AZ) Weekly Journal Miner*, Dec. 23, 1871.

6. Mills, quoted in Twitchell, *Leading Facts of New Mexican History*, 3:80.

7. Mills quoted in Anderson, *History of New Mexico*, 2:683–84.

8. Hart, testimony in Transcript of Record: Charles Bent et al. v. Guadalupe Miranda et al., 117.

9. *Santa Fe Weekly Post*, Sept. 18, 1869. The *Daily Rocky Mountain News* reported that the approved change of venue was to Mora County, rather than Taos as reported by the *Post*. *Daily Rocky Mountain News*, Sept. 8, 1869.

10. Joseph Kinsinger, interviewed in the *Southwest Sentinel* (Silver City, NM), Nov. 24, 1885. Joseph Kinsinger was a brother of Peter Kinsinger, one of the three men involved in the discovery of gold in the Baldy Mountain–Moreno Valley region.

11. *Raton Range*, Feb. 28, 1925. The popular tale of Clay Allison's involvement in the Kennedy hanging, and of the public display of Kennedy's severed head, appeared in print in Agnes Morley Cleaveland's *Satan's Paradise*, and may have originated as a bedtime story told by Fred Lambert's grandmother, as referenced by Cleaveland.

12. Attributed to the *Elizabethtown Press and Telegraph*, quoted in Bryan, *Robbers, Rogues and Ruffians*, 8.

13. *Daily Central City (CO) Register*, Oct. 18, 1871.

14. *Daily Central City Register*, Nov. 1, 1871.

15. *Santa Fe Weekly New Mexican*, Nov. 14, 1871.

16. *News and Press*, July 11, 1878.

17. *Daily New Mexican*, Nov. 15, 1871. *Cimarron News and Press*, July 11, 1878.

18. *News and Press*, July 11, 1878. The informant killed in the bar may have been William Ward or a man identified as "Meehan," both reported killed in such an incident at Cimarron in February 1872. *Colorado Transcript*, Feb. 28, 1872. The *News and Press* article's implication was that the fight was contrived as a pretext for a revenge killing, or perhaps to prevent the witness's further testimony.

19. *Daily Central City Register*, March 16, 1872.

20. *Colorado Daily Chieftain* (Pueblo), May 21, 1872.

21. *Daily Rocky Mountain News*, July 24, 1874.

22. *Denver Daily Times*, July 24, 1872 (quote); *Daily Rocky Mountain News*, Jul 24, 1872.

23. Maddox, *Porter and Ike Stockton*, 25. Maddox's detailed study of Texans and their activities in Colfax County in the 1870s was an indispensable resource for this section.

24. Maddox, 3–53.

25. Porter, *Pencillings of an Early Western Pioneer*, 29.

26. Maddox, *Porter and Ike Stockton*, 6.

27. See Kenner, "Great New Mexico Cattle Raid." Also see Maddux, *John Hittson*, 153–70.

28. The best source of information on Hittson's New Mexico operation may be an interview with him, conducted a few months after the 1872 raid; Hittson said his force was comprised of three parties of approximately thirty men each. *Daily Rocky Mountain News*, April 29, 1873. The *Weekly New Mexican*, Sept. 24, 1872, estimated Hittson's force at sixty men. The high mark was set by the *Colorado Weekly Chieftain*, Oct. 17, 1872, reporting that Hittson's outfit consisted of "three parties, numbering eighty men each."

29. Criminal Docket, 1869–1875, Colfax County Territorial District Court Records, NMSRCA, 81–84.

30. Otero, *My Life on the Frontier, 1864–1882*, 61–62. The father's name was also Miguel Antonio Otero, and his son, the author of this anecdote, was designated "Miguel Antonio Otero II."

31. John Hittson to Hon. William Veale, chairman of the Committee on Indian Affairs, House of Representatives of the State of Texas, Feb. 10, 1873. Hittson's letter was published in numerous newspapers, including the *Austin (TX) Daily Democratic Statesman*, Feb. 19, 1873.

32. For a concise summary of Hittson's operation, see Kenner, "Great New Mexico Cattle Raid."

33. Lomax, *Songs of the Cattle Trail and Cow Camp*, 11. Maddox, *Porter and Ike Stockton*, 23.

34. See *Pueblo (CO) Daily Chieftain*, July 9, 1874; and *Daily Rocky Mountain News*, July 8, 1874.

35. Numerous papers across the nation carried reports of the July 1874 depredations in Colfax County. See, for instance, the *San Francisco Evening Bulletin*, July 24, 1874.

36. *Daily Inter-Ocean*, Aug. 19, 1874.

37. *Colorado Springs Gazette*, May 2, 1874. "Mr. Houx" referred to in the brief note probably was Benjamin F. Houx, who was identified in other references at other times as sheriff and justice of the peace.

38. Letter from the Acting Secretary of the Interior, transmitting *Petition of Citizens of Colfax County, for Removal of Jicarilla Apache and Ute Indians to Their Reservation, to Be Considered in Connection with the Treaty or "Agreement," with Said Indians Presented to Congress, with Letter to the Speaker of the House, February 3, 1874*. Ex. Doc. No. 138, U.S. House of Representatives, 43d Cong., 2d Sess., Records of the U.S. House of Representatives, NARA.

CHAPTER 6. UNSETTLED

1. Frank Springer to Francis Springer, July 27, 1873, FS/CS.
2. Collinson, *Report of the President to Holders of Stocks and Bonds*.
3. *Colorado Daily Chieftain*, March 14, 1873.
4. *Las Animas (CO) Leader*, Sept. 3, 1875.
5. See Cleaveland, *Morleys*, 75.
6. See Caffey, *Chasing the Santa Fe Ring*.
7. Caffey, 53.
8. Pearson, *Maxwell Land Grant*, 110–11.
9. See Cleaveland, *Morleys*, 72–73.
10. Horgan, *Figures in a Landscape*, 9–12.

11. Taylor, *O. P. McMains and the Maxwell Land Grant Conflict*, 127. See also Charles E. Gast to Committee of Share and Bondholders of the Maxwell Land Grant and Railway Company, Sept 1., 1877, MLG.

12. All three women are referenced in written testimony appended to Frank Warner Angel's report of his investigation of charges against Samuel B. Axtell, governor of New Mexico, growing out of Axtell's involvement in controversies in Colfax and Lincoln Counties between 1875 and 1878. Documents written by Mary E. McPherson and Emma Hunt are among evidentiary statements included with the report. *In the Matter of the Investigation of the Charges against S. B. Axtell.*

13. Of 1,725 non-Indian residents of Colfax County in the 1870 census, 1,160 were designated as, "Born in the Territory." The majority of these are likely to have been of Spanish-Mexican, or Hispanic, origin. Francis Walker, Superintendent of the Census, *Statistics of the Population of the United States. Ninth Census—Vol. I*, 1872.

14. See *Las Vegas Daily Optic*, Sept. 2, 1884; and *Las Cruces (NM) Borderer*, Jan. 10, 1872.

15. See *Colorado Weekly Chieftain*, May 16, 1872. The *Chieftain* usually supported Colfax citizens in their struggle against Santa Fe Ring influence. The paper apparently regarded Palen favorably on his merits as judge.

16. See the *Holt County Sentinel* (Oregon, MO), Oct. 29, 1875, quoting from the *Cimarron News and Press.*

17. See *Daily Inter-Ocean*, July 14, 1874; and July 16, 1874.

18. F. J. Tolby to My Dear Niece, July 29, 1874. Copy in Collection of the Old Mill Museum, Cimarron, NM.

19. See Taylor, *O. P. McMains and the Maxwell Land Grant Conflict*, 9–34.

20. Evans, "Old Bum," 239.

21. *Colorado Weekly Chieftain*, Jan. 28, 1875. See also *Las Animas Leader*, Feb. 5, 1875.

22. Maddox, *Porter and Ike Stockton*, 44. Maddox surmises that the Spiller referenced in reports was James Spiller.

23. Maddox, 43.

24. *Denver Mirror*, March 14, 1875.

25. *Weekly New Mexican*, May 18, 1875.

26. *Daily Rocky Mountain News*, June 4, 1875.

27. Kingman, *Kingman Family History*, 152–54.

28. *News and Press*, May 29, 1875.

29. *Las Vegas Gazette*, May 22, 1875.

30. *Colorado Weekly Chieftain*, June 3, 1875.

31. Deposition of Frank Springer, Aug. 9, 1878, Department of the Interior: Appointment Papers, Governor of the Territory of New Mexico, 1848–1907, RG 48, NARA.

32. Alexander G. Irvine to Lt. Col. Thomas C. Devlin, May 10, 1875, RG 98, NARA, AC/NMHU.

33. T. C. Devlin to A. G. Irvine, May 11, 1875, RG 98, NARA, AC/NMHU.

34. *Las Vegas Gazette*, June 19, 1875.

35. *New York Evening Post*, Aug. 9, 1875. The correspondent's dispatch from a camp near Taos, New Mexico, was dated July 13, 1875. The expedition was part of the "Wheeler

Survey," an extensive study of the American West beyond the one hundredth meridian, conducted in multiple expeditions between 1871 and 1879. The survey was primarily engaged in mapping, but also produced a wealth of scientific, cultural, and economic data. Envisioned and led by Maj. George Montague Wheeler, the effort ended when Congress created the United States Geological Survey and assigned many of the Wheeler Survey's functions to the new agency.

36. Westphall, *Thomas Benton Catron and His Era*, 116.

37. *Las Animas (CO) Leader*, Aug. 27, 1875.

38. Brevoort, *New Mexico: Her Natural Resources and Attractions*, 18. Brevoort estimates Colfax County's population at 4,290 persons, probably not including the Utes and Jicarillas, who were part-time residents and unrecognized in census counts of American political units. Women did not vote in this time.

39. Deposition of Frank Springer, Aug. 9, 1878.

40. *New York Sun*, July 5, 1875.

41. A. M. Morley, "One Cowboy Captain," *Albuquerque Morning Journal*, March 27, 1910.

42. Taylor, *O. P. McMains and the Maxwell Land Grant Conflict*, 36. In reporting this information, Taylor relied in part on Colfax County deed records indicating that promissory notes had been given to effect a purchase of land. Efforts by Tolby and associates to secure a home for Indians in the area likely were tentative and aspirational.

43. This portrayal relies on the author's experience of some twelve fall seasons in or near the northern New Mexico mountains. The *Golden (CO) Weekly Globe*, Oct. 2, 1875, described a scene about three hundred miles north of Cimarron: "The dark pine slopes are varied with the golden foliage of the quaking aspen. The traveler comes across a mountain side one mass of dazzling gold, orange, scarlet, or light green like the plumage of a parrot. In other places he rides through colonnades of shimmering gold leaf."

CHAPTER 7. THE TOLBY MURDER AND ITS AFTERMATH

1. *Las Animas Leader*, Oct. 8, 1875.

2. Deposition of Frank Springer, Aug. 9, 1878, Department of the Interior: Appointment Papers, Governor of the Territory of New Mexico, 1848–1907, RG 48, NARA. *In the Matter of the Investigation of the Charges against S. B. Axtell.*

3. *New York Sun*, Dec. 3, 1894. The *Sun*'s article was picked up by numerous other papers around the country.

4. See *Daily New Mexican*, Sept. 18, 1875.

5. Harwood, *History of New Mexico Spanish and English Missions*, 266.

6. See Culley, *Cattle, Horses and Men of the Western Range*, 220. The information came to Culley through Mrs. Crocker's daughter, Annie Crocker Kingman, who recalled the incident as a memory from her girlhood in Cimarron.

7. Culley, 220.

8. *Delphi (IN) Journal*, Nov. 3, 1875.

9. *New York Times*, Nov. 14, 1875.

10. Mary Tolby lived in Indiana until her death in 1923, and remained a member of the Methodist Church for life. She married Erastus H. Smith in 1884. *Lafayette (IN) Journal*

and Courier, Jan. 20, 1923. Rachel Tolby married John Colfax Mahin, and they settled in California, where Rachel's sister, Grace, lived also for a time. U.S. Census, 1900.

11. *Indianapolis Sentinel* (Indianapolis), Aug. 31, 1876.

12. Harwood, *History of New Mexico Spanish and English Missions*, 267–69. Reverend Harwood offers a genteel version of this theory, naming no names; but for readers familiar with the circumstances, his conjecture points clearly enough to Griego.

13. *Saguache (CO) Chronicle*, May 27, 1876. In support of McMains's defense against charges in the killing of Vega, the *Chronicle* recalls that Ring men had earlier accused McMains of murdering Tolby. *Lafayette (IN) Daily Journal*, Oct. 18, 1875. The *Journal* postulated that an Indiana man had conspired to steal Tolby's salary.

14. Records of the Territorial Governors, TANM, Roll 98. The citizens' petition and Axtell's proclamation are found in the Territorial Archives, in records of Axtell's tenure as governor. The petition is undated, but the governor's proclamation was issued Oct. 7, 1875, and appeared in the *Daily New Mexican* of Oct. 8, 1875, and the *Las Vegas Gazette* of Oct. 9, 1875.

15. See Culley, *Cattle, Horses and Men of the Western Range*, 218–19.

16. Deposition of Frank Springer, Aug. 9, 1878.

17. *News and Press*, Aug. 30, 1877. The *News and Press* published a complete account of testimony at the trial of McMains at Mora, New Mexico, Aug. 22–23, 1877, for his role in Cruz Vega's death. Included were accounts of witnesses with whom McMains spoke to arrange the "interview" with Vega, and who were present for some part of the ill-fated interrogation.

18. *News and Press*, Aug. 30, 1877. Reported testimony of William Low at the trial of O. P. McMains. Irvin W. Lacy, testifying after Low, stated that the campfire had been prearranged as a signal to the party coming to detain Vega.

19. Hughes, *Give Me Room!*, 70. The information apparently was from an interview with Mary Lail of Cimarron.

20. *News and Press*, Aug. 30, 1877. Testimony of I. W. Lacy.

21. The party accosting Vega was said by some to have been organized by Clay Allison, a recognized leader among the Texas herders and cowmen of northern Colfax County. Crocker, *Memories of Cimarron*, unpaginated. In his sketch of Clay Allison in *Cattle, Horses and Men of the Western Range*, John H. (Jack) Culley relies on the story that Crocker had heard in his youth.

22. *News and Press*, Aug. 30, 1877. Testimony of William Low at the trial of O. P. McMains.

23. *News and Press*, Aug. 30, 1877. Testimony of Irvin W. Lacy.

24. *Las Animas Leader*, Nov. 5, 1875.

25. *Daily New Mexican*, Nov. 4, 1875.

26. From early newspaper accounts, Francisco Griego is referred to as Vega's relative. Later accounts often refer to Griego as Vega's uncle. Attribution of this relationship appears traceable to two early sources. One is a sketch of Henri Lambert, who lived in Cimarron during events surrounding the Tolby murder, in Anderson, *History of New Mexico*, 2:696–97. Information conveyed to James Steven Peters by Mary Lail indicated that Vega and Manuel Cardenas were cousins raised by Griego, their uncle. Peters, "Postmortem of an Assassination: Parson Tolby and the Maxwell Land Grant," 357. Neither source is conclusive, and there are indications that Griego may have been related by blood not to Vega, but to his wife, Joaquina Griego de Vega.

27. *Las Animas Leader*, Nov. 5, 1875.
28. Culley, *Cattle, Horses and Men of the Western Range*, 217.
29. *Llano (TX) News*, March 26, 1942. The article is credited to the *Houston Post*.
30. Otero, *My Life on the Frontier, 1864–1882*, 121.
31. See Parsons, *Clay Allison*, 2–3.
32. Clifford, *Deep Trails in the Old West*, 28. Frank Clifford was born John Menham Wightman in 1860, in Wales, and went by several aliases after his time in Cimarron. His story, recorded in 1940, is edited with commentary by Frederick Nolan. The author's father, James Temple Wightman, died in September 1874, but the son was in the area until about 1877.
33. Richens Lacy Wootton Jr. related two such incidents to a writer for the *Albuquerque Journal*, Jan. 29, 1920, one occurring at a dance hall in El Moro, Colorado, in which Allison reportedly paid $125 for damaged woodwork and broken glassware after pleading guilty to a related offense and promising to "settle up" to avoid jail time. In an 1879 dance hall incident at Trinidad, Colorado, Allison avoided arrest by agreeing to pay the proprietor $50.
34. Clark, *Clay Allison of the Washita*, 15. Ferd Davis, an acquaintance during wild times in southern Colorado, remarked, "I never knew Allison to give up his gun but once, and that was to Dick Wootton, Jr., former sheriff of Las Animas county. He knew Dick didn't want to murder him."
35. See Sonnichsen, *Ten Texas Feuds*, 3–8.
36. Coe, *Frontier Fighter*, 15.
37. Schoenberger, *Gunfighters*, 10.
38. Coe, *Frontier Fighter*, 13.
39. *Trinidad (CO) Enterprise and Chronicle*, April 6, 1877. There are several accounts of the killing of Pancho Griego, varying in detail, but similar as to basic facts. The account most used here appeared in the *Trinidad Enterprise and Chronicle*, based on an interview with Allison. The writer spoke with Allison several times during his trial for killing Charles Faber in 1877. The writer had invited Allison to tell his story concerning three shooting deaths attributed to him.
40. *Enterprise and Chronicle*, April 6, 1877.
41. Soldiers and Sailors Database; and Fort Union Historic Research Study. See also U.S. Census, 1860–1890. *Daily New Mexican*, March 1, 1895.
42. Brevet Brigadier General William N. Grier to R. H. Longwell, Acting Assistant Surgeon, March 9, 1870, RG 98, NARA. Grier to Brevet Major William A. Kobbe, March 10, 1870, RG 98, NARA, AC/NMHU. "Longwill" and "Longwell" are common spellings in references to Robert Longwill and his family. In quoted material in this text, both spellings are used as published.
43. Stock Ledger, Maxwell Land Grant and Railway Company, Aug. 30, 1870, MLG. *Daily New Mexican*, Oct. 19, 1870.
44. *Daily Rocky Mountain News*, Nov. 5, 1870; *Democratic Advocate*, Jan. 5, 1871.
45. 1st Lt. Edmund Luff to Lt. J. H. Mahnken, Oct. 28, 1870, RG 98, NARA, AC/NMHU.
46. *Daily New Mexican*, Oct. 28, 1870.
47. *News and Press*, June 20, 1878.
48. Deposition of Frank Springer, Aug. 9, 1878. See also *Laws of the Territory of New Mexico*.

49. Deposition of Frank Springer, Aug. 9, 1878.

50. Longwill was in charge of the agency from approximately October 1872 to March 1873. *Las Vegas Gazette*, Nov. 2, 1872; *Daily New Mexican*, March 24, 1873. He was again in charge, with the modest title of "Farmer in Charge," between April 1874 and December 1874. *Report of the Commissioner of Indian Affairs*, 1874, 305.

51. In publications of the University of Pennsylvania, the eldest Longwill son appears as "Stephen Benton Elkins Longwell." *University Bulletin; Catalogue of the University of Pennsylvania, 1899–1900*. Otherwise, the first name is generally dropped in favor of a simpler version: "Benton Elkins Longwell." The son preferred the alternative spelling "Longwell."

52. *New York Sun*, Dec. 3, 1894.

53. *News and Press*, June 20, 1878.

54. Affidavit of William R. Morley, sworn before Harry Whigham, Notary Public, June 15, 1878. Copy in the files of Frank Springer, FS/CS.

55. *New York Sun*, Nov. 29, 1885.

56. Deposition of Frank Springer, Aug. 9, 1878; Affidavit of William R. Morley, June 15, 1878. Holographic copies of correspondence among Longwill, Elkins, Lemuel Jones, and W. B. Hogan concerning the death of John Glass are in the Frank Springer Papers, FS/CS. Copies of these items are in files of the author.

CHAPTER 8. A TOWN IN TURMOIL

1. *Daily New Mexican*, Nov. 9, 1875.

2. *Daily New Mexican*, Nov. 10, 1875.

3. The timeline for events occurring between Nov. 5 and Nov. 11, 1875, is derived primarily from an account titled "City and County," originally published in the *Cimarron News and Press*. A transcription of the article is in Records of the Office of the Secretary of the Interior, Governor Appointment Papers for the Territory of New Mexico, 1873–1907, Microcopy 750, Roll 1, RG 48, NARA. The transcribed article is undated, but presumably was published in mid-November 1875, shortly after the reported events and testimony occurred. Other accounts covering this period vary as to the dates of particular events; this document appears to provide the most detailed, internally consistent, and accurate account.

4. "City and County." Cardenas's sworn statement is included in the article as part of a recital of testimony and evidence given in a hearing at Cimarron on Nov. 10, 1875.

5. "City and County." The *News and Press* reported the arrests of Donoghue and Mills, as well as the foiled pursuit of Longwill, as included in the handwritten transcription in Department of the Interior files.

6. Lt. George A. Cornish to Col. Gordon G. Granger, Santa Fe, Nov. 8, 1875, U.S. Army District of New Mexico, telegrams sent and received, RG 98, NARA, AC/NMHU.

7. M. W. Mills to C. N. Blackwell, Feb. 13, 1924, copy in Collection of the Old Mill Museum, Cimarron, NM.

8. Lt. George A. Cornish to A.A.A. General, Santa Fe, Nov. 9, 1875, U.S. Army District of New Mexico, telegrams sent and received, RG 98, NARA, AC/NMHU.

9. Lt. George A. Cornish to A.A.A. General, Santa Fe, Nov. 11, 1875, U.S. Army District of New Mexico, telegrams sent and received, RG 98, NARA, AC/NMHU.

NOTES TO CHAPTER 8

10. Trauer apparently called on Capt. John C. McFerran at Fort Union, in June 1862, on business of "the firm." M. Trauer to Capt. J. C. McFerran, Fort Union, June 26, 1862, War Department Collection of Confederate Records: Papers Relating to Citizens, 1861–1867, RG 109, NARA. William A. Keleher also places Trauer at Fort Stanton in 1862, noting that Trauer saw Christopher "Kit" Carson and formed an impression of him. Keleher, *Maxwell Land Grant*, 65.

11. *Daily New Mexican*, Nov. 5, 1874; *Colorado Weekly Chieftain*, Jan. 28, 1875.

12. Citizens' petition, Records of the Territorial Governors, TANM, Roll 98.

13. *Daily New Mexican*, Feb. 9, 1875; *Las Vegas Gazette*, Oct. 23, 1875.

14. "City and County."

15. "City and County."

16. Culley, *Cattle, Horses and Men of the Western Range*, 216.

17. Lt. George A. Cornish to recipients at U.S. Army command, District of New Mexico, Nov. 8, Nov. 9, and Nov. 11 (two messages), 1875, RG 98, NARA, AC/NMHU.

18. *New York Sun*, Nov. 25, 1894.

19. "City and County."

20. "City and County."

21. *Silver City (NM) Eagle*, March 20, 1895.

22. Lt. George A. Cornish to Col. G. Granger, Santa Fe, Nov. 8, 1875, RG 98, NARA, AC/NMHU.

23. For the rationale for identifying each of these individuals in connection with the Santa Fe Ring, see Caffey, *Chasing the Santa Fe Ring*, 241–58.

24. "City and County." The account of witness testimony is from the *News and Press* transcription unless otherwise noted.

25. *New York Sun*, Dec. 3, 1894.

26. *New York Sun*, Dec. 3, 1894. The *Sun* article appears to be based on an interview with "the man from New Mexico," who is not identified, and provides the only detailed eyewitness account of the event. The narrator apparently had attended the hearing, and the route to his destination put him near the jail in time to witness the killing.

27. Lt. George A. Cornish to C.O., District of New Mexico, Santa Fe, Nov. 11, 1875, RG 98, NARA, AC/NMHU.

28. *New York Sun*, Dec. 3, 1894.

29. A mention of Herberger as the possible assassin of Cardenas appears in the biographical note on Melvin W. Mills in Twitchell, *Leading Facts of New Mexican History*, 2:82n31.

30. Lt. George A. Cornish to A.A.A. General, Santa Fe, Nov. 11, 1875, RG 98, NARA, AC/NMHU.

31. Culley, *Cattle, Horses and Men of the Western Range*, 218–19. Culley relates the narrative of George E. Crocker concerning Allison's alleged role in the killing of Manuel Cardenas.

32. Harwood, *History of New Mexico Spanish and English Missions*, 267.

33. "Proceedings of the Citizens' Meetings," transcribed from the *News and Press*, ca. Nov. 11, 1875, Records of the Office of the Secretary of the Interior, Governor Appointment Papers for the Territory of New Mexico, 1873–1907, Microcopy 750, Roll 1, RG 48, NARA.

34. "Proceedings of the Citizens' Meetings."

35. Lt. George A. Cornish to A.A.A. General, Santa Fe, Nov. 11, 1875.

36. Reprinted from the *Western Christian Advocate* in the *Lafayette Daily Journal*, Nov. 18, 1875.

CHAPTER 9. RUMORS OF AN INDIAN WAR

1. Thomas Blair, A.A.A.G., Santa Fe, to Lt. George Cornish, Nov. 13, 1875, RG 98, NARA, AC/NMHU. Lt. Blair was designated "Acting Assistant Adjutant General," representing Col. Gordon Granger, commanding officer for the District of New Mexico.

2. *Report of the Commissioner of Indian Affairs*, 1874, 5. This point is raised by Reeve in "Federal Indian Policy in New Mexico," 146–91.

3. Veronica Velarde Tiller, comment to the author in personal correspondence, Oct. 2021.

4. *Las Vegas Gazette*, Feb. 20, 1875.

5. *Daily New Mexican*, Feb. 18, 1875, reprinted from the *Cimarron News and Press*. See also *Daily New Mexican*, March 24, 1875.

6. Jicarilla leaders had never conceded ownership of lands of which they had been dispossessed by non-Indian settlers. The U.S. Indian Claims Commission, created in 1946, determined that large masses of land had been owned by, and taken from, the Utes and Jicarillas and other tribes. See Nordhaus, *Tipi Rings*, especially 117–41.

7. Wooster, *Nelson A. Miles*, 72.

8. *Daily New Mexican*, Nov. 17, 1875. Other accounts of the incident vary somewhat in their recitals of the facts. See, for example, Crocker, *Memories of Cimarron*, unpaginated.

9. *New Orleans Times-Picayune*, Dec. 9, 1875, reprinted from the *Cimarron News and Press*.

10. Goddard, *Jicarilla Apache Texts*, 254. Goddard collected his texts in interviews with Jicarilla informants between August and October 1909.

11. Alexander G. Irvine, U.S. Indian Agent, to Gen. Gordon Granger, Commanding Officer, District of New Mexico, Nov. 17, 1875, RG 98, NARA, AC/NMHU.

12. Lt. John Lafferty to A.A.A. General, Dist. of N.M., Santa Fe, Nov. 19, 1875, RG 98, NARA, AC/NMHU.

13. A. G. Irvine to A.A.A. General, Santa Fe, Nov. 20, 1875, RG 98, NARA, AC/NMHU.

14. *Times-Picayune*, Dec. 9, 1875, reprinted from the *Cimarron News and Press*.

15. *Weekly New Mexican*, Nov. 30, 1875. The source was a dispatch from Cimarron dated Nov. 26, 1875.

16. *Times-Picayune*, Dec. 9, 1875, reprinted from the *Cimarron News and Press*.

17. *Times-Picayune*, Nov. 27, 1875, reprinted from the *Cimarron News and Press*.

18. *Saint Louis Globe-Democrat*, Dec. 1, 1875. The source was a report from Denver, published previously in the *Kansas City Times*.

19. *Times-Picayune*, Dec. 9, 1875, reprinted from the *Cimarron News and Press*.

20. *Las Vegas Gazette*, Dec. 4, 1875.

21. John Pope, Bvt. Maj. Genl., Commanding., Dept. of the Missouri, Ft. Leavenworth, KS, to Col. G. Granger, Commanding, Dist. of New Mexico, Santa Fe, Nov. 27, 1875 (two messages); and T. A. McParlin, Surgeon and Chief Medical Director, Dist. of New Mexico, Santa Fe, to Hd. Qrs., Dept. of the Missouri, Ft. Leavenworth, KS, Nov. 27, 1875, RG 98, NARA, AC/NMHU.

22. *News and Press*, Nov. 27, 1875.
23. R. Williams, A.A.G., by command of Gen. Pope, to Commanding Officer, Dist. of Santa Fe, Dec. 1, 1875, RG 98, NARA, AC/NMHU.
24. *Las Vegas Gazette*, Dec. 4, 1875.
25. Miles, *Personal Recollections and Observations*, 182–84.
26. Miles, 184.
27. *Las Vegas Gazette*, Dec. 25, 1875.
28. A law providing for compensation to settlers and entrepreneurs for losses in Indian depredations also fueled efforts to sustain a state of conflict and incentivized fraudulent claims, including some involving the Utes and Jicarillas. Michno, *Depredation and Deceit* (see especially 249–53).
29. *Leavenworth Times*, Jan. 6, 1876.
30. *Helena (MT) Weekly Herald*, Dec. 9, 1875.
31. Lt. S. S. Stafford, Dist. of New Mexico, to Capt. William McCleave, 8th Cavalry, Fort Union, Dec. 23, 1875, RG 98, NARA, AC/NMHU.
32. See Tiller, *Jicarilla Apache Tribe*, 81–82.

CHAPTER 10. THE WHIRLWIND

1. *News and Press*, as reprinted in the *Daily New Mexican*, Dec. 29, 1875.
2. *New York Sun*, Dec. 16, 1875.
3. *Daily New Mexican*, Jan. 21, 1876. *Las Animas Leader*, Jan. 28, 1876.
4. *Las Animas Leader*, Jan. 28, 1876.
5. Porter, *Pencillings of an Early Western Pioneer*, 29.
6. "Clay Allison's Edition" may first have been mentioned in print in the *Live Stock Journal of New Mexico*, July 22, 1887, as quoted and cited in Stanley, *Grant That Maxwell Bought*, 156. The *Live Stock Journal of New Mexico* was published with the *Raton Range* of this date. The incident is retold without attribution in numerous accounts of Allison's life and exploits.
7. *Steamboat Springs (CO) Pilot*, June 14, 1916. Cleaveland, *No Life for a Lady*, 8.
8. Concerning Dawson's informative sketches of towns and places in territorial New Mexico written after his relocation to Santa Fe, see Tórrez, *New Mexico in 1876–1877*.
9. *Daily New Mexican*, Feb. 8, 1876.
10. *News and Press*, Feb. 18, 1876.
11. M. W. Mills to C. N. Blackwell, Feb. 13, 1924, collection of the Old Mill Museum, Cimarron, NM.
12. Orange Phelps succeeded Samuel Trauer as justice of the peace for Colfax County, Precinct 3. Oath of Office for Orange Phelps, Justice of the Peace, Precinct 3, March 4, 1876, Oaths and Bonds of County Officials, Roll 36, TANM.
13. *Daily New Mexican*, Jan. 22, 1876.
14. Military correspondence Jan. 4, 1876 to March 13, 1876, culminating in confirmation from Fort Union that troops were being dispatched to Colfax County. Maj. James F. Wade, Fort Union, to Gen. Edward Hatch, Santa Fe, March 13, 1876, RG 98, NARA, AC/NMHU.
15. S. B. Axtell to O. K. Chittenden, Feb. 21, 1876, holographic copy, FS/CS.

16. House Journal, 22nd Legislative Assembly, Territory of New Mexico, 1875–1876, TANM. See also *Las Vegas Gazette*, Feb. 19, 1876, in which Mills elaborates on his rationale in opposing the legislation.

17. Cleaveland, *Morleys*, 113.

18. *News and Press*, Feb. 4 and Feb. 11, 1876.

19. Affidavit of Frank Springer, June 10, 1878, U.S. Department of the Interior: Appointment Papers, Governor of the Territory of New Mexico, 1848–1907, RG 48, NARA.

20. Affidavit of Frank Springer, June 10, 1878.

21. S. B. Axtell, Governor of New Mexico, to Maj. James F. Wade, Fort Union, Jan. 24, 1876, U.S. Army District of New Mexico, telegrams sent and received, RG 98, NARA, AC/NMHU.

22. Affidavit of Frank Springer, June 10, 1878.

23. Affidavit of Frank Springer, June 10, 1878.

24. *Saint Louis Republican*, March 1, 1876; *Leavenworth (KS) Daily Commercial*, March 2, 1876.

25. See Billington, *New Mexico's Buffalo Soldiers*, 67.

26. Deposition of Frank Springer, Aug. 9, 1878, Department of the Interior: Appointment Papers, Governor of the Territory of New Mexico, 1848–1907, RG 48, NARA.

27. Deposition of Frank Springer, Aug. 9, 1878. Maj. J. F. Wade, 9th Cavalry, to Acting Assistant Adjutant General, District of NM, Santa Fe, April 9, 1876, Fort Union Letter Books, Letters sent, vol. 16, 462–63, RG 98, NARA, AC/NMHU.

28. Crocker, *Memories of Cimarron*. Crocker moved to Cimarron with his family at age five, in 1871, and lived there until 1882. He was ten years old at the time of the shooting incident referenced. Stories are presumed to be as he heard them from others, remembered and written decades later before his death in 1953.

29. *Las Vegas Gazette*, April 1, 1876.

30. Crocker, *Memories of Cimarron*.

31. *Moab (UT) Times Independent*, May 31, 1934.

32. *Daily New Mexican*, Aug. 16, 1876. Cited as the source was the *Cimarron News and Press*, Aug. 11, 1876.

33. *Las Vegas Gazette*, Sept. 23, 1876.

34. *Las Vegas Gazette*, Oct. 7, 1876. Orange Phelps was the justice of the peace criticized for leniency in the case.

35. *Las Vegas Gazette*, Oct. 7, 1876.

36. Utley, *High Noon in Lincoln*, 175–77.

37. Billington, *New Mexico's Buffalo Soldiers*, 67.

38. *Weekly New Mexican*, May 2, 1876.

39. See Pagán, *Valley of the Guns*, 14–15.

40. Peters, "Allison Brothers of Tennessee," 8–9.

CHAPTER 11. THE COMING OF THE LAW

1. See Ebright, *Land Grants and Lawsuits in Northern New Mexico*, 70.

2. During the relatively brief period of Mexican administration following the Mexican Revolution of 1821, the governor was, for a time, known as the *jefe politico*, or political chief,

and larger communities were governed by a local *ayuntamiento*, or council, in preference to the *alcalde mayor* designated during the Spanish ascendancy. Twitchell, *Leading Facts of New Mexican History*, 2:8–9.

3. Ebright, *Land Grants and Lawsuits in Northern New Mexico*, 67–68.

4. Twitchell, *Leading Facts of New Mexican History*, 2:13. See also Ebright, *Land Grants and Lawsuits in Northern New Mexico*, 60.

5. Swarthout, *Skeletons*, 68.

6. Pomeroy, *Territories and the United States*, 51.

7. See Caffey, *Chasing the Santa Fe Ring*, 244–45. See also Speer and Brown, *Encyclopedia of the New West*, 36.

8. Poldervaart, *Black-Robed Justice*, 1.

9. Lt. John S. Loud, Acting Asst. Adjt. Gen., Santa Fe, to Capt. Chambers McKibbin, 15th Infantry, Fort Marcy, March 30, 1876, RG 98, NARA, AC/NMHU.

10. See Deposition of Frank Springer, Aug. 9, 1878, Department of the Interior: Appointment Papers, Governor of the Territory of New Mexico, 1848–1907, RG 48, NARA.

11. *Colorado Daily Chieftain*, May 20, 1876.

12. Deposition of Frank Springer, Aug. 9, 1878.

13. *Colorado Daily Chieftain*, May 20, 1876.

14. Henry Waldo's middle name appears in varied forms, as Ludlow, Linn, and Lynn.

15. Twitchell, *Leading Facts of New Mexican History*, 2:484–85n395.

16. Though they were associated in business and politics from the mid-1860s until Elkins's death in 1911, Catron and Elkins were partners in a private law practice only briefly, between January 1874 and May 1876. Westphall, *Thomas Benton Catron and His Era*, 399.

17. *Daily New Mexican*, May 1, 1876.

18. *Daily New Mexican*, May 1, 1876.

19. *Daily New Mexican*, May 1, 1876.

20. See *Daily New Mexican*, July 12, 1876.

21. Affidavit of Frank Springer, June 10, 1878, Department of the Interior: Appointment Papers, Governor of the Territory of New Mexico, 1848–1907, RG 48, NARA.

22. Schoenberger, *Gunfighters*, 11. Sources refer to Cooper as "Tom," "Bill," or simply "a man named Cooper." In documents of the territorial government, his name is Charles Cooper.

23. Ritch, "Honor vs. Coddling: Springer Redivivus," holographic manuscript, n.d., Papers of William Gillet Ritch. See also "R. C. Allison Proclamation for Reward," Feb. 21, 1876, Executive Record Books, 1851–Jan. 15, 1912, Reel 21, TANM.

24. Peters, "Allison Brothers of Tennessee," 9.

25. Crocker, *Memories of Cimarron*.

26. Ritch, untitled note of the June 1876 meeting between Allison and Axtell, holographic manuscript, n.d., Papers of William Gillet Ritch.

27. *Enterprise and Chronicle*, April 6, 1877. The article, "A Texas Desperado," giving Allison's account, was found in Frank Springer's scrapbook of clippings from the 1870s. Copy in files of the author. The *Las Animas Leader* offered a report more favorable to the local lawman, Charles Faber, and less favorable to the Allisons (Dec. 22, 1876).

28. *Las Vegas Gazette*, March 31, 1877.

29. Deposition of Frank Springer, Aug. 9, 1878.
30. *Daily New Mexican*, May 15, 1876.
31. M. W. Mills to C. N. Blackwell, Feb. 13, 1924, Collection of the Old Mill Museum, Cimarron, NM.
32. Knudsen, "Mills Mansion Has Become a Shell of Its Former Self."
33. Mills to Blackwell, Feb. 13, 1924.
34. *Colorado Daily Chieftain*, May 20, 1876.
35. "City and County," *Cimarron News and Press*. Transcription in files of the Department of the Interior, Governor Appointment Papers for the Territory of New Mexico, 1873–1907, Microcopy 750, Roll 1, RG 48, NARA.
36. *Colorado Daily Chieftain*, June 4, 1876.
37. *Colorado Daily Chieftain*, June 4, 1876.
38. *Colorado Weekly Chieftain*, May 10, 1877.
39. *Las Vegas Gazette*, Aug. 25, 1877; *Weekly New Mexican*, Sept. 4, 1877.
40. *Colorado Weekly Chieftain*, Sept. 6, 1877.
41. *News and Press*, Aug. 30, 1877.
42. *Colorado Weekly Chieftain*, April 11, 1878.

CHAPTER 12. A MOST AUDACIOUS RING

1. See Caffey, *Chasing the Santa Fe Ring*, 53.
2. *New York Sun*, Aug. 16, 1875. Franklin Tolby and William Morley fell under suspicion as likely authors or informants for this and other such pieces appearing in the *Sun* in the summer of 1875.
3. *Las Vegas Gazette*, April 6, 1878.
4. Mary McPherson's father, William Tibbles, was described as a "circuit rider" for the church. One brother, William Harvey Tibbles, was a lifelong, regularly appointed Methodist minister; and brother Thomas Henry Tibbles was ordained in the Methodist Church, but later served in Presbyterian and Unitarian churches. In the last year of her life, McPherson was involved in a Ladies Aid Association tribute to the "Founders of Methodism." *Washington (DC) Evening Star*, March 17, 1897.
5. Cleaveland, *Morleys*, 91.
6. Cleaveland, 89.
7. Cleaveland, 91. Cleaveland was clear, perhaps based on his mother's word, that Mary Tibbles McPherson had written the letter taken from the post office by Ada Morley, and that it concerned alleged corruption among territorial officials.
8. Deposition of Frank Springer, Aug. 9, 1878, Department of the Interior: Appointment Papers, Governor of the Territory of New Mexico, 1848–1907, RG 48, NARA. Cleaveland, *Morleys*, 91. In his biography of Catron, Victor Westphall referred to the letter in question as having been mailed by Ada Morley's sister, but there is no apparent basis for this notion, and Westphall appears to have dropped the reference by 1988, when he presented in a symposium on the Santa Fe Ring. Westphall, *Thomas Benton Catron and His Era*, 116. Also, Westphall, "Colfax County War and the Santa Fe Ring."

9. Westphall, *Thomas Benton Catron and His Era*, 116–20. Westphall probably offers the most complete account of the incident, including charges and official responses from records of the Justice Department (RG 60) and reports of U.S. Attorneys in the U.S. National Archives. The principal source concerning the writer and content of the letter taken from the Cimarron post office is Cleaveland, *Morleys*, 91–94.

10. Deposition of Frank Springer, Aug. 9, 1878.

11. Statement of Asa Middaugh, March 31, 1876, *In the Matter of the Investigation of the Charges against S. B. Axtell*.

12. Westphall, *Thomas Benton Catron and His Era*, 117–19. T. B. Catron to Alonso Taft, Feb. 24, 1877, Records of the Department of Justice, RG 60, NARA.

13. Cleaveland, *Morleys*, 125. Cleaveland provides a useful account of Mary McPherson's efforts to assist O. P. McMains and raise awareness in the administrations of U. S. Grant and Rutherford B. Hayes, regarding corruption among officials in New Mexico. He details McPherson's contacts and activities, using correspondence from family records. Substantial family archives are in the special collections of the New Mexico State University Library.

14. Cleaveland, *Morleys*, 125.

15. Taylor, *O. P. McMains and the Maxwell Land Grant Conflict*, 52–53.

16. Mrs. Mary E. McPherson to Attorney General Taft, Feb. 7, 1877, Records of the Department of Justice, RG 60, NARA.

17. Westphall, *Thomas Benton Catron and His Era*, 119–20. Catron to Taft, Feb. 24, 1877, Records of the Department of Justice, RG 60, NARA.

18. W. R. Morley to Mary E. McPherson, March 6, 1877, Records of the Department of the Interior, RG 48, NARA.

19. Ada McPherson Morley to Mary E. McPherson, March 7, 1877. A transcription of the letter appears in Cleaveland, *Morleys*, 129–32.

20. W. B. Matchett and M. E. McPherson to Secretary of the Interior Carl Schurz, March 1877, Records of the Department of the Interior, RG 48, NARA.

21. W. B. Matchett and M. E. McPherson to President Rutherford B. Hayes, April 1877, Records of the Department of the Interior, RG 48, NARA.

22. Samuel B. Axtell to Secretary of the Interior Carl Schurz, June 14, 1877, Records of the Department of the Interior, RG 48, NARA.

23. *San Francisco Chronicle*, April 1, 1877.

24. *Colorado Weekly Chieftain*, April 19, 1877.

25. *Daily New Mexican*, April 7, 1877.

26. W. B. Matchett and M. E. McPherson to Hon. Secretary of the Interior [Carl Schurz], May 5, 1877, Records of the Department of the Interior, RG 48, NARA.

27. McPherson and Matchett, *In the matter of the Charges Vs. Governor Samuel B. Axtell and Other New Mexican Officials*.

28. *Deseret News* (Salt Lake City), July 16, 1877.

29. W. R. Morley to Charles Devens, Attorney General, Sept. 3, 1877, Records of the Department of Justice, RG 60, NARA.

30. Bowden, "Private Land Claims in the Southwest," 4:842–43.

31. H. Merriam to Hon. Sec. of the Interior, n.d., Records of the Department of the Interior, RG 48, NARA. As the referenced and attached affidavits are dated July 31 and Aug. 30, 1877, it is reasonable to surmise that Merriam's letter reached Washington in September 1877 or thereabout.

32. *Washington Evening Star*, Sept. 29, 1877.

33. M. E. McPherson to Carl Schurz, Sept. 30, 1877, Records of the Department of the Interior, RG 48, NARA.

CHAPTER 13. A RECKONING

1. Hough, *Story of the Outlaw*, 200. Hough's thirty-one-page chapter on the Lincoln County War tracks reasonably well with later, more comprehensive treatments. It was "the first of many, many accounts of the Lincoln County War," wrote the ultimate scholar of the affair, Frederick Nolan. Nolan, *Lincoln County War*, 437. The summary account related here relies on these two sources.

2. Mullin, *Fulton's History of the Lincoln County War*, 111–12.

3. See Nolan, *Lincoln County War*, 199–212. Billy also used other names, at times identifying himself as Henry Antrim or Henry McCarty.

4. See Jacobsen, *Such Men as Billy the Kid*, 114.

5. Nolan, *Lincoln County War*, 508.

6. Edward Thornton to William M. Evarts, March 9, 1878, Records of the Department of Justice, File 44-4-8, RG 60, NARA.

7. Montague R. Leverson to Rutherford B. Hayes, president, March 16, 1878, in Angel, *In the Matter of the Lincoln County Troubles*; and *In the Matter of the Cause and Circumstances of the Death of John H. Tunstall*. Evidence supporting both reports was submitted on Nov. 27, 1878, with the report on the death of Tunstall. Leverson to Edward Thornton, March 16, 1878, British Foreign Office File F05–1965, transcribed in Nolan, *Life and Death of John Henry Tunstall*, 292–95. Leverson to John C. Sherman, March 20, 1878; see Nolan, *Lincoln County War*, 238–39. Leverson to Carl Schurz, March 25, 1878, cited in Nolan, *Lincoln County War*, 241.

8. Henry M. Arms to William M. Evarts, March 23, 1878, Records of the Department of Justice, RG 60, NARA.

9. For an informed discussion of the Uña de Gato claim, Catron's involvement in it, and the roles of Lewis Kingman and Henry Arms, see Westphall, *Mercedes Reales*, 185–89.

10. Frank Springer to Rush Clark, April 9, 1878, Records of the Department of War, RG 165, NARA. Copy seen in Chase Ranch Records, New Mexico State University.

11. Nolan, *Lincoln County War*, 254.

12. Nolan, 253.

13. Carl Schurz to Frank W. Angel, April 16, 1878, Records of the Office of the Assistant Attorney General for the Department of the Interior, RG 48, NARA.

14. See Nolan, *Lincoln County War*, 297.

15. *Weekly New Mexican*, May 4, 1878.

16. For these dates, Victor Westphall cites letters in files of the Justice Department from Angel to U.S. Attorney General Charles Devens on July 10 and 16, 1878, in *Thomas Benton Catron and His Era*, 126, 411n5.

NOTES TO CHAPTER 13

17. Angel, *Lincoln County Troubles*. Referring to the two sides in the dispute, Angel writes in the introduction to his report, "Both have done many things contrary to the law; both have violated the law." Nonetheless, he observes that McSween acted conscientiously, while Murphy and his successors acted for private gain and revenge.

18. Frank Warner Angel to E. C. Watkins, U.S. Indian Inspector, July 2, 1878. This letter is included in the official report, Angel, *In the Matter of the Examination of the Charges against C. F. Godfroy*, Records of the Bureau of Indian Affairs, U.S. Department of the Interior, RG 75, NARA.

19. Angel, *Death of John H. Tunstall*.

20. According to records of Angel's report on the *Lincoln County Troubles*, he took a total of four affidavits from witnesses in Doña Ana County on June 16 and 17, 1878, returning to Lincoln County to obtain additional affidavits. While no other statements identified as having been taken in Doña Ana are included in his reports, the *Mesilla Valley (NM) Independent* of July 6, 1878, reported Angel's arrival in Las Cruces the previous evening. By Westphall's account, based on Angel's communications with the Department of Justice, Angel was back in Santa Fe by July 16, awaiting funds requested for travel to Las Vegas and Cimarron in pursuit of additional testimony; Westphall, *Thomas Benton Catron and His Era*, 127.

21. Deposition of Frank Springer, Aug. 9, 1878, Department of the Interior: Appointment Papers, Governor of the Territory of New Mexico, 1848–1907, RG 48, NARA; Angel, *In the Matter of the Investigation of the Charges against S. B. Axtell, Governor of New Mexico*.

22. See Westphall, *Thomas Benton Catron and His Era*, 128.

23. Theisen, "Frank Warner Angel's Notes on New Mexico Territory," 336–37. *Denver Daily Tribune*, Aug. 17, 1878.

24. Crocker, *Memories of Cimarron*. Crocker was five years old when his family moved to Cimarron in 1871. He was an older adult when he wrote his memoir of Cimarron in the 1870s.

25. *News and Press*, Sept. 6, 1878.

26. *Salt Lake City Deseret News*, Sept. 11, 1878.

27. *Troy (KS) Bulletin*, Sept. 14, 1878.

28. *Indiana State Sentinel* (Indianapolis), Sept. 11, 1878.

29. See Henry M. Arms to William M. Evarts, Sec. of State, referred to Carl Schurz, Sec. of the Interior, March 13, 1878, File 44-4-8, RG 60, NARA.

30. See S. B. Elkins to George C. Wing, chief clerk, U.S. Dept. of Justice, n.d.; Wing to S. B. Elkins, Sept. 7, 1878; S. B. Elkins to Charles Devens, Sept. 13, 1878; and S. B. Elkins to Charles Devens, Sept. 24, 1878, all in File 44-4-8, RG 60, NARA.

31. Catron to Devens, Oct. 10, 1878, File 44-4-8, RG 60, NARA.

32. Devens to Catron, Nov. 12, 1878, copy of telegram sent, File 44-4-8, RG 60, NARA.

33. *Santa Fe Sentinel*, Aug. 22, 1878. Clippings included in Angel, *In the Matter of the Investigation of the Charges against S. B. Axtell*.

34. T. B. Catron to S. B. Elkins, Sept. 26, 1892, TBC.

35. S. D. Miller to T. B. Catron, Oct. 3, 1892, TBC.

36. Catron to Elkins, Feb. 5, 1893, TBC.

37. Westphall, *Mercedes Reales*, 86–88.

38. Taylor, "Uña de Gato Grant in Colfax County," 142–43n58.

39. See Wilson, *Merchants, Guns, and Money*, 210; and Utley, *High Noon in Lincoln County*, 118–19.

40. Utley, 119.

41. Jacobsen, *Such Men as Billy the Kid*, 285.

CHAPTER 14. SETTLING THE MAXWELL GRANT CONFLICT

1. Delaney, *Southern Ute People*, 57.

2. *Weekly New Mexican*, Nov. 1, 1879. Of the Jicarillas' removal from the Cimarron country to their proposed reservation, the *New Mexican* remarked, "Agent [Benjamin M.] Thomas started with them from Cimarron last Sunday, much to the relief of the people of Colfax County."

3. See Tiller, *Jicarilla Apache Tribe*, 96. See also *Report of the Commissioner of Indian Affairs*, 1887, lxxii–lxxiv.

4. Tiller, *Jicarilla Apache Tribe*, 81–98. Concerning the location of the reservation in relation to the traditional Jicarilla homeland, see Nordhaus, *Tipi Rings*, 14–26.

5. Porter, *Pencillings of an Early Western Pioneer*, 31.

6. Maddox, *Porter and Ike Stockton*, 84–85.

7. Peters, "Allison Brothers of Tennessee," 10. Because Clay Allison returned to the area several times, a date for his departure from Colfax County seems to be elusive. Stanley Francis Louis Crocchiola—"Father Stanley"—says he left the summer after his trial at Taos. The trial ended in April 1877. Stanley, *Clay Allison*, 154.

8. *Compendium of the Ninth Census*, 1870 (Washington, DC: Government Printing Office, 1872), in Records of the U.S. Census. Also, Brevoort, *New Mexico: Her Natural Resources and Attractions*, 18. Elias Brevoort at one time was receiver in the federal land office at Santa Fe. He was a whistleblower of sorts, calling the attention of federal officials to the prevalence of fraud in the distribution of public lands in New Mexico in 1881.

9. *Compendium of the Tenth Census*, 1880 (Washington, DC: Government Printing Office, 1882), in Records of the U.S. Census.

10. Chase, *Editor's Run in New Mexico and Colorado*, 62.

11. Loosbrock, "Changing Faces of a Mining Town," 362.

12. For a summary of regiments assigned to Fort Union, see Oliva, *Fort Union and the Frontier Army in the Southwest*, 699.

13. Pearson, *Maxwell Land Grant*, 77–79.

14. Pearson, 82.

15. Pearson, 96–102.

16. Henning, *George Curry*, 46–57. Curry, later a territorial governor of New Mexico, provided one of the more reliable accounts of the confrontation, a major source for this telling. He was not a disinterested observer, however, since he was involved in some of the proceedings and his brother, John Curry, was one of three men killed in the shoot-out at Springer.

17. Henning, 48–49. See also Keleher, *Maxwell Land Grant*, 99–101.

18. Frank Springer to Josephine Springer, June 4, 1879, FS/CS.

19. Henning, *George Curry*, 48–49.

20. See Mattson, *Story of an Immigrant*, 276–89.

21. Henning, *George Curry*, 49.

22. At least three newspapers, the *New Mexican* in Santa Fe, and the *Optic* and the *Gazette* in Las Vegas, covered the events extensively. Miguel Antonio Otero, a slight participant in the affair, wrote about it in one of his memoirs, *My Life on the Frontier, 1882–1897*, 151–64. These and later historical narratives are inconsistent concerning facts, dates, and sequences. Multiple sources have been consulted in an attempt to produce the most accurate account possible.

23. *Las Vegas Daily Optic*, March 30, 1885.

24. *Santa Fe Weekly New Mexican Review*, March 19, 1885.

25. *Santa Fe Weekly New Mexican Review*, March 19, 1885.

26. *Santa Fe Weekly New Mexican Review*, March 19, 1885.

27. *Las Vegas Daily Optic*, March 20, 1885.

28. *Las Vegas Daily Optic*, Aug. 28, 1888. The commentary was almost certainly written by Russell A. Kistler, founder and longtime editor of the *Optic*, an outstanding New Mexico newspaper in territorial times.

29. For a summary of the patent suit and legal proceedings, see Caffey, *Frank Springer and New Mexico*, 71–81.

30. Caffey, 73–81.

31. *New York Times*, June 28, 1887; and Oct. 12, 1887.

32. Correia, *Properties of Violence*, 9–10.

33. *Las Vegas Daily Optic*, July 25, 1888.

34. See Taylor, *O. P. McMains and the Maxwell Land Grant Conflict*, 194. Taylor provides an extensively researched and well-told account of the "Stonewall War," an indispensable source for this summary.

35. Taylor, 168.

36. Taylor, 169, 173, 194.

37. *Pueblo Daily Chieftain*, Aug. 24 and Aug. 25, 1888.

38. *Pueblo Daily Chieftain*, Aug. 24 and Aug. 25, 1888 (quotes).

39. *Pueblo Daily Chieftain*, Aug. 26, 1888.

40. *Daily New Mexican*, Aug. 27, 1888. In response, the *Northwest New Mexican* of Chama protested that no one living on the Tierra Amarilla tract had been away from home during the recent hostilities. *Weekly New Mexican Review*, Sept. 13, 1888.

41. Taylor, *O. P. McMains and the Maxwell Land Grant Conflict*, 217–19.

42. Russell, *Land of Enchantment*, 128, 139. For reasons unknown, the author's name is spelled "Marian" in print editions of the memoir but appears as "Marion" in family papers and on her gravestone. See Marc Simmons, afterword, in reprint edition, 1981, 162.

43. Taylor, *O. P. McMains and the Maxwell Land Grant Conflict*, 250.

44. Taylor, 247.

45. Pearson, *Maxwell Land Grant*, 132.

46. Pearson, 132. See also *Las Vegas Daily Optic*, Feb. 23, 1891.

47. *Boise City (OK) News*, Oct. 13, 1899.

48. *Colorado Springs Weekly Gazette*, April 24, 1901.

49. *Santa Fe New Mexican*, Oct. 21, 1899.

CHAPTER 15. TIME AND CHANGE

1. Twitchell, *Military Occupation of New Mexico*, 49.
2. Limerick, *Legacy of Conquest*, 27. See also Montoya, *Translating Property*.
3. Statistical calculation for events of the late 1800s is fraught with uncertainties and judgments. Where judgments have been required, the intent of the author has been to interpret the data conservatively, so as to produce homicide and lynching rates that cannot reasonably be seen as inflated. Counts are likely to be low, since some homicides, perhaps especially murders of Indian and Hispanic people, may have gone unrecorded. Some but not all quantitative studies of homicide in the nineteenth-century West restrict examination to an adult population by excluding persons under age sixteen; no such exclusion was made here. Data used to calculate homicide rate for Colfax County is in the files of the author and available for examination upon request.
4. "Rate of Homicide Offenses by Population."
5. Roth, Maltz, and Eckberg, "Homicide Rates in the Old West," 183.
6. Roth, "Are Modern and Early Modern Homicide Rates Comparable?"
7. Dykstra, "Quantifying the Wild West."
8. Abbey, *Fire on the Mountain*, 39.
9. Jacobs, *After One Hundred Winters*, 17.
10. Westphall, *Mercedes Reales*, 228. For more detail concerning the Tierra Amarilla grant saga, See Ebright, *Tierra Amarilla Grant*, 1–29.
11. Nordhaus, *Tipi Rings*, 126–27.
12. Tameling v. United States Freehold and Emigration Company 93 US 644 (1877).
13. Nordhaus, *Tipi Rings*, 8–11.
14. Delaney, *Southern Ute People*, 83.
15. Nordhaus, *Tipi Rings*, 210.
16. Nordhaus, 141.
17. Quoting Freiberger, *Lucien Maxwell*, 48. The widely accepted notion of settler rights was elaborated in comments of Malcolm Ebright to the author, Feb. 22–25, 2022.
18. See Montoya, *Translating Property*, 78–79.
19. Columbus Delano, secretary of the interior, put it a bit too elegantly, remarking, "The rapid disappearance of game from the former hunting grounds must operate largely in favor of our efforts to confine the Indians to smaller areas, and compel them to abandon their nomadic customs, and establish themselves in permanent homes." *Report of the Secretary of the Interior*, 1872, 5. Concerning the decimation of buffalo, Carl Coke Rister wrote, "By the fall of 1879, the Southern herd had been destroyed." *Fort Griffin on the Texas Frontier*, 196.
20. *Report of the Commissioner of Indian Affairs*, 1875, 328.
21. *Report of the Commissioner of Indian Affairs*, 1875, 328–29.
22. See Eiselt, *Becoming White Clay*, 178–79. Development or expansion of a pottery trade benefiting the tribe was suggested by Veronica E. Velarde Tiller, as a contribution of women to the well-being of the Jicarillas in a time of scarcity and distress. Personal communication to author, Jan. 26, 2022.
23. *Winfield (KS) Daily Courier*, Dec. 1, 1886.
24. *Weekly New Mexican Review*, Dec. 1, 1886.

25. Tiller to author, Jan. 26, 2022.
26. Montoya, *Translating Property*, 53–54.
27. Montoya, 55.
28. See Montoya, 137–43, 218. Relatively few Hispano families could purchase lands that they occupied without lease or title, partly because of the company's aversion to selling small or irregular plots; and few Hispanic settlers could afford to buy regular tracts of 40 or 160 acres or more.
29. *Las Vegas Daily Optic*, Nov. 1, 1900.
30. Pension Application of Juaquina Griego de Vega, Feb. 7, 1895, Civil War Pension Files, Veterans Service Records, RG 94, NARA.
31. *Weekly New Mexican*, Aug. 24, 1869.
32. "Olive Ennis Hite," 97–98.
33. Russell, *Land of Enchantment*.
34. Chavez, *My Penitente Land*, 255.
35. Architectural Research Consultants, *Colfax County Comprehensive Plan*, IV-2 and IV-3. The landholders cited are named and shown on a map in this plan.
36. Quick Facts, Colfax County, New Mexico, U.S. Census, 2021, Population Estimates. Persons designated here as Native Americans are identified by the Census Bureau as "American Indians and Alaskan Natives."

Bibliography

ARCHIVAL AND MANUSCRIPT SOURCES

Arrott Fort Union Collection. District of New Mexico: Letters Sent and Received, Telegrams Sent and Received. RG 98. NARA. Copied and arranged in sixty-seven volumes. Special Collections. New Mexico Highlands University, Las Vegas, NM. (AC/NMHU)

Chase Ranch Records. Rio Grande Historical Collections. New Mexico State University Special Collections. Las Cruces, NM. (RGHC/NMSU)

Civil War Pension Files. Veterans Service Records. Records of the Adjutant General's Office. RG 94. NARA.

Collection of the Old Mill Museum. Cimarron, NM.

Criminal Dockets and Case Files, 1869–1900. New Mexico State Records Center and Archives, Santa Fe. (NMSRCA)

Frank Springer Papers. Collection of the CS Cattle Company. Cimarron, NM. Private collection, unprocessed. Copies of items referenced are in the files of the author. (FS/CS)

Maxwell Land Grant Collection. University of New Mexico Center for Southwest Research and Special Collections, Albuquerque. (MLG)

Papers of William Gillet Ritch. Huntington Library, San Marino, CA. Full or partial microfilm copies are also available at University of New Mexico Center for Southwest Research and Special Collections; and Special Collections, Donnelly Library, New Mexico Highlands University.

Records of the Bureau of Indian Affairs. RG 75. NARA, Washington, DC.

Records of the Department of Justice. RG 60. NARA, College Park, MD.

Records of the Department of War. General Records. RG 165. NARA, College Park, MD.

Records of the Office of the Secretary of the Interior. RG 48. NARA, College Park, MD.

Records of U.S. Army Commands. RG 98. NARA, Washington, DC.

Territorial Archives of New Mexico, 1846–1912. Microfilm edition. New Mexico State Records Center and Archives, Santa Fe. (TANM)

Thomas B. Catron Papers. Center for Southwest Research, University of New Mexico, Albuquerque. (TBC)

War Department Collection of Confederate Records: Papers Relating to Citizens, 1861–67. RG 109. NARA, Washington, DC.

GOVERNMENT DOCUMENTS

Angel, Frank Warner. *In the Matter of the Cause and Circumstances of the Death of John H. Tunstall, A British Subject.* November 27, 1878. Records of the U.S. Department of Justice. RG 60. NARA.

———. *In the Matter of the Examination of Charges against Dr. B. M. Thomas, U.S. Indian Agent, Pueblo Indians of New Mexico.* October 7, 1878. Records of the Bureau of Indian Affairs. U.S. Department of the Interior. RG 75. NARA.

———. *In the Matter of the Examination of the Charges against C. F. Godfroy, U.S. Indian Agent, Mescalero Apaches, N.M.* October 2, 1878. Records of the Bureau of Indian Affairs. U.S. Department of the Interior. RG 75. NARA.

———. *In the Matter of the Investigation of the Charges against S. B. Axtell, Governor of New Mexico.* October 3, 1878. Records of the Office of the Secretary of the Interior. RG 48. NARA.

———. *In the Matter of the Lincoln County Troubles.* October 7, 1878. Records of the U.S. Department of Justice. RG 60. NARA.

———. *In the Matter of the Uña de Gato Grant.* August 1878. Records of the U.S. Department of Justice. RG 60. NARA.

Colfax County Territorial District Court Records. 1869–1877. New Mexico State Records Center and Archives, Santa Fe.

Laws of the Territory of New Mexico. Passed by the Legislative Assembly, Session of 1860–1861. Santa Fe: John T. Russell, 1861.

Records of the U.S. Census. Including enumerator data collection sheets, compiled reports, and interim and special reports, 1850–2021.

Records of the U.S. House of Representatives. 41st–43d Cong. 1869–75. RG 233. NARA.

Report of the Commissioner of Indian Affairs. Washington, DC: U.S. Government Printing Office, 1861–87.

Report of the Secretary of the Interior. Washington, DC: U.S. Government Printing Office, 1872.

Raymond, Rossiter W. *Statistics of Mines and Mining in the States and Territories West of the Rocky Mountains.* 41st Cong. 2d Sess. House Ex. Doc 207. Washington, DC: U.S. Government Printing Office, 1870.

Treaty of Guadalupe Hidalgo: Findings and Possible Options Regarding Longstanding Community Land Grant Claims in New Mexico. Washington, DC: General Accounting Office, 2004.

White, Koch, Kelley and McCarthy, Attorneys at Law. *Land Title Study.* Santa Fe: New Mexico State Planning Office, 1971.

COURT DECISIONS

Charles Bent et al. v. Guadalupe Miranda et al. Supreme Court of the Territory of New Mexico. 8 NM 78, 1895.

Tameling v. United States Freehold and Emigration Company. 93 U.S. 644, 1877.

Transcript of Record. Charles Bent et al. v. Guadalupe Miranda et al. Supreme Court of the Territory of New Mexico. July 1894. Las Vegas, NM: La Voz del Pueblo, 1894.
United States v. Maxwell Land-Grant Co. et al. 121 U.S. 325, 1887.

NEWSPAPERS AND NEWSLETTERS
Albuquerque Journal, 1920
Albuquerque Morning Journal, 1910
Albuquerque Republican Review, 1871
Arizona Citizen (Tucson), 1871
Austin (TX) Daily Democratic Statesman, 1873
Boise City (OK) News, 1899
Boston Herald, 1868
Chicago Daily Inter-Ocean, 1874–76
Cimarron (NM) News and Press, 1875–79
Cincinnati (OH) Commercial, 1871
Colorado Chieftain (Pueblo), 1871–75
Colorado Daily Chieftain (Pueblo), 1871–88
Colorado Miner (Georgetown), 1870
Colorado Springs Gazette, 1874
Colorado Springs Weekly Gazette, 1901
Colorado Transcript (Golden), 1870–71
Colorado Weekly Chieftain (Pueblo), 1871–77
Congressional Globe (Washington, DC), 1870–71
County Observer and Monmouthshire Central Advertiser (Usk, Wales, UK), 1871
Daily Central City (CO) Register, 1871–72
Daily Ohio Statesman (Columbus), 1858
Daily Rocky Mountain News (Denver), 1864–75
Delphi (IN) Journal, 1875
Deming (NM) Headlight, 1901
Denver Daily News, 1874
Denver Daily Times, 1872
Denver Daily Tribune, 1878
Denver Mirror, 1875
Deseret News (Salt Lake City), 1877–78
Elizabethtown (NM) Press and Telegraph 1870–71
Elizabethtown (NM) Railway, Press and Telegraph, 1872–74
Galveston (TX) Daily News, 1875
Golden (CO) Weekly Globe, 1875
Hartford (CT) Courant, 1867
Helena (MT) Weekly Herald, 1875
Holt County Sentinel (Oregon, MO), 1875
Idaho World (Idaho City), 1871
Indianapolis Sentinel, 1876

Indiana State Sentinel (Indianapolis), 1878
Kansas Tribune (Lawrence), 1875
Lafayette (IN) Daily Journal, 1875
Lafayette (IN) Journal and Courier, 1923
Las Animas (CO) Leader, 1875–76
Las Cruces (NM) Borderer, 1872
Las Vegas (NM) Daily Gazette, 1874
Las Vegas (NM) Daily Optic, 1884–88
Las Vegas (NM) Gazette, 1872–76
Leavenworth (KS) Bulletin, 1868
Leavenworth (KS) Daily Commercial, 1876
Leavenworth (KS) Times, 1871–76
Llano (TX) News, 1942
Mesilla Valley (NM) Independent, 1878
Moab (UT) Times Independent, 1934
Ness County News (Ness City, KS), 1891
New Orleans Times-Picayune, 1875
New York Evening Post, 1875
New York Sun, 1875–94
New York Times, 1875–87
Omaha (NE) Morning World Herald, 1895
Prescott (AZ) Weekly Journal Miner, 1871
Pueblo (CO) Daily Chieftain, 1874–88
Raton (NM) Range, 1925
Raton (NM) Reporter, 1922
Saguache (CO) Chronicle, 1876
Saint Louis Globe-Democrat, 1875
Saint Louis Republican, 1876
San Francisco Chronicle, 1877
San Francisco Evening Bulletin, 1874
San Francisco Examiner, 1875
Santa Fe Daily New Mexican, 1870–75
Santa Fe New Mexican, 1899
Santa Fe Sentinel, 1878
Santa Fe Weekly Gazette, 1868
Santa Fe Weekly New Mexican, 1869–79
Santa Fe Weekly New Mexican Review, 1885–88
Santa Fe Weekly Post, 1869
Silver City (NM) Eagle, 1895
Southwest Sentinel (Silver City, NM), 1885
Topeka (KS) Daily Commonwealth, 1870
Trinidad (CO) Enterprise and Chronicle, 1877
Troy (KS) Bulletin, 1878

Washington (DC) Evening Star, 1877–97
Western Home Journal (Lawrence, KS), 1871
Winfield (KS) Daily Courier, 1886

BOOKS AND ARTICLES

Abbey, Edward. *Fire on the Mountain*. New York: Dial Press, 1962.
Anderson, George B. *History of New Mexico: Its Resources and People*. 2 vols. Los Angeles: Pacific States Publishing, 1907.
Architectural Research Consultants. *Colfax County Comprehensive Plan*. Raton, NM: Colfax County Board of Commissioners, 2015.
Bell, William A. *New Tracks in North America: A Journal of Travel and Adventure*. London: Chapman and Hall, 1870. Reprint, Albuquerque: Horn and Wallace, 1965.
Billington, Monroe Lee. *New Mexico's Buffalo Soldiers, 1866–1900*. Niwot: University Press of Colorado, 1991.
Bowden, J. J. "Private Land Claims in the Southwest." 6 vols. Master of Laws thesis, Southern Methodist University, 1969.
Brayer, Herbert Oliver. *William Blackmore: The Spanish-Mexican Land Grants*. Denver: Bradford-Robinson, 1949.
Brevoort, Elias. *New Mexico: Her Natural Resources and Attractions*. Self-published, 1874.
Bryan, Howard. *Robbers, Rogues and Ruffians*. Santa Fe: Clear Light Publishers, 1991.
Caffey, David L. *Chasing the Santa Fe Ring: Power and Privilege in Territorial New Mexico*. Albuquerque: University of New Mexico Press, 2014.
———. *Frank Springer and New Mexico: From the Colfax County War to the Emergence of Modern Santa Fe*. College Station: Texas A & M University Press, 2006.
Catalogue of the University of Pennsylvania, 1899–1900. Philadelphia: University of Pennsylvania, December 1899.
Chase, C. M. *The Editor's Run in New Mexico and Colorado*. Montpelier, VT: Argus and Patriot Book and Job Printing House, 1882.
Chavez, Fray Angelico. *My Penitente Land: Reflections on Spanish New Mexico*. Albuquerque: University of New Mexico Press, 1974.
Chavez, John R. *The Lost Land: The Chicano Image of the Southwest*. Albuquerque: University of New Mexico Press, 1984.
Christiansen, Paige W. *The Story of Mining in New Mexico*. Socorro: New Mexico Bureau of Mines and Mineral Resources, 1974.
Clark, O. S. *Clay Allison of the Washita, First a Cow Man and then an Extinguisher of Bad Men*. Self-published, 1922.
Cleaveland, Agnes Morley. *No Life for a Lady*. Boston: Houghton Mifflin, 1941.
———. *Satan's Paradise*. Boston: Houghton Mifflin, 1952.
Cleaveland, Norman. *The Morleys: Young Upstarts on the Southwest Frontier*. With George Fitzpatrick. Albuquerque: Calvin Horn, 1971.
Clever, Charles P. *New Mexico: Her Resources; Her Necessities for Railroad Communication with the Atlantic and Pacific States; Her Great Future*. Washington, DC: McGill, Witherow, 1868.

Clifford, Frank. *Deep Trails in the Old West*. Edited by Frederick W. Nolan. Norman: University of Oklahoma Press, 2011.
Coe, George W. *Frontier Fighter: The Autobiography of George W. Coe*. Boston: Houghton Mifflin, 1934.
Collinson, John. *Report of the President to Holders of Stocks and Bonds of the Maxwell Land Grant and Railway Company*. Dutch edition. Amsterdam: Blikman and Sartorius, 1871.
Collinson, John, and W. A. Bell. *The Maxwell Land Grant, Situated in Colorado and New Mexico, United States of America*. London: Printed by Taylor and Co., 1870.
Conard, Howard Louis. *"Uncle Dick" Wootton, the Pioneer Frontiersman of the Rocky Mountain Region*. Chicago: W. E. Dibble, 1890.
Correia, David. *Properties of Violence: Law and Land Grant Struggle in Northern New Mexico*. Athens: University of Georgia Press, 2013.
Crocker, George E. *Memories of Cimarron, 1871–1882*. Albuquerque: self-published, ca. 1952.
Culley, John H. (Jack). *Cattle, Horses and Men of the Western Range*. Los Angeles: Ward Ritchie Press, 1940. Reprint, Tucson: University of Arizona Press, 1984.
Delaney, Robert W. *The Southern Ute People*. Phoenix: Indian Tribal Series, 1974.
Dykstra, Robert R. "Quantifying the Wild West: The Problematic Statistics of Frontier Violence." *Western Historical Quarterly* 40, no. 3 (Autumn 2009): 321–47.
Ebright, Malcolm. *Land Grants and Lawsuits in Northern New Mexico*. Albuquerque: University of New Mexico Press, 1994.
———. *The Tierra Amarilla Grant: A History of Chicanery*. Santa Fe: Center for Land Grant Studies, 1993.
Ebright, Malcolm, Rick Hendricks, and Richard W. Hughes. *Four Square Leagues: Pueblo Indian Land in New Mexico*. Albuquerque: University of New Mexico Press, 2014.
Eiselt, B. Sunday. *Becoming White Clay: A History and Archaeology of Jicarilla Apache Enclavement*. Salt Lake City: University of Utah Press, 2012.
Evans, Max. "Old Bum." In *Spinning Sun, Grinning Moon*. Santa Fe: Red Crane Books, 1995.
Fergusson, Harvey. *Grant of Kingdom*. New York: William Morrow, 1950.
Freiberger, Harriet. *Lucien Maxwell: Villain or Visionary*. Santa Fe: Sunstone Press, 1999.
Fulton, Maurice Garland. *New Mexico's Own Chronicle*. Dallas: Banks Upshaw, 1937.
Goddard, Pliny Earle. *Jicarilla Apache Texts*. Anthropological Papers of the American Museum of Natural History 8. New York: American Museum of Natural History, 1911.
Guild, Thelma S., and Harvey L. Carter. *Kit Carson: A Pattern for Heroes*. Lincoln: University of Nebraska Press, 1984.
Gunnerson, Dolores A. *The Jicarilla Apaches: A Study in Survival*. DeKalb: Northern Illinois University Press, 1974.
Harwood, Thomas. *History of New Mexico Spanish and English Missions of the Methodist Episcopal Church from 1850 to 1910*. Vol. 1. Albuquerque, 1908.
Henning, H. B., ed. *George Curry, 1861–1947: An Autobiography*. Albuquerque: University of New Mexico Press, 1958.
Hilton, Tom. *Nevermore, Cimarron, Nevermore*. Fort Worth: Western Heritage Press, 1970.
Horgan, Paul. *Figures in a Landscape*. New York: Harper and Brothers, 1940.

Hough, Emerson. *The Story of the Outlaw: A Study of the Western Desperado.* New York: Outing Publishing, 1907.
Howbert, Irving. *Memories of a Lifetime in the Pike's Peak Region.* New York: G. P. Putnam's Sons, 1925.
Hughes, Delbert Littrell, and Lenore Harris Hughes. *Give Me Room!* El Paso, TX: Hughes Publishing, 1971.
Inman, Colonel Henry. *The Old Santa Fe Trail: The Story of a Great Highway.* New York: Macmillan, 1897.
Jacobs, Margaret D. *After One Hundred Winters: In Search of Reconciliation on America's Stolen Lands.* Princeton, NJ: Princeton University Press, 2021.
Jacobsen, Joel. *Such Men as Billy the Kid: The Lincoln County War Reconsidered.* Lincoln: University of Nebraska Press, 1994.
Johnson, David M., Chris Adams, Larry Ludwig, and Charles C. Hawk. "Taos, the Jicarilla Apache, and the Battle of Cieneguilla." In *Taos: A Topical History*, edited by Corina A. Santistevan and Julia Moore, 137–51. Santa Fe: Museum of New Mexico Press, 2013.
Jones, Fayette Alexander. *New Mexico Mines and Minerals.* World's Fair edition. Santa Fe: New Mexican Printing, 1904.
Keane, John L. "The Towns That Coal Built: The Evolution of Landscapes and Communities in Southern Colorado." *Yearbook of the Association of Pacific Coast Geographers* 62 (2000): 70–94.
Keleher, William A. *Maxwell Land Grant.* Santa Fe: Rydal Press, 1942.
Kenner, Charles L. "The Great New Mexico Cattle Raid—1872." *New Mexico Historical Review* 37, no. 4 (1962): 243–59.
Kingman, Lewis. *Kingman Family History.* Mexico City: Imprenta de Hull, 1907.
Kiser, William S. *Borderlands of Slavery: The Struggle Over Captivity and Peonage in the American Southwest.* Philadelphia: University of Pennsylvania Press, 2017.
La Farge, Oliver. "New Mexico." *Holiday* 11, no. 2 (February 1952): 34–37.
Lamar, Howard Roberts. *The Far Southwest, 1846–1912: A Territorial History.* New Haven, CT: Yale University Press, 1966.
Lambert, Oscar Doane. *Stephen Benton Elkins: American Foursquare.* Pittsburgh: University of Pittsburgh Press, 1955.
Limerick, Patricia Nelson. *The Legacy of Conquest: The Unbroken Past of the American West.* New York: W. W. Norton, 1987.
———. "The Trail to Santa Fe: The Unleashing of the Western Public Intellectual." In *Trails: Toward a New Western History*, edited by Patricia Nelson Limerick, Clyde A. Milner II, and Charles E. Rankin, 59–77. Lawrence: University Press of Kansas, 1991.
Loosbrock, Richard D. "The Changing Faces of a Mining Town: The Dual Labor System in Elizabethtown, New Mexico." *New Mexico Historical Review* 74, no. 4 (October 1999): 353–73.
Lomax, John A., ed. *Songs of the Cattle Trail and Cow Camp.* New York: MacMillan, 1920.
Maddox, Michael R. *Porter and Ike Stockton.* Self-published, 2014.
Maddux, Vernon R. *John Hittson: Cattle King on the Texas and Colorado Frontier.* Niwot: University Press of Colorado, 1994.

Manypenny, George W. *Our Indian Wards*. Cincinnati: Robert Clarke, 1880.

Mattson, Hans. *The Story of an Immigrant*. Saint Paul: D. D. Merrill, 1891.

Mauzy, Wayne L. *A Century in Santa Fe: The Story of the First National Bank of Santa Fe*. Santa Fe: First National Bank of Santa Fe, 1970.

McKanna, Claire V., Jr. *Homicide, Race, and Justice in the American West, 1880–1920*. Tucson: University of Arizona Press, 1997.

McPherson, M. E., and W. B. Matchett. *In the Matter of the Charges Vs. Governor Samuel B. Axtell and Other New Mexican Officials: Submitted to the Departments of the Interior and Justice*. Privately printed, August 1877.

Merriam-Webster's Collegiate Dictionary. Tenth edition. Springfield, MA: Merriam-Webster, 1993.

Michno, Gregory F. *Depredation and Deceit: The Making of the Jicarilla and Ute Wars in New Mexico*. Norman: University of Oklahoma Press, 2017.

Miles, Nelson A. *Personal Recollections and Observations of General Nelson A. Miles*. Chicago: Werner, 1896.

Miller, Darlis A. *The California Column in New Mexico*. Albuquerque: University of New Mexico Press, 1982.

Montoya, María E. *Translating Property: The Maxwell Land Grant and the Conflict over Land in the American West, 1840–1900*. Berkeley: University of California Press, 2002.

Mullin, Robert N., ed. *Maurice Garland Fulton's History of the Lincoln County War*. Tucson: University of Arizona Press, 1968.

Murphy, Lawrence R. "Boom and Bust on Baldy Mountain, New Mexico, 1864–1942." Master's thesis, University of Arizona, 1965.

———. *Frontier Crusader—William F. M. Arny*. Tucson: University of Arizona Press, 1972.

———, ed. *Indian Agent in New Mexico: The Journal of Special Agent W. F. M. Arny, 1870*. Santa Fe: Stagecoach Press, 1967.

———. *Lucien Bonaparte Maxwell: Napoleon of the Southwest*. Norman: University of Oklahoma Press, 1983.

———. *Philmont: A History of New Mexico's Cimarron Country*. Albuquerque: University of New Mexico Press, 1972.

———. "Rayado: Pioneer Settlement in Northeastern New Mexico, 1848–1857." *New Mexico Historical Review* 46, no. 1 (1971): 37–56.

Nolan, Frederick W. *The Life and Death of John Henry Tunstall*. Albuquerque: University of New Mexico Press, 1965.

———. *The Lincoln County War: A Documentary History*. Norman: University of Oklahoma Press, 1992.

Nordhaus, Robert J. *Tipi Rings: A Chronicle of the Jicarilla Apache Land Claim*. Albuquerque: BowArrow, 1995.

Oliva, Leo. *Fort Union and the Frontier Army in the Southwest*. Santa Fe: Division of History, National Park Service, 1993.

"Olive Ennis Hite." *Old Santa Fe: A Magazine of History, Archaeology, Genealogy and Biography* 3, no. 9 (April 1916): 97–98.

Osburn, Katherine M. B. *Southern Ute Women: Autonomy and Assimilation on the Reservation, 1887–1934*. Albuquerque: University of New Mexico Press, 1998.
Otero, Miguel Antonio. *My Life on the Frontier, 1864–1882*. New York: Press of the Pioneers, 1935.
———. *My Life on the Frontier, 1882–1897*. Albuquerque: University of New Mexico Press, 1939.
Pagán, Eduardo Obregón. *Valley of the Guns: The Pleasant Valley War and the Trauma of Violence*. Norman: University of Oklahoma Press, 2018.
Parsons, Chuck. *Clay Allison: Portrait of a Shootist*. Seagraves, TX: Pioneer Book Publishers, 1983.
Paul, Rodman W. *Mining Frontiers of the Far West*. New York: Holt, Rinehart and Winston, 1963.
Pearson, Jim Berry. *The Maxwell Land Grant*. Norman: University of Oklahoma Press, 1961.
Peters, James Steven. "The Allison Brothers of Tennessee." *Quarterly of the National Outlaw and Lawman Association* 6, no. 4 (July 1981): 2–12.
———. "Postmortem of an Assassination: Parson Tolby and the Maxwell Land Grant." *Texana* 11, no. 4 (1973): 328–61.
Poldervaart, Arie W. *Black-Robed Justice*. Publications in History 13. Santa Fe: Historical Society of New Mexico, 1948.
Pomeroy, Earl S. *The Territories and the United States, 1861–1890*. Philadelphia: University of Pennsylvania Press, 1947.
Porter, Henry M. *Pencillings of an Early Western Pioneer*. Denver: World Press, 1929.
Quintana, Frances Leon. *Pobladores: Hispanic Americans of the Ute Frontier*. Aztec, NM: self-published, 1991.
Reeve, Frank D. "The Federal Indian Policy in New Mexico, 1858–1880." Pt. 3. *New Mexico Historical Review* 13, no. 2 (April 1938): 146–91.
Report to Holders of Stocks and Securities of the Maxwell Land Grant and Railway Company, 1870. Dutch edition. Amsterdam: Blikman and Sartorius, 1871.
Report to Holders of Stocks and Securities of the Maxwell Land Grant and Railway Company, 1871. Dutch edition. Amsterdam: Blikman and Sartorius, 1871.
Rhodes, Eugene Manlove. *Bransford in Arcadia*. New York: Henry Holt, 1914.
Richardson, Rupert Norval. *The Comanche Barrier to South Plains Settlement: A Century and a Half of Savage Resistance to the Advancing White Frontier*. Glendale, CA: Arthur H. Clark, 1933.
Rister, Carl Coke. *Fort Griffin on the Texas Frontier*. Norman: University of Oklahoma Press, 1956.
Rosenbaum, Robert J. *Mexicano Resistance in the Southwest: "The Sacred Right of Self-Preservation."* Austin: University of Texas Press, 1981.
Roth, Randolph. "Are Modern and Early Modern Homicide Rates Comparable? The Impact of Modern Non-Emergency Medical Care on Homicide Rates." Paper presented at the Social Science History Association Conference, 2007.
Roth, Randolph, Michael D. Maltz, and Douglas L. Eckberg. "Homicide Rates in the Old West." *Western Historical Quarterly* 42, no. 2 (Summer 2011): 173–95.

Russell, Marian. *Land of Enchantment: Memoirs of Marian Russell along the Santa Fe Trail.* With the assistance of Mrs. Hal Russell. Evanston, IL: Branding Iron Press, 1954. Reprinted with afterword by Marc Simmons. Albuquerque: University of New Mexico Press, 1981.

Ryus, William H. *The Second William Penn: Treating with Indians on the Santa Fe Trail, 1860–66.* Kansas City, MO: Frank T. Riley, 1913.

Santistevan, Corina A., and Julia Moore, eds. *Taos: A Topical History.* Santa Fe: Museum of New Mexico Press, 2013.

Schoenberger, Dale T. *The Gunfighters.* Caldwell, ID: Caxton Printers, 1971.

Sherman, James E., and Barbara H. *Ghost Towns and Mining Camps of New Mexico.* Norman: University of Oklahoma Press, 1975.

Simmons, Virginia McConnell. *The Ute Indians of Utah, Colorado, and New Mexico.* Boulder: University Press of Colorado, 2000.

Sonnichsen, C. L. *I'll Die Before I'll Run: The Story of the Great Feuds of Texas.* New York: Harper and Brothers, 1951.

———. *Ten Texas Feuds.* Albuquerque: University of New Mexico Press, 1957.

Speer, William S., and John Henry Brown, eds. *The Encyclopedia of the New West.* Marshall, TX: United States Biographical Publishing, 1881.

Stanley, F. [Stanley Francis Louis Crocchiola]. *Clay Allison.* Denver: World Press, 1956.

———. *The Grant That Maxwell Bought.* Denver: World Press, 1952.

Swarthout, Glendon. *Skeletons.* Garden City, NJ: Doubleday, 1979.

Taylor, Morris F. *O. P. McMains and the Maxwell Land Grant Conflict.* Tucson: University of Arizona Press, 1979.

———. "The Uña de Gato Grant in Colfax County." *New Mexico Historical Review* 51, no. 2 (April 1976): 121–43.

Theisen, Lee Scott. "Frank Warner Angel's Notes on New Mexico Territory, 1878." *Arizona and the West* 18, no. 4 (Winter 1976): 333–70.

Tiller, Veronica E. Velarde. *The Jicarilla Apache Tribe: A History, 1846–1970.* Lincoln: University of Nebraska Press, 1983.

———, ed. *Tiller's Guide to Indian Country: Economic Profiles of American Indian Reservations.* Second edition. Albuquerque: BowArrow Publishing, 2005.

Tórrez, Robert J., ed. *New Mexico in 1876–1877, A Newspaperman's View: The Travels and Reports of William D. Dawson.* Los Ranchos, NM: Rio Grande Books, 2007.

Twitchell, Ralph Emerson. *Leading Facts of New Mexican History.* Vol. 2 Cedar Rapids, IA: Torch Press: 1912.

———. *Leading Facts of New Mexican History.* Vol. 3. Cedar Rapids, IA: Torch Press: 1917.

———. *The Military Occupation of New Mexico, 1846–1851.* Denver: Smith-Brooks, 1909.

University Bulletin. Philadelphia: University of Pennsylvania, October 1898.

Utley, Robert M. *High Noon in Lincoln: Violence on the Western Frontier.* Albuquerque: University of New Mexico Press, 1987.

West, Elliott. *The Contested Plains: Indians, Goldseekers, and the Rush to Colorado.* Lawrence: University Press of Kansas, 1998.

Westphall, Victor. "The Colfax County War and the Santa Fe Ring." Paper prepared for a symposium in Cimarron, New Mexico, April 30, 1988. Typescript privately published by Frank R. "Skitt" Trujillo, August 2001.

———. *Mercedes Reales: Hispanic Land Grants of the Upper Rio Grande Region*. Albuquerque: University of New Mexico Press, 1983.

———. *Thomas Benton Catron and His Era*. Tucson: University of Arizona Press, 1973.

Whitford, William Clarke. *Colorado Volunteers in the Civil War: The New Mexico Campaign in 1862*. Denver: State Historical and Natural History Society, 1906.

Wilson, John P. *Merchants, Guns, and Money: The Story of Lincoln County and Its Wars*. Santa Fe: Museum of New Mexico Press, 1987.

Wooster, Robert. *Nelson A. Miles and the Twilight of the Frontier Army*. Lincoln: University of Nebraska Press, 1995.

Young, Richard K. *The Ute Indians of Colorado in the Twentieth Century*. Norman: University of Oklahoma Press, 1997.

DIGITAL RESOURCES AND OTHER MATERIALS

Blevins, Jason. "A Rare New Coal Mine in Southern Colorado Adds to Trinidad's Economic Revival." *Colorado Sun*, June 21, 2021. https://coloradosun.com/2021/06/24/new-elk-coal-mine-trinidad-economic-development.

Fort Union Historic Research Study. Appendix B: Surgeons at Fort Union. http://www.santafetrailresearch.com/fort-union-nm/fu-oliva-t.html.

Knudsen, Jon. "Mills Mansion Has Become a Shell of Its Former Self." *New Mexico Marketplace*. October 2018. https://www.nmmarketplace.com. Search Mills Mansion.

Manuscript review by Veronica E. Velarde Tiller, October 2021. At the author's request, Tiller reviewed chapters 1 and 9, and excerpts of other chapters concerning Native American involvement in the narrative. Dr. Tiller provided written comments and verbal response.

"New Elk Coal Commences Coal Mining Operations in Colorado." *Coal World*, June 15, 2021. https://www.worldcoal.com/coal/15062021/new-elk-coal-commences-coal-mine-operations-in-colorado.

"Rate of Homicide Offenses by Population." New Mexico and the United States. Federal Bureau of Investigation Crime Data Explorer. Accessed September 14, 2021. https://crime-data-explorer.app.cloud.gov/pages/explorer/crime/crime-trend.

Soldiers and Sailors Database. The Civil War. National Park Service. https://www.nps.gov/civilwar/soldiers-and-sailors-database.htm.

Zimmer, Stephen A. "The Colfax County War." Presentation at the Raton Museum, Raton, NM, July 7, 2018.

Index

References to illustrations appear in italic type.

Abbey, Edward, 196
Abiquiu, N.Mex., 15, 16, 121, 177, 178
Abreu, Jesús and Petra Beaubien (and family), 23, 200, *201*
Adams, Alva, 189
After One Hundred Winters (Jacobs), 196–97
agents, Indian. *See under* Indian Affairs, Office of
alcohol and violence: and Allison's behavior, 94, 96; and frontier violence, 63, 82–83, 92, 94, 109, 132, 146; illegal sales to Natives, 114, 118; and "running the town," 65, 80, 96, 103–4, 131–32, 183
Alexander, A. J., 31
Allison, John, 102, 143
Allison, Robert Clay "Clay": Axtell's determination to convict, 128–29, 130, 141–42, 150; blamed for Vega's death, 93; and Chunk Colbert shootout, 95; court proceedings against, 142–43; departure from Colfax County area, 178; hearing and discharge for Griego shooting, 104–5; under influence of alcohol, 94; killing of Griego, 96–97; and lynching of Charles Kennedy, 61; meeting with Mary Tolby, 87–88; as one of "the Texans," 65, 78–79; as possible killer of Cardenas, 109; response to threat of Indian violence, 83; and retreat of Longwill, 102; role in Colfax County War, 95–96; support for Ring resistance, 123–24

American occupation and legal system, 12–13, 135–38, 137–38, 193–94
Anderson, George B., 37
Angel, Frank Warner, 165. *See also* Lincoln County War
Angel Fire ski resort, 207
Angel investigation and reports. *See* Lincoln County War
Antrim, Henry (William Bonney), 93, 163
anvils, shooting off of, 169
Apaches (other than Jicarilla), 13, 18, 68, 121
Arapahos, 11, 68
Armijo, Manuel, 12, 193
Arms, Henry W., 158, 159, 164–65
Army, U.S.: decreasing presence in Colfax County, 179; fort installations and interactions with indigenous, 13–15, 35; Fort Stanton, 121, 162, 166; Fort Sumner, 33, 34, 46; maintaining order at first Colfax-Taos court session, 138; responsibility for settling Indian issues, 117–21. *See also* Fort Union
Arny, William Frederick Milton, 10, 17, *20*, 214n7
assassinations in Colfax County, 62–63, 92, 97–100, 102, 107–10, 138. *See also under* Tolby, Franklin James
Atchison, Topeka and Santa Fe Railroad, 182, 205

249

Axtell, Samuel B.: allegations against, 156–59; appointed governor, 77–78; as Chief Justice, 176, 184; Colfax County sheriff appointments by, 126; determination to convict Allison, 128–29, 130, 141–42, 150; Justice Department investigation of, 165, 167, 172; later political activities, 176; Matchett and McPherson complaint against, 156; and McMains case, 154; removal as governor, 168–71; and Tolby murder case, 89
Aztec Mine, 30, 38

Baird, Martin, 129
Baldy Mountain, 37–41, 39–41, 42, 48, 54, 76, 179
Ballard, Jean (book character), 44
Barela, Juan, 115–17, 117
Beardsley, Ezra, 159
Beaubien, Charles Hipolite Trotier "Don Carlos," 12, 22
Beaubien, María de la Luz "Luz" (Lucien Maxwell's wife), 22, 200
Beaubien and Miranda Land Grant, 3, 12–13, 22–24, 179, 200. *See also* Maxwell Land Grant
Becoming White Clay (Eiselt), 9
Bell, William A., 31, 32, 46
Bent, Charles, 24
Bent, William, 10–11
Bergman, E. H., 30, 33, 34, 38
Big Ditch project, 25, 39
Billington, Monroe Lee, 132
"Billy the Kid," 93–94, 163
Black soldiers, 130–31, 132, 179, 205
Bloomfield, Morris, 39, 57
Blosser, George, and family, 188
Bonney, William "Billy the Kid," 93–94, 163
Booth, Jack, 62
Bosque Redondo, 33, 46
Boston Herald, 32
Bowman, Thomas, 154
Breeden William, 107, 137, 139, 144, 154
Brevoort, Elias, 179
Bristol, Warren, 156, 163
British settlers/miners brought in by Maxwell Company, 52–53, 52–54, 73

British syndicate purchase and administration of Maxwell grant, 5, 33, 45, 47–48, 71–72. *See also* Maxwell Land Grant and Railway Company
Bronson, Larry, 37, 38
Buckley, James "Coal Oil Jimmy," 62
buffalo herds, decimation of, 9, 120, 199–200
buffalo soldiers. *See* Black soldiers
Burch, Eli, 185
Burleson, Pete, 102

California Column (Union volunteer group), 36–37
Canadian River (Red River), 1, 18, 34, 64
Cardenas, Manuel, 89, 90, 91, 101–2, 105–9, 144
Carleton, James H., 13–14, 36
Carson, Christopher "Kit," 12, 13, 17, 18, 22, 31
Carter, James, 183, 184
Catron, Thomas B.: and Ada Morley case, 153, 155; and emergence of Santa Fe Ring, 49; investigation and resignation of, 169, 171, 173; involvement in Lincoln County, 163–64; land grant fraud involvement, 159, 165, 172–73; later political activities, 176; Matchett and McPherson complaint against, 155–56, 156; and networking with Ring coalition, 73–75; sale of First National Bank to, 33; as U.S. attorney, 78, 107, 137
cattlemen/ranchers, 5, 64–66, 161–63, 178, 206–7
"Cedar Bark people," 8. *See also* Mouache Utes
Chaffee, Jerome Bunty, 33, 45
Chavez, Angelico, 205
Cheyennes, 11
Chicago Daily Inter-Ocean, 1, 68, 79
Chisum, John, 162
Chittenden, Orson K., 126
Christy, F. C., 53–54
Cimarron, N.Mex., 72–73, 80–81, 82–83, *108*, 205
Cimarron Agency, 17, 19, 114–15, 121, 200
Cimarroncito Mining District, 213n6
Cimarron country, overviews, 1–2, 4, 5, 9, 219n43
Cimarron News/Cimarron News and Press: animosity of Allison toward, 95; call for

confinement of Natives on reservations, 118; and Catron's retaliation against Morley, 153, 155; denial of violence in Cimarron, 81; on Fisher murder, 55, 63; internal friction and Ring support/resistance, 122–25; media profiles and propaganda wars, 110–11; Morley and Springer editing, 77; move to Raton and name change, 206; on murder of Black soldiers, 130–31; on power of county probate judge, 98–99; on removal of Axtell as governor, 169, *170*; on survey of Maxwell grant, 82; vandalism and destruction of, 126
Cincinnati Commercial, 51–52
Civil War, impact of, 4, 35, 36, 67
Clark, Rush, 165
Cleaveland, Agnes Morley, 25, 25–26, 27, 48, 124, 203, 216n11
Cleaveland, Norman, 152, 229n13
Clemes, H. C., 53–54
Cleveland, Grover, 176, 182, 187
Clever, Charles P., 38
Clifford, Frank, 94, 221n32
Clifton House hotel and stage station, 64–65, 66, 95
Coe, George W., 95–96
Colbert, Chunk, 95, 105, 142
Coleman, L. G., 65, 81
Colfax County, N.Mex.: Cimarron, N.Mex., 72–73, 80–81, 82–83, 205; current overview and future outlook, 207–8; Elizabethtown, N.Mex., 38, 40, 41–43, 57–61, 99–100, 179; government positions controlled by Ring, 49–51, 74, 77–78, 78, 104, 122, 137–38; judicial attachment to Taos County, 127, 150; Justice Department investigations and end of, 173–74. *See also* violence in Colfax County
"Colfax County War," 3, 76, 93, 95, 173
Collinson, John, 45, 46–47, 52–53, 55, 71–72, 179–80
Colorado Chieftain, 110, 138–39, 146, 147–48
Colorado Fuel and Iron Company, 192
Colorado portion of Maxwell grant, 187–91, 192, 207
Colorado Transcript, 48–49

Colorado Weekly Chieftain, 157
Comancheros (New Mexicans engaged in illegal trade), 65–66
Comanches, 11, 13, 18, 65–66, 68
Cooper, Charles, 133, 142
Cornish, George A., 102, 103, 108–9, 112, 119, 121
Cornish miners, 53–54
Correia, David, 187
Cortez, Manuel, 139
Cossairt, John, 54, 55
"cowboy" behavior and character, 183–85
Cox, Hiram Washington, 65, 178
Cox, Jacob, 44
Crocker, George, 105, 130, 143, 169, 226n28
Crocker, Jane, 87
Crockett, David, 65, 130–32, 131–32
Culley, John H. "Jack," 89, 93
cultural prejudice. *See* racial/cultural prejudice
Cummings, Dallas, 102, 104, 107
Cunningham, W. O., 127
Curry, George, 182, 184, 232n16
Curry, John, 232n16
Curtis, Zenas, 91

Daily Rocky Mountain News, 25, 28, 29, 50. *See also* Goldrick, O. J.
Davis, Ferd, 221n34
Davis, Hallie, 76
Davis, Henry G., 76
Davis, Nicholas S., 39
Dawson, John B., 65
Dawson, Will, 110, 122, 123, 123–25, 126, 127, 178
Delano, Columbus, 234n19
demographics, 40, 41, 77, 194–96, 207, 214n7, 219n38
Denver Mirror, 81
Denver Times, 63
Department of the Interior, U.S., 81–82, 117. *See also* Indian Affairs, Office of; Schurz, Carl
Deseret News (Salt Lake City), 158
Devens, Charles, 154, 155, 158, 165, 167, 171
Devlin, Thomas G., 83
Dobie, J. Frank, 93–94
Dodds, John, 183, 184
Dolan, James J., 162–63, 166
Dold, John, 38, 39
Doña Ana County, 127, 167

Donoghue, Florencio, 102, 106, 107, 126, 138, 144–45
Dorsey, Stephen W., 159, 173
drinking and violence. *See* alcohol and violence
Dutch financial backers of Maxwell Companies, 33, 64, 71, 81, 180, 186, 188, 192
Dykstra, Robert R., 196

Eagle Nest Dam, 206
Eiselt, B. Sunday, 9
ejectments. *See* eviction actions
elections and Ring control, 49–50, 74, 77, 78, 86–87, 98–99
Elizabethtown, N.Mex., 38, 40, 41–43, 57–61, 99–100, 179
Elizabethtown Press and Telegraph, 61
Elizabethtown Railway, Press and Telegraph, 49, 110
Elkins, Stephen B.: as congressional delegate, 73, 107, 139–40; involvement with Longwill, 99–100; leadership roles in Maxwell Company, 50–51, 73–75, 76; as Maxwell's lawyer in land grant sale, 33; move into national politics, 76, 148; purchase of Maxwell's banking interest, 33; as Santa Fe Ring founder/leader, 49, 73–74, 77, 84, 123–25, 137, 149–50; support for Catron, 171, 172; as U.S. attorney, 78
"English company." *See* Maxwell Land Grant and Railway Company
Ennis, Joseph, 24, 202, 211n8
Ennis, Olive (Hite), 24–25, 26–27, 202, 211n8
Ernest, Finis, 95–96
"E-Town." *See* Elizabethtown, N.Mex.
Evans, Max, 80
Evarts, William M., 158, 164
eviction actions, 50–51, 71, 75, 181–84, 186–92

Faber, Charles, 143, 221n39, 227n27
federal contracts, Maxwell's, 16, 25, 29, 31
Fergusson, Harvey, 44
Figures in a Landscape (Horgan), 76
First Judicial District court, 136–39
First National Bank of Santa Fe, 33, 99, 163
Fisher, John, 62–63, 99
Foley, Tim, 38
forgery of Uña de Gato grant, 158–59, 172–73

Fort Stanton, 121, 162, 166
Fort Sumner, 33, 34, 46
Fort Union: establishment of, 13; inferior rations and Jicarilla unrest, 114–19; Maxwell's supply contract for, 25; posse comitatus act and closure of, 179; responses to local conflicts, 50, 54–55, 98, 101–3, 108, 128–29, 184; shooting of three Black soldiers, 130–32
Frémont, John C., 22, 30
Fritz, Emil, 163
frontier, concepts of, 4–6
"frontier justice," 58–61. *See also* guns and frontier culture of violence; vigilantism

Garcia, Emanuel, 82
Getty, George, 31
Glass, John, 62, 99–100, 107–8
Goddard, Pliny Earle, 115
Godfroy, Frederick, 166–68, 171
gold discoveries, 10–11, 25, 32, 36, 37–38, 39–41
Goldrick, O. J., 25, 26, 28, 29
Gonzales, Francisco, 91–92
Gonzales, Manuel, 192
Goodman, Henry, 130, *131*
Grand Cañon War (Colorado), 2
Granger, Gordon, 115, 117–18
Grant administration, 155
Grant of Kingdom (Fergusson), 44
grants, land. *See* land grant systems
Griego, Francisco "Pancho," *78*; arrest for shooting soldiers, 82; blaming Allison for Vega's death, 92–93; implicated in Tolby murder case, 102; killing of, 96–97, 104–5, 142, 144; support for Ring figures, 77; Tolby witnessing assault by, 89
Griego de Vega, Joaquina, 201–2, 220n26
Grier, William, 97
Griffin, William, 167–68
Grover, James, 82
Gunnerson, Dolores, 8–9
guns and frontier culture of violence, 5–6, 59, 82–83, 130–31, 136, 141, 184–85. *See also* "running the town"

Harwood, Thomas, 87, 109
Hayes, Rutherford B., 154, 156, 164, 165

INDEX

Heffron, Augustus "Gus," 65, 130, 131–32
Herberger, Joseph, 101, 106, 109
Hispanics: *Comancheros*, 65–66; demographics, 77, 207; on Maxwell's property, 27, 29, 32; racial/cultural prejudice against, 66–67, 90, 92; and support for Ring, 49, 77; women's experiences, 200–202
History of New Mexico (Anderson), 37
Hite, Olive Ennis, 202. *See also* Ennis, Olive (Hite)
Hite, Wallace, 202
Hittson, John, 65–66
Hixenbaugh, "Duce," 183
Hogan, W. B., 99–100
Holland, John, 24
Holly, Charles F., 45
homicide records, 194–96, 199
"Hoodoo War" (Texas), 2
Horgan, Paul, 76
Horrell War (N.Mex.), 2
"House, the," 162–63, 167
Howbert, Irving, 26
Hunn, William, 190
Hunt, Emma, 77
hydraulic mining operations, 39–40

Indian Affairs, Office of: agent roles and challenges, 15, 17, 19–21, 83, 112–13, 114; Cimarron Agency, 17, 19, 114–15, 121, 200; Mescalero Indian Reservation and Agency, 121, 162, 166–68, 177; transfer to War Department, 118
Indian Citizenship Act (1924), 198
Indian Claims Commission, 198, 224n6
Indian tribes. *See* indigenous peoples of Cimarron country
indigenous peoples of Cimarron country: dispossession of lands, 9–17, 114, 196–99, 198, 224n6; historical overview, 7–9; humanitarian support of, 13, 17, 19–21, 84–85; relationship with Maxwell, 30–31, 33–34, 47–48; Spanish and English names for, 209n2; women, 199–200. *See also* Indian Affairs, Office of; raiding by Indians; rations and supplies for Indians; relocation of Indians to reservations; *names of individual tribes/bands*

Inman, Henry, 25
Interior Department. *See* Department of the Interior, U.S.
intermarriage between tribes/bands, 8, 11
Irvine, Alexander G., 83, 113–18, 121

Jacobs, Margaret, 196–97
Jacobsen, Joel, 173
Jenkins, Henry, 54
Jicarilla Apaches: adaptability of, 8–9; compensation claim for land, 198–99; historical overview, 7–11; inferior rations incident at Cimarron Agency, 114–18; interaction with U.S. Army, 13–15; Manco Burro Pass incident, 23; relations/alliance with Utes, 8, 11–13; response to Maxwell's sale of grant, 33–34, 67. *See also* indigenous peoples of Cimarron country; relocation of Indians to reservations
Jones, Fayette Alexander, 37
Jones, Lemuel, 99–100
judicial system (territorial), overview, 137–39
Julian, George W., 51
Julian, Juan, 114–15

Kearny, Stephen Watts, 193
Keithly, Levi J., 17
Kennedy, Charles, 60–61
Kimberly, William, 183, 184
Kingman, Lewis, 82, 158, 159
Kinsinger, Joseph, 61
Kinsinger, Peter, 37, 38
Kiowas, 11, 13, 18, 68
Kistler, Russell A., 233n28
Klee, Benjamin, 189
Kroenig, William, 36, 37–38, 38, 39

Labadie, Lorenzo, 15
Lacy, Irwin W., 65, 81, 91, 178
La Farge, Oliver, 2
Lafferty, John, 115–16, 117
Lambert's (Henri) Saloon (Cimarron, N.Mex.), 61, 96, 109, 130
land grant systems: fraud and government corruption, 157, 158–59, 164–65, 172–73; under Spanish and Mexican law, 11–12, 67, 185–86, 197–98

land ownership and law, concepts and interpretations, 9–10, 133, 187–88, 193–94, 196–99
Las Animas County, Colo., 143, 189, 203
Las Animas Leader, 84, 92, 92–93
Las Gorras Blancas ("White Caps"), 191
Las Vegas Daily Optic, 185
Las Vegas Gazette, 82, 117, 119–20, 130, 150, 169
leases on Maxwell grant, miner/settler opposition to, 47, 49, 53, 181–82, 182, 186–89, 191–92, 194. *See also* squatters, evictions and settlements of
Lee, Jesse, 183, 184
Lee, William D., 159
Leverson, Montague R., 164, 165
Lewelling, J. W., 189
Limerick, Patricia, 4
Lincoln County War: background and events of, 2–3, 161–65; and "Billy the Kid," 93–94; conclusions of investigation, 163; federal judgments, 168–71; investigations of by Angel, 165–68; reports filed by Angel, 171–74
Littrell, Marion, 184
Littrell, Sam, 183–84
livestock, thefts of, 33, 42, 65–66, 68, 114. *See also* rustling
Llanero band of Jicarillas, 7–8, 11. *See also* Jicarilla Apaches
Lomax, John A., 67
Longwill, Robert Hamilton: background and military assignments, 97; and emergence of Ring, 49–50; exoneration of in Tolby murder, 144; implicated and charged in Tolby murder, 102, 106–7, 138; on livestock theft by Natives, 42; as managing director of Maxwell Company, 50, 99; political ambitions, 97–98; as probate judge, 49–51, 77; and Ring in Colfax County, 74; suspected of ordering assassinations, 97–100
Losch, Samuel, 184
Low, William, 90–91, 105
Luna, Antonia, 105
Lynch, Matthew, 38
lynchings, 60–61, 90–93, 130, 133, 136, 195 (table), 196. *See also* vigilantism

Maddox, Michael, 67
Manco Burro Pass incident, 23
Manypenny, George, 13
Marcy, Randolph, 28
Martin, Charles, 183
Masterson, James, 182–83
Matchett, William B., 155, 158, 159–60
Mattson, Hans, 182
Maxwell, Lucien Bonaparte, 27, 45; background and early days in New Mexico, 22–23; character, manner, and style of, 27–28, 30; death of, 33; decision to sell grant and relocate, 32–34; and distribution of supplies to Natives, 15–17, 26, 29, 114; ownership in mining interests, 38, 39; public service/politics, 28; relationship with Natives, 30–31, 33–34, 47–48; splendor and hospitality of ranch home, 24–25, 29; wealth and financial issues, 29–30. *See also* Maxwell Land Grant
Maxwell Cattle Company, 180
Maxwell Company. *See* Maxwell Land Grant and Railway Company; Maxwell Land Grant Company
Maxwell grant disputes: final resolution of claim ownership, 206, 215n23; surface and mineral rights, 32, 48, 48–49; survey initiated to settle claims, 81–82; title and ownership disputes, 34, 46–48, 50, 62–64, 76, 181. *See also* leases on Maxwell grant, miner/settler opposition to
Maxwell Land Grant: Maxwell's acquisition of Beaubien and Miranda Grant, 23–24; sale of, 33–34, 44–46, 47; use of name by Lucien Maxwell, 24. *See also* Maxwell grant disputes
Maxwell Land Grant and Railway Company: continuing challenges for, 56; Dutch financial backers of, 33, 64, 71, 81; failure and reorganization of, 180; origins, 4–5; strategies and plans, 46–48, 52–53. *See also* British syndicate purchase and administration of Maxwell grant; Maxwell grant disputes
Maxwell Land Grant Company, 180, 181–85, 186, 188, 192, 206. *See also* Maxwell grant disputes

McBride, Patrick, 50, 62, 99
McCleave, William, 116, 117, 121
McCullough, John B., 153, 158
McKanna, Claire V., Jr., 195
McMains, Oscar P.: "Citizens' Meeting" on Tolby killing, 109–10; final years and death of, *191*, 192; on Glass assassination, 100, 138; indictment and trial for Vega murder, 145–48; as leader of resistance to Maxwell land takeover, 185, 186–91; McPherson's support for, 154, 156; as Tolby's assistant, 79; Vega's murder and hearings, 89–92, 105
McPherson, Marcus, 150–51
McPherson, Mary Tibbles: background and family, 150–52; efforts to fight corruption, 154–59, 159–60; first visit to Morley home, 77; postal theft case against Ada Morley, 152–54
McSween, Alexander, 162–63, 166
media and propaganda wars, 110–11
Meriwether, David, 15
Merriam, Horace, 159
Mescalero (Apache) Indian Reservation and Agency, 121, 162, 166–68, 177
Mesilla Valley Independent, 169
Messervy, William, 14
Methodist Church, 1, 79, 87–88, 111, 152, 154
Mexico rule, era of, 11–12
Middaugh, Asa, 124, 153
Miles, Nelson A., 119–21
militia organized at request of Maxwell Company, 181, 182–83
Mills, Melvin Whitson: accused in Tolby murder, 102–3, 105–6, 105–7, 144; on disorder and violence in Elizabethtown, 58–61; on early mining frenzy, 40–41, 58; final years and death of, 125–26; later life in Colfax County, 145; on Maxwell's appearance, 28; on Maxwell's relationship with Natives, 30–31, 34; as Ring associate, 49, 74, 77, 86
miners: decline of in Colfax County area, 178–79; evolution of mining in New Mexico, 36–37; influx in late 1860s, 39–41; outspoken manner and aggression of, 32–33; and ownership disputes, 48–49; petition to Congress over title dispute, 51; resistance and violence of, 3, 50–51, 54–55. *See also* leases on Maxwell grant, miner/settler opposition to
Miranda, Guadalupe, 12, 23
Missouri, Ring associates from, 73, 137, 139
Monkkonen, Eric H., 195
Monmouthshire County Observer (Wales), 52
Montezuma Mine, 54–55
Montoya, María, 193, 200
Moore, John, 41
Moore, William H., 38, 39, 213n8
Moreno Valley, mining in, 1, 5, 32, 39–43, 48–51, 76, 179
Moreno Water and Mining Company, 39
Morley, Ada McPherson, 77, 83–84, 124, 150–54, 155–56, 158, 202–3
Morley, William R.: on Longwill's culpability, 99–100, 125, 126, 150; media control and propaganda wars, 110–11, 122, 123, 125; opposition to Colfax County attachment to Taos, 127; opposition to Ring, 75, 76–77, 155–56
Morleys (N. Cleaveland), 229n13
Mormons, 156–57
Morris, Charles, 63
Morrison, George, 81
Mouache Utes: compensation claim for land, 198; historical overview, 7–11; interaction with U.S. Army, 13–15; relations/alliance with Jicarillas, 8, 11–13; response to Maxwell's sale of grant, 33–34, 67. *See also* indigenous peoples of Cimarron country; relocation of Indians to reservations
"mountain-valley people" (Ollero band of Jicarillas), 7–8, 11. *See also* Jicarilla Apaches
Mullen, Kevin J., 195
Murphy, Lawrence Gustave, 162
Murphy, Lawrence R., 24

National Rifle Association, 206
Native peoples. *See* indigenous peoples of Cimarron country
Navajos, 18, 26–27, 28
New Mexican. See Santa Fe New Mexican
News and Press. See Cimarron News/Cimarron News and Press
newspapers in Cimarron country, 110–11, 208

New York Sun, 84, 99, 107–9, 123, 125, 149
nomadic *vs.* village-dwelling Indians, 9–10
Norton, A. B., 19–21
Norton, J. B., 159

Old Santa Fe Trail, The (Inman), 25
Ollero band of Jicarillas, 7–8, 11. *See also* Jicarilla Apaches
Orth, Godlove, 169
Osterlow, Henry, 50–51
Otero, Miguel Antonio, 66, 94

Palen, Joseph G., 78, 84, 122, 137
Palen, Rufus J., 137
Palmer, William J., 72, 75, 151
Pearson, Jim Berry, 213n8
Pecos River, 46, 162
Pels, Martinus Petrus, 186, 188, 192
peonage system, 26–27
Peters, James S., 142
Pile, William, 54–55
placer mining, 25, 38
"Plains people" (Llanero band of Jicarillas), 7–8
Plains tribes, raiding by, 18, 33, 46, 65–66, 68, 79, 83, 195 (table)
Pley, José, 23
Pollock, Thomas, 50
Ponil Creek, 17, 90
Pope, John, 117–18, 118–19
Porter, Henry, 65, 124, 127
postal theft incident, 83–84, 152–54
Pratt, John, 107
Pritchard, George, 52
Pueblo Daily Chieftain, 189
Pueblo Indians, 9, 10, 14, 139, 166, 167
"pueblo league" (land measure), 10
Pyle, John E., 121

quartz mining, 25, 39, 54, 55

racial/cultural prejudice: against Black people, 67, 130, 179; against Hispanic people, 66–67, 90, 92; against indigenous people, 9, 13–14, 67–69, 83; by *Las Vegas Gazette*, 119–20; overviews, 3, 5–6, 12, 132–33, 204–5
raiding by Indians: and fraudulent settler claims, 120; by Plains tribes, 18, 33, 46, 65–66, 68, 79, 83, 195 (table); and "steal or starve" conundrum, 14–15, 42, 71, 121
railroads, 5, 30, 47, 53, 182, 205
ranchers. *See* cattlemen/ranchers
Randolph, E. J., 189
rations and supplies for Indians: federal system fraud, 166–67; Maxwell's distribution of, 16, 26, 29, 47, *114*; quality and deficiency issues, 70, 113, 114–20, 121; and role of Indian agents, 15, 17, 114
Raton, N.Mex., 182
Raton Range, 206
Rayado River, 19, 22–23
Raymond, Rossiter W., 37
recreation and tourism, 206–7
Red River (Canadian River), 1, 18, 34, 64
Red River (not Canadian River), 64
Reed, J. Langham, 65–66
"Regulators, the," 167
relocation of Indians to reservations: efforts and plans for, 19–21, 43, 120–21; final settlement of Mouache and Jicarilla, 12–13, 16, 177–78; public/media demands for, 68, 71, 118; "starving out" strategy, 199–200
Richardson, Rupert Norval, 18
Riley, John H., 162, 163, 166
Rinehart, Isaiah, 90, 131, 143
Ring. *See* Santa Fe Ring (the Ring)
"Ring rule" concept, 4, 55. *See also* Santa Fe Ring (the Ring)
Rister, Carl Coke, 234n19
Ritch, William G., 142
Rocky Mountain News. See Daily Rocky Mountain News
Rogers, Dick, 183–84
Roth, Randolph, 195–96
"running the town," 65, 80, 96, 103–4, 131–32, 183. *See also* guns and frontier culture of violence
Russell, John T., 28
Russell, Marion Sloan, 190, 203
Russell, Richard, 189, 190, 203
Russell, Zeb, 192
rustling, 2, 63, 162. *See also* livestock, thefts of
Rynerson, William, 163
Ryus, William, 26

Salt War (Texas), 2
Sanchez, Pedro, 49–50, 127, 138–39
San Francisco Chronicle, 157
Sangre de Cristo Mountains, 8
San Pablo (Jicarilla chief), 117
Santa Fe New Mexican: on allegations against Axtell, 157; on exonerations for Tolby murder, 144; on Fisher murder, 63; on Glass assassination, 99; Governor Pile's rebuke of over mining conflict, 55; on Griego killing inquiry/hearing, 104–5; on indigenous and land ownership disputes, 47–48; media profiles and propaganda wars, 110–11; opposition to removal of Axtell, 169; on pending arrests for Tolby murder, 102; on sale of Maxwell Company Colorado holdings, 192; on state of Colfax County in late 1875, 101; on vandalism after Tolby's murder, 123–24; on Vega lynching, 82; Waldo on resolution of Tolby murder, 110
Santa Fe Ring (the Ring): alliance and relationship with Maxwell Company, 73–74; associations/involvement with Lincoln County, 163–64; departure from Colfax County, 3, 176; emergence and rise to power, 49–51; and Longwill's political ambition, 99; national recognition of, 149–50; overviews, 3; political associations and control, 74–75, 77–78, 78, 104, 122, 137–38; resistance/opposition to, 75, 76–77, 123–24, 125, 126, 150; suppression of after Justice Department investigations, 173
Santa Fe Sentinel, 172
Santa Fe Trail, 4, 13, 29, 65
Santa Fe Weekly New Mexican, 116–17
Satan's Paradise (A. Cleaveland), 216n11
Schoenberger, Dale, 142
Schurz, Carl, 156, 158, 164–65, 165, 168–69
scouts, Indian, 18
Shelby, Valentine S., 38, 39
Sheldon, Lionel, 181
Sherman, John, 164
Sherwin, Frank Remington, 180, 186
"shooting up the town" incidents, 65
Sierra Blanca Mountains, 161–62
"six shooter law," 59, 136

slavery of captive Indians, 26–27
smallpox, Natives' fear of, 42
Smith, Edward P., 113
Smith, Erastus H., *203*, 219n10
Smith, Mary Tolby (and children), *203*, 204. *See also* Tolby, Mary (Smith) (and children)
Songs of the Cattle Trail and Cow Camp (Lomax), 67
Sonnichsen, C. L., 95
Southern Ute Reservation, 177
Spanish-Mexican settlers and land losses, 199
Spanish settlement era, 11
Spiller, James, 81
Springer, Frank, 192; actions and allegations against Axtell, 159, 165, 168; on Axtell's obsession with Allison, 142; criticism of Maxwell Company management, 71–72; media control and propaganda wars, 110–11, 122, 123, 125; and meeting about Tolby murder, 109; and opposition to Ring, 75, 76–77, 86, 125–26, 127; outrage against Axtell's schemes, 128, 129; as president of Maxwell Company, 180, 205–6; representation of McMains in murder trial, 146; support for McMains against Ring, 154
Springer (New Mexico) "courthouse fight," 182–85
Springer Stockman, 183
squatters, evictions and settlements, 50–51, 71, 75, 181–84, 186–92
Statistics of Mines and Mining in the States and Territories West of the Rocky Mountains (Raymond), 37
"steal or starve" conundrum for Indians, 14–15, 42, 71, 121
Stevens, Benjamin "Ben," 128, 129, 150
Stewart, William M., 51
Stockton, Isaac "Ike," 65
Stockton, Mathias "Thike," 65, 178
Stockton, Porter "Port," 65
Stockton, Thomas "Tom," 64–65, *65*. *See also* Clifton House hotel and stage station
Stonewall, Colo., 188
"Stonewall War," 187–91
Supreme Court, U.S., 187, 198

Taft, Alphonso, 153, 155
Taos, Maxwell's early days in, 22
Taos County, Colfax judicial attachment to, 127
"Taos Revolt/Massacre," 139
Taylor, Morris, 173
Taylor, Thomas "Tom," 62
"Texans, the," 5, 64–65, 65, 65–67, 78–79, 80–81, 178
Texan–Santa Fe Expedition (1841), 64
Texas, Republic of, 11
Texas and Pacific Railroad, 30
Thomas, Benjamin, 166, 167, 168
Thornton, Edward, 164
Thunderbolt (Elizabethtown), 58
Tibbles, Thomas Henry, 152
Tierra Amarilla, N.Mex., 177
Tierra Amarilla grant, 187, 197
Tiller, Veronica E. Velarde, 9
Tolby, Franklin James: background and work in New Mexico, 1, 79, 84–85; "Citizens' Meeting" on murder, 109–10; implications/accusations and charges in murder of, 101–2, 105–9, 138; investigation and aftermath of murder, 88–93; murder/assassination of, 2, 86–88; trial conclusions and exonerations, 144
Tolby, Mary (Smith) (and children), 1, 79, 87–88, *203*, 204
tourism and recreation, 206–7
translation of property, 193–97. *See also* land ownership and law, concepts and interpretations
Trauer, Albert and Kate, 103–4
Trauer, Louis, 104, 126
Trauer, Maurice, 80, 103–4, 126
Trauer, Samuel S., 77, 102, 104, 107, 116, 126
Trauer, Sigmund, 104, 126
Treaty of Guadalupe Hidalgo, 67, 185–86, 197, 198
Trinidad Enterprise and Chronicle, 63, 221n39
Trujillo, Juan, 129–30
Tunstall, John Henry, 162–63, 164, 165, 167, 171
Turner, John, 80
Turner thesis (American frontierism), 4
Twitchell, Ralph Emerson, 38

Uña de Gato grant, 158–59, 164–65, 166, 172–73
Uniform Crime Reporting Program, 195
Utes. *See* Mouache Utes
Utley, Robert M., 132, 173

Valerio, Rafael, 190
Vega, Cruz, 77, 89–93, 101–2, 138, 201–2, 220n26
Vermejo area, 65, 183, 191–92, 206
vigilance. *See* vigilantism
vigilantism: defense or justification for, 95; lynchings, 60–61, 90–93, 130, 133, 136, 195 (table), 196; and racial prejudice, 132–33, 205; and "Springer court house fight," 182; vigilance committees, 59–60, 92, 101–2
village-dwelling Natives, 10
violence in Colfax County: "Colfax County War," 3, 76, 93, 95, 173; comparison study of, 194–96; incident over quality of Indian rations, 114–19; miners, 3, 50–51, 54–55; overviews, 2–3, 56, 132–34; Springer's rebuttal against claims of, 127; "Stonewall War," 187–91; Waldo's efforts against, 139–41. *See also* raiding by Indians; violence in West
violence in Lincoln County. *See* Lincoln County War
violence in West, 2–3, 194–96. *See also* alcohol and violence; guns and frontier culture of violence
Virginia City (Maxwell venture), 41

Waldo, Henry L.: background, 139; as chief justice, 122, 133, 137; as defense lawyer in Tolby murder, 103, 110; efforts against frontier violence, 139–41; Matchett and McPherson complaint against, 156; and McMains's trial, 146, 147; resignation as chief justice, 147
Waldo, Lawrence Ludlow, 139
Walker, Francis A., 19
Wallace, Lew, 169
Washington Evening Star, 159
water resources, scarcity of, 25, 36, 39–41, 53, 206
Watkins, Edwin C., 167–68
Watts, John Sebrie, 38, *45*

INDEX

Welding, Erastus, 91
Welsh miners, importation of by Maxwell Company, 53–54
Western Christian Advocate, 111
Western Home Journal, 52
Westphall, Victor, 153–54, 172–73, 197
Whealington, Tom, 184
Wheeler Survey, 218–19n35
Whigham, Harry, 159, 182, 186
"White Caps" movement, 191–92

Widenmann, Robert, 163, 164
Wightman, James Temple, 52, 54, 63, 65, 100, 221n32
"wild" designation for tribes, 10, 14
Williams, Jack, 184
Willow Creek, 37–38
women in Cimarron country, 41, 77, 199–204, 200, 200–202
Wootton, Richens Lacy "Uncle Dick," 31, 221n33

Printed in the USA
CPSIA information can be obtained
at www.ICGtesting.com
CBHW020049140924
14499CB00005B/621